SOCIO-ECONOMIC AND POLITICAL DEVELOPMENT IN SOUTH ASIA

SOCIO-ECONOMIC AND POLITICAL DEVELOPMENT IN SOUTH ASIA

(In 3 Volumes)

SOCIAL DEVELOPMENT IN SOUTH ASIA

(Volume-1)

Editors

Dr. T.R. Sareen,

Dr. S.R. Bakshi

ISHA BOOKS

DELHI-110 033

Socio-Economic and Political Development in South Asia

Rs. 2500 (Set)
Rs. 835 (each volume)

ISBN: 81-8205-074-X (Set)
ISBN: 81-8205-075-8 (Vol. 1)

Published in 2004 in India by
Isha Books, D-43, Prithviraj Road,
Adarsh Nagar, Delhi-110 033

Laser Typesetting at : Shree Vaishnavi Creations, Delhi
Printed at : Chawla Offset Press, Delhi

Contents

Preface

The countries in South Asia are united by shared culture and history, and divided by contested state boundaries that pit two nuclear powers against each other, and by religion, language, ethnicity, caste, class and a myriad other divisions. One of the largest developing region in the world in terms of land mass and population, it is home to more than a third of the world's poor. The nexus between poverty, environment and development is apparent in the region.

In South Asia, the levels of social development, though improved since the 1960s, have started to stagnate or even decline. This decline had been caused by problems which were common to all social sectors across the region. These included: weak planning and budgeting; inadequate and irregular supply of key inputs required for regular and quality service delivery; lack of trained staff aggravated by recruitment bans; weak supervision, monitoring and accountability leading to poor governance; extensive gender biases, resulting in low coverage of female population; and absence of any involvement of clients in the design and management of services. Underlying all these issues were lack of political commitment and inadequate focus on social services.

By the early-1990s all the countries in South Asia had embarked on the process of globalisation by liberalising their economies, opening up their markets and implementing reforms to improve economic management. Most countries failed to maintain a balance between economic and social development policies during globalisation. So that there has not been much improvement in high population growth rates, high levels of illiteracy, poor health attainments, pervasive poverty and inequitable distribution of income and assets.

South Asian countries have been implementing several social development programmes over the past decades. However with the onset of globalisation resource allocations to these programmes in real terms have been declining. The most important challenge faced by South Asia is to use the forces unleashed by globalisation to improve human development. The region needs to make sustained efforts in the areas of education, improve economic management and enhance regional and global integration.

This book provides a comprehensive description about the progress and challenges of social development in South Asia. Students, teachers, researchers, administrators, policy planners and professionals from different streams of academic disciplines will find this work informative and useful.

Editor

1

Committed Poverty Reduction: Trends of Social Development

Social protection is defined as the set of policies and programmes designed to reduce poverty and vulnerability by promoting efficient labour markets, diminishing people's exposure to risks, and enhancing their capacity to protect themselves against hazards and interruption/loss of income. Social protection consists of five major elements:

(i) labour markets,

(ii) social insurance,

(iii) social assistance,

(iv) micro and area-based schemes to protect communities and

(v) child protection.

When implemented properly, these policies and programmes can make a major contribution to the overarching goal of the Asian Development Bank (ADB) of reducing poverty. Social protection, as an integral part of social development, one of the three pillars of the ADB

Poverty Reduction Strategy, aims to assist individuals to break the cycle of poverty and enhance the ADB's developing member countries (DMCs) quality of growth by investing in human capital, increasing productivity, and reducing citizen's vulnerability to risks.

Different kinds of reforms and policies are needed in different economies. Where social protection systems have become too expensive and are no longer appropriate to serve a country's vulnerable populations, they need to be restructured and consolidated. Where these systems are inadequate to deal with the major risks faced by rural and urban populations, social protection needs to be extended and expanded.

The vision of the ADB's Social Protection Strategy (SPS) is the provision of social protection to all citizens of the Asia through the development of sustainable, statutory programs with universal coverage to effectively assist DMCs to reduce poverty, achieve growth by enhancing productivity, and create opportunities for individual self-reliance.

Social protection policies will vary from one country to another owing to variations in needs, available resources, institutions, and the political economy of reforms. Once a specific intervention is chosen, or a mix of them, selected programmes will have to attend to critical principles such as coverage, targeting of vulnerable populations, sustainability, good governance, and institutional and political capacity for reforms, this topic is explored next.

A main development challenge for the South Asia to achieve sufficient sustainable growth to secure the inclusion of the poor and young new entrants in the development process. However, growth alone is not a sufficient condition for generating inclusive societies. Populations, households, and individuals face various risks that can plunge them into poverty, so societies have to take steps to reduce their vulnerability and to cope with the effects when shocks occur.

Risks may include natural disasters; civil conflicts; economic downturns, of which the 1997 Asian financial crisis is the most recent example; or idiosyncratic household reversals, such as crop failures, unemployment, illness, accident, disability, death, and old age, threatening the future of the household and its members.

Development interventions may themselves create new vulnerability and risks through involuntary effects such as less affordable goods and services, temporary job loss, loss of common property, displacement, and loss of community support networks and social capital. Generally, four main types of risk to the poor can be identified: (i) those related to the individual lifecycle, (ii) economic, (iii) environmental and (iv) social/governance related.

Some risks affect all population groups equally; others have more intense impacts on the poor. The poor are highly vulnerable to risks and are constantly preoccupied with risk-averse and coping strategies to avoid sinking further into poverty. Social risk is a dynamic concept-insecurity means exposure to risks of events that if they occur, result in further vulnerability. While anyone can be vulnerable, the poor and the near poor are particularly at risk since they have fewer assets, reserves, or other opportunities to fall back on.

There are many risk reduction mechanisms, formal and informal, public and private sector delivered. However, as urbanization and industrialization gradually undermine the effectiveness of traditional and informal protection mechanisms, new public and/or private systems need to be put in place to reduce risks to the population. Social protection presents a variety of instruments to deal with the diversification of most of these risks.

The long-term solution to vulnerability depends on good social and economic development decisions that address the structural causes of vulnerability. Development policies should therefore (i) involve proactive interventions to reduce vulnerability and support populations to overcome poverty; and (ii) try not to alter existing informal family and community-based mechanisms to cope with risk, given that these provide a level of social protection to the population, and when possible, encourage community-driven interventions (social funds, microinsurance, etc).

The large variety of risks is not addressed through social protection alone. Social protection is not the entirety of development activities. Social protection instruments are generally not considered for risk reduction; for this, other instruments are available. Sound development policies and investments are ways to reduce the probability of or even eliminate such risks (e.g., infrastructure investment for flood control). Social protection programs are built primarily to mitigate the impacts of shocks or to help people cope with risks if they occur.

The boundaries between social protection and related activities are somewhat arbitrary and have to take account of regional characteristics and practical links to distinct and well-established disciplines such as education, health, and agriculture. With these considerations in mind, ADB has developed a definition of social protection based on labour markets and small-scale agriculture, in line with ADB's overarching goal of reducing poverty in South Asia.

Asia is a largely young, rural, and poor continent: social protection programs and policies should be built to respond to Asia's needs. The Asia does not have adequate protection systems in place to reduce the impact of shocks on its population; as a result, risks will continue to have devastating implications for poverty, inequality, and the prospects of long-term growth.

Social protection schemes should be planned on the basis of a thorough assessment of needs across the entire range and the costs of meeting them in the short, medium, and long term in a sustainable manner. Demographic trends have important implications for this process. The demographic transition has started in Asia with a progressive decrease in the number of infants and a progressive increase in the elderly. However, the major issue in the years 2000-2015 will be the predominance of children and the young new entrants into the labour market.

In contrast to the developed regions and the industrialized countries in Asia, people over 65 comprise only about 5.5 percent of the total population of developing Asia. This percentage is expected to rise gradually to 7.2 percent by 2015 as fertility rates fall and life expectancy increases. At present, older people in Asia reside primarily in rural areas, but with urbanization trends the percentage of older people living in rural areas is expected to decrease.

Policy makers will need to plan for labour market and other social assistance and social insurance schemes. The considerable size of the workforce combined with decreasing fertility rates could indicate that the Asian countries will likely face serious old-age challenges in 25 to 30 years, as the dependency ratios will be negatively affected. However, old-age policies should not be precipitated but carefully evaluated; the fact that most of the population remain children and working age people allows many policy design options. Short-term priorities remain addressing the urgent social issues of supporting children and poverty reduction.

More than 60 percent of the population in Asia lives in rural areas. Most of the poverty in the region is also rural-based, although urban poverty is increasing. Social divisions of a class, caste, ethnic, or racial nature are often intensified by differing poverty levels; and recently arrived immigrants tend to be poorer than others. Further, the high levels of poverty in Asia constrain the expansion of traditional social protection instruments given that these products are not affordable or attractive to the poor.

The priorities of the poor are sustaining their sources of livelihood; securing food, shelter, and clothing; avoiding natural disasters; and maintaining the health of the breadwinner-and not, for instance, old-age insurance. The new century starts with profound changes. Globalization is shifting trade, capital, technology and information flows, changing values and social structures. The increased opportunities resulting from access to new ideas, goods, services, and technology are also accompanied by increasing risks.

Interdependence may lead to possible economic shocks and downturns; if no social policies and safety nets are in place, countries may experience mounting unemployment, poverty, marginalization, and political conflict. Most of the political opposition to globalization is due to the absence of adequate transitional compensation systems, which makes implementation of reforms very difficult given that populations may have to pay the costs of reform in the short term.

Globalization requires the development of effective social protection systems in both developed and developing countries. The world's forward-looking development agenda gives social protection a primary role to sustain growth and well-functioning markets. The main social protection sub-sectors are:

(i) labour market policies and programs designed to facilitate employment and promote the efficient operation of labour markets;

(ii) social insurance programs to cushion the risks associated with unemployment, health, disability, work injury, and old age;

(iii) social assistance and welfare service programs for the most vulnerable groups with no other means of adequate support;

(iv) micro and area-based schemes to address vulnerability at the community level; and

(v) child protection to ensure the healthy and productive development of the future Asian workforce.

The focus on labour adjustments and the efficient operation of labour markets recognizes that, as economic development proceeds, employment will become the major source of economic support for most workers and their families. Improving labour market operations is an important element of strategies to reduce poverty, facilitate human capital development, and address gender discrimination. It will also help allocate a country's human capital resources to their most productive uses, enhancing general economic welfare and encouraging growth and development.

Labour market improvements to enhance social protection include the following.

(i) Labour market assessments describing demographic trends, labour-absorbing sectors, unemployment, migration flows, and the size and causes of the informal sector can help identify a country's needs and development options.

(ii) Active labour markets programs include (a) direct employment generation (promoting small and medium enterprises, public works); (b) labour exchanges or employment services (job brokerage, counseling) linking supply of with demand for labour; and (c) skills development programs (training and retraining of labour).

(iii) Passive labour market policies include (a) unemployment insurance, (b) income support, and (c)an appropriate legislative framework that strikes a balance between economic efficiency and labour protection. An appropriate legislative framework will include provisions on issues such as minimum age, maximum hours and overtime, labour contracts, industrial relations, special protection appropriate for new mothers, and antidiscrimination provisions to protect women and minorities.

Internationally recognized labour standards, when ratified, are also part of the legislative framework of a DMC. With regard to the Core Labour Standards, no explicit ratification is needed for them to be part of the legislative framework of a country. The Core Labour Standards consist of (a) freedom of association and the effective recognition of the right to collective bargaining, (b) the abolition of all forms of forced or compulsory labour, (c) the elimination of discrimination in respect of employment and occupation, and (d) the elimination of child labour.

All Asian DMCs, by virtue of being member of the International Labour Organization (ILO), are held to respect, promote, and realize the fundamental Core Labour Standards.

Social Insurance Programmes

Participating in labour markets exposes workers to several kinds of risks. Reducing these risks allows workers who have lost their jobs to search for a good alternative, removes barriers that might otherwise discourage workers from acquiring education and training, and helps ensure that the health and education of their children are not sacrificed in an economic downturn.

Social insurance programs mitigate the risks by providing income support in the event of illness, disability, work injury, maternity, unemployment, and old age. Such programmes include (i) unemployment insurance to deal with frictional (sometimes structural) unemployment; (ii) work injury insurance to compensate workers for work-related injuries or diseases; (iii) disability and invalidity insurance, normally linked to old-age pensions, to cover for full or partial disability; (iv) sickness and health insurance to protect workers from diseases;(v) maternity insurance to provide benefits to mothers during pregnancy and post delivery lactating months; (vi) old-age insurance to provide income support after retirement; and (vii) life and survivors insurance, normally linked to old-age pension to ensure that dependents are compensated for the loss of the breadwinner;

As countries develop, some form of government intervention is needed to deal effectively with these risks. Family resources, even those of an extended family, are no longer sufficient to deal with the individual risks. A wide variety of approaches are available for structuring and operating social insurance programmes. They may be contributory, in that eligibility is based on the payment of premiums each year, or noncontributory; and handled either by public sector or private sector institutions.

Where such programs are managed by the private sector, however, government retains a major role in overseeing and regulating their operation. Traditionally, private insurance companies have had difficulty providing products affordable to low-income groups because of problems associated with high transaction costs, adverse selection, and moral hazard.

Most countries have evolved toward a multipillar mixed public-private system that contains two basic elements: (i) public programs to assure minimum income to the aged, unemployed, and other vulnerable groups; and (ii) private programs that encourage voluntary supplementation by individuals. In the case of old-age pensions, a second intermediate pillar is added: public or private programs that provide retirement benefits scaled to individual contributions.

The design of a particular social insurance intervention involves selecting the approach that seems most appropriate, considering the country's stage of development and its social traditions. A proper balance must be maintained between the social gains from improved protection and the economic losses that can occur if a system becomes too generous. Social assistance and welfare services provide protection to those who cannot qualify for insurance payments or would otherwise receive inadequate benefits.

Social assistance programs are designed primarily to enhance social welfare by reducing poverty directly. Programs targeted to younger people can also promote longer term growth and development by encouraging greater investment in human capital. Social assistance interventions may include

(i) welfare and social services, institutionalized or community-based, to highly vulnerable sections of the population, such as the physically or mentally disabled, orphans, and substance abusers;

(ii) cash or in-kind transfers such as, food stamps and family allowances to vulnerable groups;

(iii) temporary subsidies, such as energy life-line tariffs, housing subsidies, or support of lower prices of staple food in times of crisis;

(iv) safeguards: attention should be paid to possible short-term negative impacts of policy reforms: in cases of a rise in prices and/or loss of entitlements to the poor, adequate mitigation measures are needed to prevent any adverse effect on the poor and the vulnerable; in the case of infrastructure, it should be designed to allow disabled populations to benefit from public investments.

Micro and Area-based Schemes

Micro and area-based schemes provide the same sort of social protection to small-scale agriculture and the urban informal sector that the more traditional social insurance programs supply to the labour force. Microinsurance offers the option to insure the poor against their main risks at affordable prices. Crop insurance programs can provide the protection necessary to encourage the adoption of new and innovative farming techniques, thereby removing an important barrier to economic development in rural areas. Together with well-designed risk reduction initiatives such as disaster management, and community-based support programs such as social funds, these programs can reduce vulnerability at the community level and promote more sustainable rural livelihoods.

The Self-Employed Women's Association (SEWA) is a registered trade union working mainly with women in the informal sector. Since 1972, its struggle has been to ensure that the minimum wage is obtained, to provide legal recourse where necessary, and to ensure democratic representation at every level of the organization. The trade union has almost 250,000 members. They are mostly hawkers and vendors, home-based workers, and laborers.

The scheme covers health insurance (including a small maternity benefit component), life insurance (death and disability), and asset insurance (loss of damage to housing unit or work equipment). SEWA members can choose to become members of the insurance scheme (at present, approximately 14 percent of all SEWA members are insured). The asset and health components come as a package and life insurance is an option.

The total premium is approximately $ 1.5 (Rs. 60) per annum for the combined asset and health insurance package and an additional Rs. 15 provides life insurance as well. Premiums and benefits are presently being restructured. Membership and claims processing is done through the SEWA Bank, along with considerable field presence and grassroots organizing from SEWA Bank and SEWA Union staff. Mobile services are also available for premium collection (normally associated with microfinance deposits and loan repayment collections).

Microinsurance involves voluntary and contributory schemes for the community, handling small-scale cash flows to address major community risks. Often such schemes are of a local character and have a very small membership. The primary aim of many of these schemes is to help their members meet the unpredictable burden of out-of-pocket expenses, such as a hospital emergency, death, or funeral expenses.

In recent years, groups of workers in the informal economy have set up their own microinsurance schemes, normally assisted by grants or government subsidies. Such schemes may operate within the context of a microfinance scheme, which has already had experience collecting contributions and administering payments. Microinsurance is an emerging topic with high potential. Microinsurance can provide social insurance at affordable prices, expanding coverage by having a realistic understanding of the problems that communities face, and promoting community involvement.

There are good historical examples of microinsurance, for instance, mutual societies played an important developmental role in early 20th century in Europe. Options for the future include pooling existing organizations, promoting reinsurance, and providing private-public partnerships. More effort needs to be placed in marketing microinsurance, as a large percentage of the target population is not well informed of the benefits of being insured, and the credibility of microinsurance needs strengthening.

Agricultural Insurance is a form of protection could be available for farming communities. It is a financial mechanism in which the uncertainty of loss in the farms is minimized by pooling a large number of uncertainties that impact on agriculture so that the burden of loss can be distributed. The loss may be due to a number of natural perils like storms, floods, droughts, hail, frost, earthquakes, volcanic eruptions, plant pests, diseases, etc.

The risks of loss can be spread temporally or spatially. With reinsurance, the risks can be further spread across national boundaries. For instance, during natural disasters of widespread proportion when a nation's finances are at a low ebb, other countries share the burden. Agricultural insurance can be reexamined as an effective tool for the development of the rural economy when implemented as part of a package of support services in the rural areas, cautiously accompanied by adequate reinsurance mechanisms.

Social funds have evolved recently outside the Asia as mechanisms to channel public resources to meet particularly pressing social needs. Community-based social funds are agencies, typically managed at the local level, empowering communities, NGOs, and local governments that provide finance for small-scale projects, such as infrastructure schemes and livelihood programs to community groups. They provide direct poverty relief and encourage skills development while contributing to a community's social capital.

The 1997 financial crisis and the growth in the number of countries undergoing economic transition have led to an increase in social funds projects in Asia. Social fund methodology is now used by local governments to promote good local governance and pilot test decentralized management and financing of small-scale infrastructure in some Asian countries.

Disaster preparedness and management is essential to assist communities in risk coping and mitigation. Several countries in Asia have established disaster management centers for assessing hazards, planning risk reduction and monitoring programmes, providing emergency assistance, and strengthening local-level risk reduction capacity. Two principal trends have developed over the past decade in disaster management: (i) improved hazard forecasting through computer models on climatic behaviour; and (ii) an increased focus on local vulnerabilities given that community-based preparedness is the best mechanism to reduce loss of human life and the scale of damage.

Given that children and youth constitute 40 percent of DMC populations, investing in child protection is of profound significance to the development of the region. The realities of child deprivation are alarming in Asia, which holds three quarters of the world's stunted, underweight children. Lack of adequate protection can result in undernourishment, poor health, and intellectual underdevelopment which can lead to being less productive adults.

Educating children and youth is essential to allow social mobility and better job prospects, and an indispensable instrument to help DMCs maintain their international competitive advantage, raise productivity, and continue economic growth. Additionally, as defined in the United Nations Convention on the Rights of the Child, society through good governance must provide measures to ensure that the child is protected from all forms of abuse and exploitation, such as child labour, child prostitution, or the adversities faced by the girl child, streetchildren, children with disabilities, and children under armed conflict.

Investment in children is a key factor in poverty reduction and economic growth but it is usually a small proportion of national budgets, despite ample evidence that the small investments currently made bring considerable future benefits to society as a whole. High child/adult dependency ratios indicate the need to provide social protection for the young, such as

(i) early child development to ensure the balanced psychomotive development of the child through basic nutrition, preventive health, and educational programs;

(ii) school feeding programmes, scholarships, or school fee waivers;

(iii) Waiving of fees for mothers and children in health services;

(iv) streetchildren initiatives;

(v) child rights advocacy/awareness programmes against child abuse, child labour etc;

(vi) youth programs to avoid social anomia in teenagers, criminality, sexually transmitted diseases such as HIV/AIDS, early pregnancies, and drug addiction;

(vii) family allowances, either means-tested cash transfers or coupons/stamps for basic goods and services (i.e., food, clothing) to assist families with young children to meet part of their basic needs

Most DMCs have some form of institutionalized social protection system, but often these programs are ineffective due to (i) limited coverage, serving only a portion of the formal sector (often the wealthiest segments of society); (ii) insufficient funds, incorrectly distributed among programs; (iii) inadequate instruments, often copied from developed countries but not appropriate to serve specific in-country needs; and (iv) factors restricting access to statutory social protection schemes, such as legal restrictions, administrative bottlenecks, and problems with compliance.

In considering the demands for social protection within Asian subregions it is important to identify the circumstances faced by their vulnerable groups. Table 3 summarizes the social protection priority issues by subregion. The countries of East and Southeast Asia are still recovering from the regional financial crisis and high levels of unemployment, and need substantial investments in social protection to overcome poverty and reduce social risk and vulnerability.

South Asian countries have large proportions of the rural population living in poverty with high levels of illiteracy, and state-funded social protection schemes exist only nominally and are supplemented by some limited programs operated by NGOs. The region needs substantial investments in social protection and human development targeted to children and the informal sector and truly vulnerable groups. Since the Asian Crisis, the effect has been to increase poverty, insecurity, and social exclusion for many vulnerable groups.

In response to the critical need to address vulnerability in development, following the experience of poverty reduction programmes in the regions where they operate, multilateral and bilateral aid agencies produced different definitions of social protection. The World Bank definition of social protection is based on social risk management; the Inter-American Development Bank (IDB) emphasizes social protection as a means to address macroeconomic and catastrophic shocks; the United Kingdom Department for International Development (DFID) uses a rights-based approach to define social protection, with an emphasis on promoting integrated livelihoods.

ILO, which is the senior agency dealing with social protection topics, maintains a structured view of social security based mostly on social insurance and labour standards. ILO was founded in 1919 to promote social justice and ensure effective social protection systems among its member countries, provide social and economic security, implement fundamental labour rights, increase work opportunities, and strengthen social dialogue. The definition of social security and the focus of ILO's work have changed often during the last eight decades.

ILO has recently adopted as its strategic objective to enhance coverage and effectiveness of social protection for all, by focusing on income security with an emphasis on the poor, identifying cost-effective and equitable ways by which social protection can be extended to all groups, and shifting from a state-led focus to emphasis on provision of social protection to the informal sector. However, social protection is still conceived mainly in terms of labour and social insurance.

ILO provides technical assistance primarily in the fields of social security systems, social protection administration and expansion of coverage, social expenditure management, labour relations, vocational training, employment policy, labour administration, labour law and industrial working conditions, management development, cooperatives, labour statistics, and occupational safety and health.

From this perspective, ILO should be a partner in any social protection initiative. The World Bank focus uses social risk management as the conceptual framework for its Social Protection Strategy Paper, consistent with its Comprehensive Development Framework and Poverty Reduction Strategy Papers (PRSPs). Social protection is defined as public interventions oriented to human capital to (i) help individuals, households, and communities better manage risk; and (ii) provide support to the incapacitated poor.

The concept of social risk management asserts that all individuals, households, and communities are vulnerable to multiple risks from different sources, whether they are natural (such as earthquakes, floods, and illness) or man-made (such as unemployment, environmental degradation, and war). Poor people are typically more exposed to risk and have inferior access to effective risk management instruments than people with greater assets. Dealing with risks involves recognizing their sources and economic characteristics, for example, whether they affect individuals in an unrelated manner or simultaneously.

The most appropriate combination of risk management strategies (prevention, mitigation, or coping) and arrangements (informal, market-based, or publicly provided or mandated) in any given situation depends on the type of risk and on the direct and opportunity costs and effectiveness of the available instruments. On the organizational side, the World Bank has established its Social Protection Department under its Human Development Network, with units in most of the World Bank's human development regional divisions.

The key objectives of the IDB social protection strategy are to

(i) guarantee minimum consumption levels and access to basic services for those permanently unable to provide for themselves (i.e., the aged and disabled);

(ii) strengthen the asset base of the poor to reduce their vulnerability to shocks;

(iii) ensure continued investment in human capital during periods of crisis in order to avoid irreversible long-term consequences for children; and

(iv) provide security to the poor to improve their economic choices and allow them to take entrepreneurial risks and earning capacity.

To achieve the International Development Goal of halving poverty by 2015, DFID emphasizes requirements of economic growth, equity, and security. DFID supports a rights-based approach to poverty reduction. Decent living standards, access to services and security are part of the fabric of rights of poor people. These rights are enshrined in national laws, international agreements and covenants, including Core Labour Standards, and form the basis on which development organizations formulate their policies.

Participation in the formulation of such policies by poor people is an equally important part of a rights-based approach. And the issue of security, in a broad sense, is central among poor people's priorities. DFID has worked extensively on the notion of sustaining livelihoods to promote opportunities for all citizens and reduce poverty.

ADB has developed different types of social protection interventions over the years, either as stand-alone loans or as components of other loans where social protection is not the primary objective. Since 1985, where social protection projects were only about 1 percent of the total ADB lending, the portfolio has been expanding.

The demand for rapid social support projects will hopefully not be necessary in the future-instead, ADB should concentrate on developing more comprehensive and effective social protection systems to assist DMCs to reduce poverty and vulnerability. The trend, however, reflects an important increase in lending in the sector. Social protection is an emerging sector that needs to be properly addressed. As social protection took on a new urgency at ADB, the need for more effective coordination strategies became clear.

In October 1998, an interdepartmental working group was formed to explore options for ADB's future interventions in social protection. A framework for operations on social protection was developed in July 1999, after close consultations among departments, to be distributed and discussed with selected DMC governments, NGOs, and other aid agencies.

Improving national social protection systems is of major importance in all regions. However, the motivations for reform and the approaches adopted differ dramatically from one country to the other. Well-developed social protection systems are large and complex undertakings that can become an integral part of the fabric of a society and have important implications for social and economic development. Social protection strategies will vary from one country to another as a result of differences in needs, institutions, and available resources. Country preferences will also be influenced by the political support and social consensus needed to implement reforms. An analysis of these four factors determines the social protection priorities of a country.

Country Needs

The main objective of social protection is to reduce poverty and vulnerability. A summary vulnerability and risk profile will help to determine the country-specific social protection needs. A description of major risks to the population, demographic structures, levels of urban-rural population, poverty, and the size of the formal sector influence the type of social protection mechanisms that are feasible and appropriate.

Where population projections show a significant number of children and new entrants into the labour market in the near future, social protection should address the needs of the young. Where population growth rates are low or negative, there is a rapidly aging population and the child/adult dependency ratios are low, social protection systems should address the priorities of the elderly.

Where the most acute problems may be others-i.e., migrant workers, victims of disasters, or any other vulnerable population group-social protection planning should accommodate the specific country needs. The results will differ from one DMC to another. The size of the formal and informal sectors; the sectoral distribution (population engaged in agriculture, industry, and services); rural and urban active population; evolution of real wages; the role of women in the labour force; working conditions; compliance with national and international labour laws and standards including the reported existence of child or bonded labour and violations to other Core Labour Standards -all will provide additional information to help determine the country priorities.

In some countries, the priority attention will be to assist unemployed or underemployed working age population to find employment opportunities; or to fight child labour. In others, the rural areas may have been forced to shoulder a disproportionate burden of the country's social problems, and strengthening rural systems may be a priority. Labour absorption is essential to avoid poverty. The country labour market analysis should evaluate which sectors/subsectors and geographical areas have a demand for labour and identify which areas may have an unmet supply of labour, to identify the right mix of public policies.

Labour market analysis is a key element in the strategic link between economic growth and poverty reduction, and the analysis should provide recommendations to ensure efficient and inclusive development patterns. The country social protection needs assessment with a rational prioritization of the country's top social protection needs, based on quantitative evidence gathered in the vulnerability profile and labour market analysis, to ensure a rational and well-demonstrated prioritization of possible development interventions.

Available Resources

The level of resources available for social protection will also influence a country's social protection choices. Many existing social protection systems and programs are underbudgeted, receive random funding, or have mistargeted benefits. Where allocated public funds are limited and the country needs large, public programs should be targeted to those most in need.

An evaluation of the effectivity of current programs and resources to reduce poverty and vulnerability in the country will immediately point the need for reforms. If a country lacks the fiscal resources to achieve the development of a comprehensive social security system with significant coverage, it should opt to concentrate on poverty reduction and improvements in the labour force through the combination of labour market policies and programs, child protection, micro and area-based schemes, social assistance, and minimal social insurance benefits.

Social expenditures reviews are a key instrument to determine fund allocations intra and intersectorally, showing the administrative costs of social protection, the relative weight as compared to other social expenditures, the distribution of funds among social protection programs; the benefit incidence and effectivity in reaching vulnerable and poor populations; and last, but not least, distribution issues-who is paying and who benefits.

Existing Institutions

Where social protection programs already exist, conscious

decisions will have to be made about whether reform efforts should build on the existing institutions or whether new institutions should be created. Societies almost always have at least some form of formal social protection institutions, but the institutions that exist may be very weak or cover only an extremely small fraction of the population. Where the existing institutions are neither very large nor very important, they may not impose serious constraints on the reform process. Where they are large, however, their influence cannot be ignored.

Existing institutions influence policies about the structure and philosophy of social protection in several ways. They form a point of reference for comparing alternatives. Where the current approaches are generally viewed favorably among the population, the political path of least resistance will be to build on and extend them. The country's institutional history, including the relative credibility of the public and private sectors and the extent of previous government social protection commitments, inevitably affects the scope and character of any new intervention.

Given that existing institutions have staff and stakeholders who are likely to protect themselves, large government bureaucracies are not dismantled easily and private concerns that are profiting from the existing arrangements will resist change. A good stakeholder analysis of old and new providers and recipients of social protection may facilitate discussions during country programming and project design, by making the trade-offs transparent. Reforming social protection policies is likely to be easier-and the odds of success are correspondingly higher-if the new approach preserves an important role for the existing institutions.

The decision whether to invest in social protection will require an understanding of the country-specific institutional capacity to deliver reforms, including (i) the efficiency and coverage of existing social protection programs, and (ii) the possible roles and risks involved in using public, market-based, and civil society/NGO mechanisms for new social protection programs, as described in paras. Before embarking on reforms, the institutional prerequisites of different social protection approaches need to be taken into account.

The risks involved in engaging the public and private sectors need to be assessed to ensure that the proposed reforms will effectively reduce poverty and vulnerability, the main objective of a social protection system. For instance, market-based companies often find disincentives to serving the poor; unless a proper public-private arrangement is envisaged, the poor will likely remain uncovered.

Pension reform projects often involve development of privately funded mechanisms to encourage the development of sophisticated financial market institutions, but they can function effectively only if the domestic capital market has already reached a minimum level of development; where the preconditions for advance funding are absent, provident funds or basic pay-as-you-go approaches may be important transition measures to ensure that the objectives of a social protection system are accomplished.

Targeted poverty and social assistance interventions that rely on formal means-testing operate on the assumption that institutions have the sufficient capacity to collect, process, and store information; investments should ensure that either this capacity is built or other institutional arrangements are found.

The Political Economy of Reform

The potential gains must be balanced against the likely losses from reforming a social protection system. This will involve a careful review of the conditions under which benefits are provided and the ways in which subsidies are constructed or abolished, the relationship between the value of the assistance offered and prevailing wages or prices, the affordability of the services provided, the incentives established in the program for delaying taking benefits and/or returning to work as quickly as possible, and the balance between the costs and benefits of new regulations.

Reforms that may encounter large resistance need more intense consultations with relevant stakeholders. Successful programs are those supported by the serious political commitment of the country's leadership. Social protection systems normally reflect the country's social architecture. To be effective, social protection strategies should be articulated in an integrated manner and discussed with all relevant social players as reforms are an opportunity to rethink the country's social contract.

This, however, is often not the case, and reforms are precipitated by crises that have exposed or exacerbated flaws in existing policies. The experience of the transition economies and countries affected by the Asian Crisis has shown that governments should not be asked to pursue policies that will require a consensus that has not yet formed within the society. A social protection agenda should be framed taking into account DMCs national policies and priorities as well as ADB's overarching goal of reducing poverty, ensuring that social protection is integrated with other development activities and into ongoing country dialogue.

Principles for Social Protection

Once one or a combination of social protection policies within the five different components (labour markets, social insurance, social assistance, micro and area based approaches, and/or child protection) have been selected in a determined DMC, the design of the specific program selected should attempt to balance several trade-offs to effectively reduce poverty and vulnerability and promote human development. The assessment should focus on the following considerations: (i) the program's coverage and benefits, (ii) its effectivity in targeting vulnerable groups and specific gender issues, (iii) the sustainability of the program (except perhaps for certain temporary interventions motivated by an economic crisis) and the adequacy of its institutional arrangements, and (iv) the program's integrated approach. Investments in program design may not to be worthwhile where the program does not contribute to reduce poverty and vulnerability, sustainability is open to question, coverage is likely to be limited, and population groups in need are not served.

In most DMCs, both public and private sectors have failed to provide effective social protection to the population. The rate of expansion will vary across countries in the region and depend on the financial and institutional resources available. Coverage gaps occur due to statutory exclusions, poor enforcement, or the lack of attractive benefits despite high contributions for particular groups.

Labour market regulations and standards and contributory social insurance programs designed for universal coverage in the medium/long term, have serious coverage gaps in Asia. These programs normally cover the larger enterprises in the formal sector. Smaller employers, particularly in industries that compete with the informal sector, are often excluded from many of the provisions, as are household workers, daily laborers, farmers, fishermen, and many urban self-employed.

The informal sector thus operates outside the scope of regulations, with low and unstable levels of income, and poor working conditions. The result of the statutory exclusions is that many of the most vulnerable people are not protected. The first priorities for the poor and the informal sector are strengthening prospects of survival and improving incomes, rather than investing scarce resources in social insurance schemes.

Additionally, old people in the informal sector who are fortunate enough to live beyond that age do not retire but are likely to remain economically active as long as they can, to support themselves and help their families survive. Efforts to expand coverage should start by addressing the needs of the poor and informal sector clientele: improvement of their productive potential and their employment and income-generating capacity, improvement of the household's welfare, and mitigation of risks that keep households in poverty.

A major area of development for informal sector groups in both urban and rural areas is microinsurance for health care, death of the breadwinner, and short-term risks, through voluntary schemes established by mutual benefit societies, cooperatives, and similar organizations, or civil society groups that rely on trust engendered through occupational groupings or community solidarity.

Even where most formal employees and self-employed people are covered according to the statute, the reality may be quite different due to poor enforcement. Lax enforcement often has the same impact as a statutory exclusion. Where enforcement is lacking or lax, labour market regulations are likely to have little impact even for those who are nominally covered. Poor enforcement can also undermine the protection offered under contributory social insurance, since benefit entitlements usually depend to some degree on how contributions have been collected.

A close link between contribution payment and subsequent benefit entitlement helps to insulate a contributory programme from the financial consequences of poor enforcement, but does this by reducing benefits and restricting protection. Effective enforcement requires institutions that have the necessary statutory authority to establish liabilities and enforce collections.

These institutions must also have adequate operating budgets, the willingness and ability to use their resources and authority to enforce the law, and the political support necessary to sustain the enforcement effort. For this reason, assessing social protection coverage necessarily involves assessing the effectiveness of the implementing institutions.

Market-based schemes have often found servicing low-income communities unattractive, as compared to the higher returns received from servicing higher income groups. The poor have discontinuous income and are more prone to risk, thus the higher transaction costs are unattractive to insurance companies and customers. Efforts should be made by governments to arrange public-private partnerships that offer low-income communities access to social protection services.

Many systems in Asia are underbudgeted or receive erratic yearly funds so that the benefits they provide do not achieve their intended social objective. Often, the transaction costs are larger than the benefits provided. It is critical that social protection systems are built to effectively provide protection given available resources. On the other hand, benefits should not be so generous that they generate disincentives.

Continuity and predictability about the conditions under which benefits are to be provided and the approximate amount to be made available is also necessary in order to realize the social gains promised by social protection programs. Where formal systems do not have sufficient human and financial resources to cover identified needs, the priority will be to target available resources to vulnerable groups.

Progressively, comprehensive social protection systems will be developed but, in the short term, resources will be channeled to those most in need. Matching the results of the social expenditure reviews and vulnerability analysis will show the need to either pursue the development of a formal social protection system or concentrate scarce resources into priority needs.

When the vulnerability analysis shows high child/adult dependency ratios and children exposed to risks, the country's social protection system should target children. When most vulnerable people live in the rural areas, resources should be decentralized and programs be put in place to target these priority population groups.

Although half of the population of all population are women, they receive much less assistance and opportunities than do men. Many poverty reduction and social development programs are focused on households and do not consider intrahousehold differences. Assets and labour are normally distributed in a different and unequal manner between men and women, boys and girls within a same household.

Unless particular attention is paid to women's unique problems and life patterns when social protection policies and programs are developed, approaches that might appear to be gender-neutral may actually disadvantage women. Positive discrimination maybe needed to ensure women's development in Asia. For example, labour market reforms must go beyond a purely traditional agenda to adequately address such special concerns of women as a higher incidence of home work, competing demands from household responsibilities, and the particular needs surrounding child bearing.

In child protection, the benefits of investing in the girl child are large-educated girls become more responsible and better informed mothers. Social insurance programs need to be designed to take into account the longer life expectancies of women in most societies; the additional implications for women of the risk of loss of support due to death, abandonment, or divorce; and the less stable earning patterns commonly found among women.

The design of any social protection scheme is directly linked to an analysis of how it can be financed and how it can best be delivered. There is no prescription or preferred social protection model, as the structure and operations will change from country to country depending on the available financial and institutional resources. Social protection interventions should include assessments of how to ensure efficient and sustainable operations to deliver the proposed coverage of social protection needs.

The variety of social protection programs may be financed through budgetary support, income-related contributions, charitable donations, or a mix of all these. Enforcement of revenue collection may result in higher tax collections, particularly in countries with young demographic pyramids. Higher tax revenues can in turn support the promotion of statutory programs. In addition to encouraging adequate tax collection, there is merit in systems in which individuals cofinance services, contributing individually or though community-based arrangements.

This is the case for social insurance, micro and area-based schemes, social funds, and selected labour market and child protection programs. However, most programs, particularly those targeted to lower income groups, require a degree of public support. Financing from charitable or aid organizations is discontinuous and does not allow sustainable social protection programs. Such financing may help to fill the gaps on a temporary basis only. In social insurance programs, accumulated savings/ contributions can be invested in financial markets.

Diversification of income sources is desirable to spread risks and ensure the overall sustainability of the program. Potential financial commitments under a program need to be evaluated to be sure that they can be borne from the resources likely to be available, including the program's contingent liabilities. Financing issues are directly linked to distribution aspects.

The design of any social protection program should carefully evaluate its distribution impacts to (i) ensure that vulnerable and poor benefit; and (ii) above all, avoid regressive redistribution issues, e.g., building systems with public resources that mostly benefit upper income groups. Since the main objective of a social protection system is to support vulnerable populations to overcome their exposure to risks, it results in more equitable societies.

Financing social protection systems implies some transfer of resources, either from taxed citizens to those outside the formal sector, or from the working age generation to younger and older people. Even when building contributory social insurance schemes, the normally expensive transition costs are passed to the public sector and thus financed by taxpayers. This does not imply that the purpose of a social protection system is merely income redistribution-the purpose is to build mechanisms that assist individuals to overcome vulnerability; for this, a degree of redistribution and support is needed.

Identifying the adequate mix of financing resources to ensure, if needed, adequate redistribution and support to vulnerable populations should be assessed after careful cost-benefit evaluation of the proposed social protection program. Social protection success depends on the effective administration of adequately designed programs.

Common operational problems among agencies include corruption, cronyism, and favouritism; inadequate information processing, storage and retrieval systems; and organizational cultures that are hostile to customer service. Good governance is crucial for sound macroeconomic management, progressive taxation, and equitable allocations of funds for social development.

The impact of basic social services is reduced by governance defects such as inadequate budgets and wasteful, inefficient, and unresponsive administrations. The poor suffer most due to poor access, low bargaining power, and little influence on local officialdom and service providers. The effects of such deficiencies in governance are exemplified by the highly unsatisfactory coverage in social insurance schemes.

These schemes have been in force for decades in many countries but have failed to reach those most in need of protection. Fundamental governance issues that should be considered when designing any social protection scheme include identifying (i) the most appropriate social protection system to serve all citizens, (ii) the most suitable institutional arrangements for the administration of schemes, and (iii) the best way to achieve operational efficiency.

Often, public social protection programs do not have sufficient human and financial resources to cover identified needs. Most DMCs need to allow flexible and innovative institutional arrangements, bringing all possible development partners together under well-regulated sectoral policies, government's administrative oversight to ensure good governance and affordable services.

The four main social protection delivery mechanisms are (i) public-based, normally best to achieve expansion of coverage; (ii) market-based, normally best for efficient delivery for the formal sector of the economy and voluntary schemes for higher income groups; (iii) NGOs and charitable institutions, normally good to target low-income communities; and (iv) a mix of these. However, each mechanism has important limitations.

The public sector should not crowd out the potential role of the private sector in delivering social protection. Instead, the public sector should concentrate its efforts to serve areas and populations that are not covered by the private sector. Decentralization of public programs offers the great potential to improve effectiveness of social programs and bring decision making closer to communities.

The private sector is often not attracted to lower income groups and/or remote areas because the associated transaction costs are high and returns low. Private-public partnerships can be agreed between governments and private companies to secure inclusion of those excluded from any form of protection. Where NGOs are already significant providers of social protection programmes, they can be encouraged to continue.

However, NGOs often have limited and discontinuous funding and their presence is scattered, and normally not broad enough to ensure equal expansion of coverage, limiting their ability to reduce vulnerability. A mixed delivery system may be best to diversify risks and address social protection priorities. Avoiding excessive administrative charges is a major challenge for certain kinds of social protection programs. Administrative charges siphon away resources from the intended beneficiaries, needlessly increasing the cost of social protection and reducing society's capacity for providing protection.

In addition to the threat they pose to program integrity, inefficient and unresponsive government bureaucracies often cause excessive administrative costs. The result is administrative resources wasted due to duplicative and inefficient service delivery structures.

Social protection should be seen as one of several measures that work together to promote socially inclusive human development, reduce poverty, and support enhanced productivity and growth.

Close collaboration is needed to ensure that social protection and other development policies are consistent and mutually supportive. Many problems of existing social protection programs are due to lack of cohesion in social and economic planning or inconsistencies between different parts of the social protection system. For instance, serious difficulties in the labour market may lead to proposals for early retirement on advantageous terms as a part of the solution to over-employment in public enterprises, but without sufficient consideration of the long-term implications for pension funds. Another example of malpractice could be social protection interventions displacing necessary health and education investments.

Integrated and coordinated national policies on social protection must be established. Sound policy formulation in social protection requires less emphasis on short-term priorities and the creation of medium- and long-term social development plans. Close coordination in policy formulation is vital when several government departments and agencies are involved.

The role of ministries of finance and national planning authorities is crucial in working out balanced views on realistic and affordable priorities with the ministries directly responsible for the management and development of programs. Dialogues on these matters can improve mutual understanding of the wide range of issues involved, and the right sequencing of reforms.

Aid agencies could provide necessary advise and help generate a consensus. Integrated planning is complex but essential for policy cohesion and the efficient use of resources. Controversial issues, including the extent of redistributive policies, changes in policies on subsidies in particular sectors, and increases in pension ages should be settled through this process.

Social protection programs and policies should be built to respond to its needs. The region is still experiencing the effects of the demographic explosion and 40 percent of its population is below 19. The region's population is 3.1 billion, half of the world's total, and of this, 900 million people are poor. About 60 percent of the total population live in rural areas and most of the population belongs to the informal sector.

The majority of DMCs have some form of institutionalized social protection system; however, most social protection programs have low effectivity due to limited coverage, insufficient funds, and inadequate instruments. Most employees in the informal sector are unable or unwilling to contribute a relatively high percentage of their incomes to financing social protection benefits that do not meet their priority needs.

In general, the informal sector prioritizes immediate needs, such as health, employment or the source of livelihood, shelter, food, clothing, and survival from natural disasters, rather than traditional social security schemes such as old-age insurance. A host of other factors restrict access to statutory social protection schemes, including legal impediments, administrative bottlenecks, and problems with compliance.

Welfare systems have not been a priority for most DMC policy-makers in Asia; social protection has been largely neglected, or at best addressed with inadequate resources. Investing in social protection was an essential part in the modernization programs of these wealthier societies at the early stages of their development. Precisely, higher levels of social security allowed high productivity gains in the workforce, expanded domestic demand, and increased economic growth.

Social protection is a logical extension of ADB's overarching objective to reduce poverty because the benefits of economic growth will not automatically reach to all poor. Lack of adequate social protection may actually put a severe limit on future economic growth. In children, malnutrition and poverty damage health, cause death, harm reproduction, reduce intelligence, and lower productivity and opportunities for the future adult, a high tax on future economic development.

Social Protection Index for Poverty Reduction

In 2001, the Asian Development Bank (ADB) approved its Social Protection Strategy. Currently, ADB is preparing steps to implement the strategy by including social protection projects and programs in the country strategy programs of developing member countries (DMCs).

Given the pivotal role of a Social Protection Index (SPI) in monitoring poverty reduction, ADB endorsed in December 2002 a concept paper to develop an SPI which was endorsed for funding by the (i) Poverty Reduction Cooperation Fund (PRF) by the Department of International Development of the Government of the United Kingdom, and (ii) Cooperation Fund in Support of the Formulation and Implementation of National Poverty Reduction Strategies by the Netherlands.

Currently, ADB is preparing or carrying out social protection studies in several countries (Indonesia, People's Democratic Republic of Lao, Nepal, Pakistan, Papua New Guinea) and a regional TA is being prepared to assess social protection systems in Marshall Islands, Papua New Guinea, and Vanuatu.

Social protection is defined as the set of policies and programs designed to reduce poverty and vulnerability by promoting efficient labor markets, diminishing people's exposure to risks, and enhancing their capacity to protect themselves against hazards and interruption/ loss of income. Social protection is moving higher on the agenda of many international, bilateral and national institutions and governments.

Due to the shock of the Asian Crisis and to ensure that economic growth in DMCs benefits the poor, social protection is needed as an element of pro-poor growth. Nearly all DMCs have social protection schemes. However, a large part of the funds dedicated to social protection is vested in formal social insurance schemes, mostly for government officials. Social protection measures are also targeted to the poor, e.g. programs for the elderly, the disabled, orphans, disaster relief, food for work, social funds, public health care provider networks, and micro-insurance schemes.

Social protection schemes include formal and informal sector social protection, financed through government budget, contributions from individuals, the private sector, nongovernment organizations, and development partners. Also, social protection concepts vary greatly among DMCs. So far, little has been done to measure quantitative dimensions of all the areas of social protection.

The International Labour Organization has done important work in compiling and analyzing formal social protection data through their social budgeting model. Hardly any aggregate quantitative information is available on other private sector activities, NGO activities, development partner contributions, and the large informal sector, which has an important role in social protection in all DMCs.

Thus, to implement the ADB Social Protection Strategy, various questions arise:

(i) How should social protection be defined in each DMC? Social protection policies, mechanisms, and instruments vary from one country to another owing to differences in needs, available resources, and priorities.

(ii) What is the situation in DMCs concerning social protection? Which tools are applied? What are the resources dedicated to social protection? Who is covered? What is the experience in poverty reduction and prevention?

(iii) How can the implementation of the Social Protection Strategy be monitored?

Information has to be collected, compiled, adapted, and analyzed with view to social protection needs. An SPI could be used to (i) to measure the situation and progress made in terms of social protection (ii) measure developments, and (iii) compare countries' efforts to reduce poverty through social protection. One of the best known indexes in the field of social development is the human development index (HDI) computed by United Nations Development Programme (UNDP).

The HDI is based on three indicators: life expectancy at birth; knowledge measured by adult literacy rate; gross primary, secondary, and tertiary enrolment; and standard of living measured by gross domestic product (GDP) per capita. The HDI is calculated for every country based on the same methodology, thus making cross-country comparisons and comparisons in time possible.

An index can also be useful for analyzing and improving data, which itself is an important step toward transparency and monitoring. In the field of social protection, a few indicators are commonly used (e.g., social expenditure as a share of GDP based on a social budget, coverage rate for formal and nonformal social insurance schemes, and poverty indicators), but no composite index is broadly accepted.

An SPI could be used to compare countries and for benchmarking, taking into account a whole set of circumstances like economic performance, size of the social problems the country faces, and achievements. Countries with low incomes could be compared in their efforts with countries with higher incomes. This might show no direct correlation between the level of social protection efforts and the economic performance of a country, and that countries with low incomes make relatively greater efforts in social protection than countries with higher incomes.

Developing an SPI will also help to define social protection (including instruments like subsidies for the poor, informal sector schemes, traditional and community-based mechanisms, and social welfare), taking into account the different concepts of social protection in each DMC. Country preferences are also influenced by the political support and social consensus needed to implement reforms. According to the ADB Social Protection Strategy, formal education and macroeconomic labor market issues, for example, are not regarded as part of social protection.

The SPI will be based on quantitative data and will be accompanied by a qualitative assessment of social protection instruments and policies through social protection studies. The SPI will be simple and transparent so that regular compilation is easy for the statistical offices of DMCs and to make it readily understandable. The index could, for example, incorporate all or some of the following elements:

(i) *affordability*: the total funds spent for formal and nonformal social protection (e.g., from the social budget, public expenditure reviews, etc.) in relation to GDP per capita;

(ii) *coverage*: percent of population covered (members and beneficiaries of social insurance, beneficiaries of social assistance, beneficiaries of non-formal protection schemes);

(iii) *equity*: distribution of social protection benefits among target groups; and

(iv) *adequacy*: poverty level (share of population to be regarded as below the poverty line); this indicator would reflect the need for social protection measures, and could, for example, use delivery of social protection benefits according to quintiles of income.

The goal of devising the SPI is to help reduce poverty by supporting social protection in the DMCs. The objectives are to

(i) define social protection for each DMC involved and develop a common standard regarding what is part of social protection (important in order to ensure comparability among DMCs),

(ii) improve statistical information on social protection (for monitoring of social protection strategy impacts), and

(iii) allow comparisons between countries and over time with view to implementation of social protection measures.

Development of Rural Roads and Markets

In Bangladesh, more than 75 per cent of the population reside in the rural areas and nearly half of them live below the poverty line. Almost one third of Bangladesh's GDP still originates in agriculture. Even the most optimistic scenario of the growth of urban manufacturing and other components of the urban economy seems unlikely to make a dent in near future on the existing widespread levels of unemployment and poverty. In the urban areas, where population has been growing at more than 3 per cent rate, the municipal services are already overstretched and delivery of basic amenities grossly inadequate.

A concern with poverty amelioration in Bangladesh, therefore, necessarily has to come to terms with some notion on the strategy of rural development. Given the dominance of agriculture in the rural economy of Bangladesh, growth of agriculture will have to play a critical role in accelerating rural development. However, the slowdown of agricultural growth throughout the eighties and early nineties coupled with the declining trend in factor productivity with respect to modern inputs such as fertilizer and irrigation suggest that technological frontiers in relation to agricultural growth under the present agrarian structure in Bangladesh may have been approached.

Accelerating the growth of agriculture and of the rural economy beyond this point will require better incentives to farmers for diversification of agriculture, increasing cropping intensity and raising productivity in non-crop production. Diversification of the overall rural economy and in particular the development of the rural non-farm sector appear, at this stage, to be sensible poverty alleviation strategies for Bangladesh.

Developments of the agricultural sector and rural non-farm activities are inextricably linked with the state of trade and transport infrastructure in the rural areas. A critical component of the trade network of Bangladesh is the set of some 2100 local assembly and secondary markets, which are the principal centres for assembly, wholesale and retail transactions of agricultural and non-agricultural goods and services in the rural areas. These markets are labelled as growth centre markets, as they are the nerve centres of rural areas and their development is likely to stimulate growth of the rural economy. As of now, most of them have deplorable infrastructure situation.

Common facilities such as paved walkways, interior roads, market yards, sales platforms and covered sheds used by the vendors etc are extremely poor. Supply of clean water, garbage disposal, drainage etc are virtually nonexistent resulting in high levels of spoilage. These secondary markets are connected with the regional and national arterial road network and with the headquarters of the lowest tier of the administrative unit called upazila (sub-district) through Feeder Roads Type B (FRBs). The poor state of the growth center markets and the FRBs suggest that the rural economy is likely to get a major stimulus if these markets are developed and are made accessible year-round through well-designed and well-maintained, improved FRBs.

In 1984, the Government of Bangladesh (GOB) spelled out its "Strategy for Rural Development" that had the objective of improving the quality of life of rural people. The Strategy was based on focussing developmental resources on physical infrastructure covering roads, markets, storage facilities, electricity, minor irrigation etc. The Strategy, has since then, provided the framework for considerable investment by the government and the funding agencies under a series of projects known as Rural Development Projects (RDPs).

Improvements of rural roads and trading infrastructures are expected to have wide-ranging social and economic impacts. The immediate effect of road improvement is felt on the transport sector. Development of earthen roads into paved roads improves pliability, particularly during the rainy seasons. This reduces transport cost of existing modes. Better pliability also facilitates use of mechanized means of transport, which further contributes towards reduction in transport cost.

The impact is also likely to be reflected in increase in the volume of traffic, freight and passenger, reduction in seasonal variations in traffic flows, changes in freight composition and changes in the pattern of ownership in the transport sector. Improvements in trade and transport infrastructure are likely to induce mutually reinforcing changes in the trade sector. Development of road is likely to lead to setting up of new shops and markets along roadside and in the vicinity of the improved roads.

Apart from this locational spread of markets there would also be increase in the size of the markets in terms of the number of buyers and sellers and turnover-leading to rise in toll revenue, changes in the composition of goods and services traded, and changes in the level of prices. Benefits from the improvement to market infrastructure would include (i) reductions in spoilage and congestion losses to traders operating in the common areas; (ii) reduced transport cost from improved circulation and parking patterns within the market area, which would benefit transporters and business located outside as well as in side the common area; (iii) health benefits from more reliable supplies of clean water, improved sanitation and drainage in the markets.

Road improvements and the consequent changes in the transport sector are likely to facilitate improvements in the institutional service sector. Major components of this sector are (i) health and family planning institutions, (ii) educational institutions, (iii) financial institutions and (iv) extension services. Apart from the likely impact of increase in the number of these institutions, both the volume and quality of service are likely to go up as a result of improvements in roads and transportation.

In the case educational institutions, favourable effects are expected with respect to the level of enrollment, attendance and dropouts. Agricultural and Non-agricultural Production Sectors Improvement in transportation facility and the concomitant reduction in transport cost transmit positive impact all around the rural economy.

Improved roads and markets will improve the availability and access to inputs at lower costs. This will raise the level of input use and thereby raise production.

Thus, for example, fertilizer used by farmers in the remote areas in Bangladesh is often sub-optimal.due to high price and procurement difficulties. Improvements of trade and transport infrastructure are likely to facilitate higher use of fertilizer in these cases. Easier access to credit and extension service.

Access to financial institutions and extension services are often restricted due to poor road communication facilities. Relaxation of these restrictions through improvement in road infrastructure is likely to encourage producers to raise investments and adopt better technology, thereby raising the level of productivity. Road improvements help reduce wastage of perishable output by providing quicker means of transport to markets and permanent storage facilities.

Lower cost of transportation and better market infrastructure also provides the producers with higher returns on output. In the case of agriculture, the cost and price incentives will encourage farmers to produce more, which may be effected through various means. One obvious way is to bring new land under cultivation. Existing land endowment and structure of operational holding in Bangladesh, however, seriously restrict the scope of bringing additional land under cultivation.

The alternative for farmers is to introduce new products, reallocate crops, intensify cultivation, and raise productivity through efficient combination of various inputs. Thus, road and market improvements are likely to result in crop diversification, higher cropping intensity and productivity growth in agriculture. The rural economy is also likely to get more diversified through improvements in trade and transport infrastructure. Apart from the direct effects through cost and price incentives, the rural non-farm sector is also likely to get a fillip from increased agricultural production.

With growing volume of agricultural surplus, the need for trade for marketing of the surplus, and transport for carrying the surplus to the market place increases. Further stimuli to trade, transport and service come from consumption demand induced linkages that accompany higher agricultural growth.

Infrastructure improves the production conditions of non-farm self-employment projects by favourably changing the relative prices between input and output. Access to larger markets helps to ease the demand constraint and stimulate new investments. All these factors have positive influence on productivity and profitability of the micro-credit projects.

The faster expansion of new technology associated with road improvements also brings favourable change in the payment system: instead of traditional time-rated labour contract (on a daily basis), piece-rated contract becomes increasingly prominent in the new situation. The hourly return on daily contract is about 57 per cent higher than in case of daily contract calculated on standard eight-hour basis. Increase in wage employment combined with the rise in wage rate leads to higher agricultural wage income aggregated over a year, which helps to raise the living standard in the extreme poor households.

First Rural Roads and Markets Improvement and Maintenance Project-1 (RRMIMP-1)

The project area covered 8 districts from the northwest region of Bangladesh. The project entailed improvement of 47 FRBs covering a length of 500 km out of the approximately 950 km of FRB in the project area by raising the crest width and paving the roads to Herringbone Bond (HBB), Waterbound Macadam (WBM) and, where justified by traffic volume, to Bituminous Carpeting (BC). Actual expenditure on this head was recorded to be about $ 40.0 million or about 42 per cent of the total project cost incurred. Average cost of each FRB improvement thus works out at $ 0.85 million or about Tk. 34 million.

The project was to improve 65 selected growth centres involving covered sheds for sale of perishables, slaughter slabs, sales platforms, internal roads and walkways within the market area and connecting with the main feeder roads serving the market, toilets, garbage pits and a small office for market administration. The actual cost of market development has been about $ 4.52 million. Average cost of each market improvement is thus estimated to be about $ 0.07 million or about Tk. 2.78 million.

The physical components of the project also included constructing and upgrading structures on rural roads, rehabilitation of roads and structures damaged by flood and construction of the headquarter building for Local Government Engineering Department (LGED), which is the main government agency for development and maintenance of the rural road network including FRBs. Two important features of the project were its emphasis on (i) improvement of design and construction standards of roads and markets structures, and (ii) developing institutional and financial arrangements to ensure better infrastructure maintenance.

In that pursuit, the project included a design and supervision consultant who would advise on the selection and design of sub-components, prepare proposals for the maintenance system and assist in implementing it, and assist government staff with supervision of works. An important component of RRMIMP-1 was monitoring and evaluation. The broad objective of monitoring and evaluation was to assess the developmental impact of the project and use the experiences gained for improving current and future project design.

An on-going system of monitoring under the name Socio-Economic Monitoring and Evaluation (SEM&E) was put in place to capture the direct effects of roads and market improvements on the transport and trade sectors covering traffic level, modal mix, transport charges, volume of passengers and goods, market size, spoilage, market utilization, toll revenue etc.

The information were to be used to estimate the direct benefits of roads and market improvements in terms of user cost savings, spoilage reduction savings, and employment and income effects. This would also provide the basis for post-project ERR calculations and comparing the same with ERR estimates made at the time of project appraisal. The SEM&E was also expected to shed light on the financial performance of the local government in revenue generation and expenditure for maintenance of rural roads and markets.

Second Rural Roads and Markets Improvement and Maintenance Project (RRMIMP-2)

RRMIMP-1 was scheduled to be completed by June 1996.

But there were some initial delays in appointing supervision consultant and disruptions caused by two major floods. Otherwise, the project progressed smoothly and was completed by June 1997. RRMIMP-1 was somewhat experimental in nature in as much as it involved new systems with regard to construction standards and procedure, and enhancing the capacity of LGED, local consultants and contractors in planning and implementing rural infrastructure projects on a sustainable basis.

The project was highly successful in achieving all its physical and most of its institutional objectives within the original cost estimates. The project thus provided the basis for replicating rural infrastructure development projects nationally, building on the experiences gained. Accordingly the Second Rural Roads and Markets Improvement and Maintenance Project (RRMIMP-2) was designed and put into implementation in 1996 as a follow up to continue the earlier program.

Upgradation and improvement of about 69 FRBs covering a length of approximately 575 km in the project area with small bridges, culverts, and tree planting alongside the roads. It also includes bridges and culverts on other FRB roads not selected for full improvement. Total budget allocated for this component was $ 58.6 million or about 44 per cent of the total project cost. Cost per FRB thus work out at 0.85 million, which is the same amount allocated per FRB in the earlier project.

Improvement of 136 growth center markets and 14 Union Parishad center markets in the project area in the same manner as was done in the earlier project. Budgetary allocation for this item is $ 10.69 or about 8 per cent of total project cost. Thus, share of market improvement in total project cost is nearly double of that in the earlier project mainly because of the doubling of the number of markets undertaken for improvement.

The successful implementation of RRMIMP-1 demonstrated the advantage of integrating road development with market development. In the new project, this idea was extended one step further by integrating inland water transport with the other two infrastructure development efforts. In particular, the project involved rehabilitation/construction of 41 priority river jetties or ghats in the project area, to improve landing/unloading facilities for country boats. Total amount allocated for this item was $2 million or about 1.5 per cent of the total project cost.

Accordingly, RRMIMP-2 provided for the construction of about 6000 culverts and small 31,600 linear bridges on existing rural roads of R1 and R2 types. Nearly 41 per cent of the total project cost or about $55.08 million has been allocated for this purpose. This.is a significant increase from 5 per cent of the total project cost allocated to this item in RRMIMP-1.

One of the distinctive features of RRMIMP-2 is its use of participatory approach in the selection, design and implementation of the various components of the project. Locations of main project components, such as, FRBs, river jetties, markets etc have been selected using active involvement of stakeholders including Union Parishad members, NGOs, and beneficiaries. Road designs are to take into consideration preferences and concerns of road users particularly the non-motorized transport operators who use these roads most intensively.

Road Users Committee consisting of various categories of road users will be involved in setting priorities for the development and maintenance of the road network. Similarly, in the case of growth center markets, the design and layout facilities are to be done in meetings with poor vendors and others who would be the main users of the market facilities.

One of the key concerns of the project is to build an adequate maintenance management system for rural infrastructure. It is important for the sustainability and ownership that the local government resources for infrastructure maintenance should progressively increase. The project will seek to do this through measures to enhance resource base of Union Parishad.

Accordingly, the project puts emphasis on better market management through user participation particularly in matters of lease auctioning. Similar systems would also be developed for river jetties under the project. The project would also complement existing best practice for maintenance, such as Rural Maintenance Program funded by CIDA/CARE. Under this arrangement, groups of disadvantaged women would be contracted to plant and take care of the trees along side FRBs and to carry out routine maintenance of the embankment slopes and earth shoulders.

The project will also aim at institutional and human resource development for increasing and strengthening managerial and technical capacity of LGED, local government agencies and the local construction industry. A sum of $ 3.54 million, i.e., 2.7 per cent of the total project cost has been earmarked for the purpose.

The project aims at maximizing employment and poverty alleviation impact by using labour intensive technology wherever viable and target the poor for receiving income-generating opportunities under the project. Use of destitute women in road maintenance is a case in point.

2

Globalisation and Social Development

In South Asia 'official' development strategies have embraced 'globalisation'. They emphasise 'opening up' of domestic economies to the global economy through liberalisation of trade and investment regimes, deregulation of domestic markets, privatisation of state enterprises and the pivotal role of the private sector in the economic growth process. This is an almost complete reversal of the dominant policy stance of the 1970s: import substitution industrialisation (ISI) strategy was thought to hold the key to rapid economic development and industrialisation, and protectionism and pervasive state intervention in the domestic economy were the order of the day.

The economic, political and social implications of this shift in development strategy will have profound implications not only for this region but also for the neighbouring regions and indeed for the entire world. After all, South Asia, united by shared culture and history, and divided by contested state boundaries that pit two nuclear powers against each other, and by religion, language, ethnicity, caste, class and a myriad other divisions, is home to more than a fifth of the world's population and a third of the world's poor.

Despite their many differences, South Asian countries have tended to follow broadly similar trajectories in their post-independence development strategies. They inherited relatively open 'liberal' economic regimes from British colonial rule, moved to progressively more stringent dirigiste policies and then to the current phase of "opening up" and "liberalisation". Though the many major differences among them preclude any simple generalisations on a topic as broad as globalisation, equity and poverty, there is merit in highlighting some features of the experience of particular countries of South Asia and placing them in a comparative and regional context.

Though South Asia in recent times developed reputation for resolutely and stubbornly resisting the opening up their economies to freer international trade, historically it has been a major participant in international trade for several millennia. It was their position in world trade that initially attracted the first of the 'modern' western colonial powers, starting with the Portuguese in the late 15 century.

But, trade had only a marginal impact on much of its economic structure and, by and large, did not disturb the established structures in the basic patterns of production and consumption remained until it was drawn into the emerging global capitalist system as part of the British Empire. The British colonial administration 'opened up' South Asia to the free flow of goods and capital with Britain.

In the region's historical memory, this exposure of South Asia to 19 century 'globalisation' is associated with outcomes like the flow of cheap British textiles to India that ruined the Indian cotton textile industry and the 'grabbing' and opening up of the forests of Sri Lanka (Ceylon) for the plantations. These not only had profound economic consequences but also gave birth to the nationalistic ideology that inspired the independence movements against colonial rule.

This early experience with foreign imposed globalisation, or more correctly, particular interpretations of that experience, continues to colour the attitudes of many South Asians today even as the region moves to grapple with the challenges of the new wave of globalisation. The nationalists, not surprisingly, viewed the opening up of the national economies of South Asia to the world economy as a tool and a mechanism for the subjugation and exploitation of the colonial nations.

The impact of British rule was seen primarily as destructive, replacing a prosperous pre-exiting social order, immiserising the country, and only benefiting a small privileged local elite. This was an oversimplified and partial view but one that helped energise the population in the struggle for independence. Certainly the early years of British rule in particular were characterised by violent repression of any challenge to their rule, taxes that burdened an already impoverished peasantry, neglect of agricultural infrastructure (such as irrigation facilities) and the decline of traditional industries unable to compete with cheap imports from Britain.

Most peasants, particularly those cultivating food grains, remained mired in chronic poverty and vulnerable to famines and near-famine conditions throughout the period of British rule. However, once British rule had been consolidated, a centralised administrative system set in place, physical infrastructure in the form of ports, road and rail networks and postal and telegraphic communications systems was developed and helped also by significant inflows of capital, an economic growth process was initiated.

From the second quarter of the 19 century to the start of the first world war, growth rates in India and Sri Lanka matched that in Britain, and significantly raised average per capita income. India's per capita income increased on average by about 0.6 percent per year during 1868-1898, rising to 1.24 percent per year during 1900-1914. Population growth rate increased from around 0.4-0.5% to 1.2 % in the post-war period. These benefits were not uniformly distributed. Regions and groups that possessed the right kind of skills and resources to exploit the new commercial opportunities did better; for example, locations where climatic conditions suited the new commercial crops prospered more than others.

As a common British administration facilitated relatively free movement of labour throughout South Asia, large numbers of Indian workers came to work in Sri Lankan plantations, making a critical contribution to the massive expansion of that sector. A large segment of the population, including those peasants who were able to take up or gain employment in cash crop agriculture and related activities probably experienced a significant improvement in the living conditions.

More importantly, by challenging (even if not overthrowing) long established caste and gender relations, the penetration of capitalist relations through the South Asian region opened up new horizons to millions who had for millennia lived at the bottom of the social and economic ladder. The eruption of the First World War ended this first phase of globalisation and the interwar years generated considerable economic distress throughout South Asia.

Integration into the global economy meant that the South Asian economies were no longer insulated from the major ups and downs of the world economy. Economic growth slowed down and average annual per capita incomes at best stagnated. The Second World War, the difficult struggle for independence, the catastrophic famine of 1943 and the political disruption caused by the partition and its bloody aftermath left bitter memories of the last years of British rule.

However, at independence South Asia was not by any means an economic basket case. The moderate nationalists who came to power throughout the region inherited functioning capitalist market economies, though many of the market institutions were weak. In per capita income terms it was not far behind most Southeast and East Asian economies.

South Asia was an important part of the global trading system and trade played an important role in the domestic economies - India, with its large economy and extensive subsistence agriculture had a trade to GDP ratio around 15% while for Sri Lanka, with a 'classic' commodity export economy, this was over 70% of GDP. Over the next two decades, a period of rapid and sustained growth of the global economy associated with even faster growth in international trade, South Asia gradually turned its back on the world trading system, erecting barriers to both international trade and investment and increasingly turning to state controls and centralised planning to 'guide' the development process towards industrialisation and growth.

Both balance of payments difficulties and ideological commitment to import substitution contributed to this policy shift. There were episodic attempts at liberalisation in the following years, but they were partial, half hearted and short-lived. By the mid-1970s the region had been reduced to a bit-player in the global trading system, with a near negligible share of global trade; India's share in world trade in the 1970s was half that of the 1950 share.

South Asia came to represent heavy protectionism, state controls and the slow 'Hindu' rate of growth. Despite quite high levels of investment, with Sri Lanka a notable exception, South Asia under-invested in human capital, particularly in education, and a large proportion of the population, particularly females, did not even gain access to basic literacy skills. Change began in the late 1970s. Relatively slow growth, recurrent balance of payments crises, and the example of the high performing East Asian economies contributed an attitudinal shift right across the mainstream political spectrum. This built up a powerful domestic constituency for reforms.

Sri Lanka was the first to undertake a decisive break with the dominant paradigm, embracing liberalisation in 1977/78, and the 1980s saw Bangladesh, Nepal and Pakistan all move towards more liberal policies. India, confronted with a major balance of payments crisis in 1991, finally joined the reform process in the early 1990s. At present the liberalisation process in South Asia is seemingly irreversible. Since the first reforms started in the 1970s, real per capita incomes in the region have grown substantially though at different rates; inter-country income disparities in incomes have widened over time.

It must be appreciated that the liberalisation process in South Asia remains limited and partial in nature - though extensive and radical in comparison with the previous policy regimes. Generally it has been a rather protracted process, with episodes of radical reforms, though late starters (like India) have tended to move faster. By the mid to late 1990s, these economies still had a considerable distance to go to become fully open economies.

When economies have been insulated for long periods of time, domestic and international markets do not become integrated overnight even if all policy barriers are removed, and certainly not when liberalisation is limited and partial. For example, despite significant progress with trade liberalisation throughout the region, domestic market imperfections have hindered integration of domestic markets with international markets.

This is even truer with respect to capital movements and hampered by continuing restrictions on capital movements, perceived high risk and the underdeveloped state of financial institutions, portfolio capital flows in particular have been discouraged. As many restrictions on FDI have been lifted and progress made with privatisation of utilities and other state economic enterprises, FDI flows have picked up in recent years. But, overall capital inflows are well below those into China and many East and Southeast Asian countries.

FDI flows into South Asia are still rather small also in terms of their significance relative to the size of the domestic economy and level of total investment. South

Asian economies are yet to be exposed to the broader currents of globalisation through international capital flows like the East and Southeast Asian countries. It is important to bear in mind that this region's recent experience with globalisation is both rather brief and limited in scope, and conclusions about the links between globalisation and equity/poverty outcomes must be drawn with much caution and care.

Further, the liberalisation measures themselves have been only a component part of broader economic policy packages implemented by governments responding to a variety of political pressures and driven by a range of motives. All this means that observed outcomes should not be directly or fully attributed to the liberalisation measures or to the globalisation process and simple pre- and post- liberalisation comparisons in particular may be quite misleading in identifying cause and effect or the likely impact of more extensive globalisation.

Given the many factors that can affect growth performance, this is not an issue that can be settled by looking at relatively short term growth outcomes, nevertheless such comparisons may still be suggestive of longer term trends. Actually, the higher growth performance of South Asia during the post-1980 as a whole tells us nothing about the impact of globalisation on growth. South Asia's average per capita growth rate during 1980-2000 was certainly significantly higher than that during the previous two decades.

As with all averages for south Asia, this figure is strongly driven by the rapid growth rate achieved by the dominant economy of the region, India, during this period, but the picture of a generally superior post-1980 growth performance is largely true for the other countries of the region too. The liberalisation process had in fact started before 1980 in some countries but serious liberalisation in India - the country that really matters for region-wide averages - started only after 1991. The average for the 1980-2000 is the average of less than a decade of liberalisation; the high average simply reflected the fact the 1980s, prior to liberalisation, was also a period of high growth for India.

India's post-liberalisation growth performance - now over a decade old - has been quite outstanding, particularly given the impact of the global slowdown in the aftermath of the 1997 Asian economic crisis, placing it among the top ten fastest growing economies in the world. But simple comparison of growth rates between 1980 and 1990 shows only a marginal difference in performance. This highlights the need to take a long term view of the impact of liberalisation and associated globalisation. The precise domestic and external circumstances, both before and after liberalisation, determine the immediate growth path.

Though the analytical problems of isolating the role of particular variables to go beyond mere growth-liberalisation correlations are formidable, as the huge literature on this topic attests, liberalisation must be judged on the extent to which it raises the sustainable level of longer term growth. The key point to take note of about the Indian growth performance of the 1980s is, as Ahluwalia points out, that it was simply unsustainable, fuelled by a build up of external debt that culminated in a balance of payments crisis in 1991.

Often, but not always, liberalisation is a response to an economy sliding into a serious crisis as was, for example, the case with India in 1991. On the other hand,

Sri Lanka's 1977/78 liberalisation was done when the country was in a very strong economic position, with high foreign reserves and low foreign debt that gave the government confidence to liberalise because it could handle the expected import boom following liberalisation even if foreign back up support was not forthcoming.

Most economies, despite some limited liberalisation during the 1970s or 1980s, really were still 'more closed than open'. For example, Sri Lanka did implement major. liberalisation in 1977/78, but it was in the 1990s, following the so-called 'second wave" of reforms that the economy really opened up to levels approaching those of Southeast Asia. Given this staggered timing, slow pace and limited scope of reforms, it is perhaps only the 1990s that can provide some reasonable indications as to how liberalisation may be affecting other economic variables.

The experience of the 1980s has been encouraging in general, with India's experience standing out. This growth also seems underpinned by stronger foundations that provide more resilience to withstand shocks and capacity for more sustainable long term growth. But, on the other hand, as the late 1990s experience of Pakistan - which had also implemented significant though partial liberalisation - and that of many other countries both in South Asia and outside shows, liberalisation reforms by themselves do not guarantee either continuing high growth or stability.

Arguably, the experience of South Asia, taken by it self, is still too short and too mixed, to assert that globalisation definitely accelerates growth. But, most South Asian analysts familiar with the complex economic and political history of the region will need a lot of convincing that the region would have performed better in the 1990s or will do better in the future with less openness to the world.

When the South Asian liberalisation experience is considered in conjunction with the longer experience of China and East Asia, it is difficult to argue convincingly that rapid and long term sustainable growth is possible in the contemporary world without participating actively in the global economy.

For most scholars and policy makers, the issue that confronts the region seems to be how to open up and exploit the growth opportunities while ensuring that other social objectives - in particular poverty alleviation and maintenance of social and national cohesion - are not undermined. Understandably, in this region with the world's largest concentration of poor and subject to much political volatility, reports of China's alarmingly rapid increase in post-liberalisation inequality and reports of rising social tensions ring alarm bells.

Trends in Poverty and Equity

Identifying trends in poverty and equity and establishing causal links between them and policy changes when many aspects of the general environment are changing is not an easy task. As is well known, measurement of poverty raises complex conceptual and methodological problems in both definition and measurement. The simplest measures of poverty with commonsense appeal are based on incomes.

But even if poverty is defined narrowly as a person's inability to obtain certain minimum levels of consumption of goods and services, income is often not a reliable predictor of a person's true capacity to command a marketed bundle of goods and services. Economists usually prefer consumption or expenditure to income as a more reliable indicator of poverty, on the basis that economic agents smooth consumption over time in line with their overall net wealth position; hence consumption tends to be more stable than income and a better indicator of household wealth but often such data series do not go far back in time for meaningful comparisons over time.

This is a major problem in every South Asian country, including India, which has the best data series among them. But even when the required income data are there, they provide at best only a partial picture of poverty and equity. Because low incomes are often correlated with poverty, using income is often taken as a reasonable indicator of poverty, though it is recognised that other factors associated with poverty (access to literacy and education, health services, absence of various forms of discrimination, even political freedoms) must also be taken into account when assessing the level or intensity of poverty and its changes over time.

Unfortunately, the many attributes of poverty or welfare cannot be satisfactorily aggregated into a single quantifiable indicator. Hence attempts to look at poverty over time with a broader definition of poverty confront even greater data and measurement problems. We will now turn to examine the evidence on poverty and inequality in the post-reform periods in South Asia.

Nevertheless, though the country experiences have been diverse, the data do point to some important common trends during the 1980s and 1990s. First, the headcount poverty - typically considerably higher in rural areas compared to urban areas - has fallen significantly during the 1990s in India - the largest economy with the most poor but the picture is mixed elsewhere in South Asia. There has been considerable concern that poverty was not falling in India after liberalisation despite growth - the 1993/94 estimates of poverty were not much different to those of the 1980s.

Bangadesh follows a rather similar pattern, with a significant fall in income poverty since the early 1980s, but poverty reduction since then has been modest. On the other hand, it has been quite successful in terms of improving broader human development indicators. Significant declines in fertility, lower infant and child mortality, reduced child malnutrition, improved literacy and primary education have been major achievements.

In Pakistan, there is at best only a minor decline in poverty rate during the 1990s; indeed, it appears that poverty actually increased in the latter half of the 1990s when the economy slowed down sharply.

Nepal too poverty appears to have worsened in the early 1990s and may well have increased further in the latter half. There are two issues of importance when looking at the poverty-growth link. One is whether growth reduces poverty, and the other is the extent to which it does so. When the trends in poverty reduction are linked to per capita growth rates of the economies, there is a reasonably clear evidence of a negative growth-poverty link, though of course the growth rate is not the only determinant of poverty reduction.

Similarly, growth continues to have a poverty reducing impact in the 1990s, suggesting that liberalisation has not fundamentally altered the nature of the growth-poverty link. But on the second issue, there are serious grounds for concern. India's growth in particular seems to be relatively less effective in reducing poverty than has been the case in other parts of Asia.

Warr has examined the degree to which growth in India has been poverty reducing, compared with that in a group of East and Southeast Asian economies. The estimated growth elasticities of aggregate poverty suggest that though growth does reduce poverty in India, its impact is much weaker than in the more open economies of Indonesia, Malaysia, Thailand and Taiwan; only the Philippines had a comparable (low) elasticity.While the results are subject to several qualifications, it is difficult to avoid being struck by the remarkably close association between the degree of openness of the country and the growth elasticity of poverty: more open economies appear to have more, rather than less, pro-poor growth.

The resulting impact was anti-labour - the single most important resource owned by the poor. There is supporting evidence at a sectoral level for this view from both Bangladesh and Sri Lanka where more open trade regimes, in combination with a more pro-FDI stance, attracted foreign investors and fuelled rapid growth in the export-oriented labour intensive garments manufacturing industries. As a result of the large expansion of these industries, both manufacturing exports and employment grew rapidly and helped maintain employment and wages levels at a time of considerable economic difficulties.

This experience highlights the complementary role of investment liberalisation for exploiting the potential gains from trade liberalisation: it was the combined trade and investment liberalisation that proved critical as either of these alone would not have produced a similar outcome. Another aspect of globalisation that has probably had a large impact on employment, and thereby on poverty, is the opening up of an international market for relatively unskilled labour, initially in the Middle East and more recently also in East Asia.

The role of domestic policy liberalisation in this case has been to ease the barriers on international travel and payments. The extensive participation of females in the migrant labour market has also had a large social impact through its impact on intra-family relations. In summary, the evidence seems strong that growth associated with liberalisation has been poverty reducing. But its effectiveness, particularly in India, seems to be less effective than in other parts of Asia and may be related to its more restrictive policies.

Deeper and more extensive reforms - in terms of faster trade liberalisation coupled with investment liberalisation - may produce growth with a greater pro-poor bias. In India (as well as in other parts of South Asia) increasing inequality in urban areas is quite visible and this moderated the decline in the urban poverty rate in response to growth; Deaton and Dreze point out that this effect is particularly pronounced in some Indian states, such as Kerala and Madhya Pradesh.

Overall, in India, if there had been no change in inequality, the head count ratio in 1999-2000 would have been 1.3 percent lower. In Bangladesh, if inequality had not worsened, poverty would have fallen at 17%, nearly twice the rate it actually did.The combination of rising inequality in urban areas and faster growth in incomes - again a common phenomenon throughout the region - is widening the urban-rural income gaps.

Regional (inter provincial and inter state) or spatial inequality too is widening throughout South Asia, often aggravating pre-existing income differences, paralleling trends seen in China that are causing much concern.The importance of ethnic, religious, caste and other divisions in South Asia implies that trends in inequality across these dimensions are also of concern.

Though the evidence is not strong that increased inequality is an direct and immediate cause precipitating conflict, poverty-related factors are often an underlying factor. Sometimes these divisions have a distinctly spatial dimension and, to that extent, widening regional disparities are relevant. They are also linked to differences in human skill attainments and endowments; education in particular is a major determinant of who benefits from post-liberalisation growth.

With respect to caste, there can be little doubt that economic changes that have undermined traditional society in India have increased the political power of traditionally depressed castes. The immediate impact of liberalisation on caste related inequality also often reflects access to human capital and marketable skills.

Datt and Ravallaion attribute the lower rate of overall reduction in poverty that is observed in the nineties to the sectoral and geographical pattern of growth that favours states with better initial conditions; states with low levels of initial rural development and human capital development were not well suited to reduce poverty in response to economic growth. This importance of human capital as a factor in widening inequality in the post-liberalisation conditions is also seen elsewhere.

For example, in Sri Lanka the 'estates' sector, which has poor human capital, appears to have experienced widening inequality and possibly rising poverty in the nineties. An important aspect of equity, particularly relevant to South Asia, is the impact of liberalisation on gender equity. The evidence on this issue is sketchy but improvements in literacy, life expectancy and overall mobility observed through most parts of South Asia are indicative of improvements, at least across some dimensions.

Where labour demand for female labour has increased substantially in some parts of South Asia, as in the case of Bangladesh and Sri Lanka with the expansion of the garments industry and access to overseas employment opportunities, there is potential for improved gender equality in incomes as well as other social dimensions affecting social relations.

On the other hand, women may now have to carry a double burden, be a bread winner at the same time as they also do the bulk of household work and care giving. Deaton and Dreze point to another issue of concern in India: with access to pre-natal sex-determination technology and sex-selective abortions, female - male ratios among children appear to have declined and this is not merely a technological phenomenon.

The overall outcomes of liberalisation and associated globalisation on these and other social inequalities will be affected by access to human capital and market opportunities but will be mediated through prevailing attitudes and preferences. The latter are of course themselves subject to change through exposure to global currents of thought and value systems. It seems difficult to assert in any case that liberalisation and globalisation have had or are bound to have only a negative impact.

Recent changes in poverty and inequality in south Asia have several common features. Growth associated with liberalisation has tended to reduce consumption poverty and often improve broader dimensions of human development. However, though inequality has not increased in any dramatic way, there are signs that across several dimensions - spatial, urban-rural etc. - inequality is increasing.

But to what extent these increases in inequality should be attributed to liberalisation, what are the long term dynamics related to growth and shorter term impacts related to stabilisation and adjustment policies, and what the counterfactual scenario would have been, is not always clear. Despite the large and growing literature on the distributional outcomes of liberalisation, there are both theoretical and empirical problems in ascertaining the relative contributions of liberalisation/globalisation and other exogenous factors to the observed patterns of change.

At the simplest level, based on some form of appeal to the basic intuition underlying the Stolper-Samuelson theorem, it is suggested that a shift to patterns of economic growth based on comparative advantage - which in the case of South Asia broadly lies in low-skilled labour intensive activities - is likely to improve distributional outcomes through its impact on relatively labour-biased factor demands.

On the other hand, it is undeniable that past patterns of educational investments that created a large pool of highly skilled labour (co-existing with the largest mass of illiterate people in the world) have been instrumental in India's dramatic successes in the skill-intensive software and broader information technology sectors.

Other distributional outcomes such as regional and spatial disparities in growth may not only reflect past urban-bias in government policies but also, and perhaps even more so, the dynamics of agglomeration forces given freer rein in more liberalised economies. But there is no persuasive case for arguing that overall, globalisation has been bad for the poor; indeed, more extensive globalisation may have had an overall positive effect on labour employment and incomes, and thereby on the poor.

But the evidence about increasing inequality is of concern. How can South Asia manage the opportunities and risks of globalisation without jeopardising social and political stability? Liberalisation reforms are unavoidably accompanied by profound distributional changes. Even when reforms lead to faster growth and higher average incomes, these gains from reforms are not distributed equally.

Indeed, often there will be, at least in the short-term, significant losers. Such transitions from rigid, insular, state-dominated economies to deregulated market economies can lead to major changes in not only actual inequality but also in perceived inequality, with perceptions magnifying changes in expected gains and losses.

Policy and institutional reforms have profound effects on the underlying determinants of asset returns (through the revaluation of skills and other human capital, social capital embodied in various networks, such as ethnic and religious networks, as well as physical capital) so the net wealth positions of households and individuals are redefined. These actual or potential distributional changes can be a potent source of social and political conflict.

Such conflicts often develop along existing social 'fault lines' - class, ethnic, religious and regional - particularly if liberalisation does not quickly generate a rapid expansion of the total economic pie. However, the social impact of policy reforms is not confined to this impact on wealth and on inequalities. It also creates new opportunities for rent extraction through access to political power and regulatory institutions and can change the scale of potential gains.

The extent to which such rents can be appropriated depends on specificities of the political and social environment. Again the experience of South Asia appears to increasingly move in the direction of the ex-planned economies, including China, where rampant corruption is aggravating social dissatisfaction with rising inequality. In a region as politically volatile as South Asia, the distributional issues cannot be lightly dismissed on the grounds that greater labour mobility and lower absolute poverty will make these changes acceptable.

Public action that enhanced human development through high levels of investment in social sectors created the basis for exploiting the huge opportunities that arose in the global trading system from the 1950s. But the turn away from openness ultimately led Sri Lanka to being left behind in both economic growth and human development by the dynamic East Asians who, coming from behind, surged ahead.

With slow growth, Sri Lanka was unable to maintain the investments in human capital, to undertake needed investments in other public goods, and to satisfy the aspirations of educated youth and the country descended into economic, political and social crisis. Social expenditures were replaced by military expenditures as violent conflict ended the peace and tranquillity that had seen as the hallmark of Sri Lanka.

As Brtuton pointed out, "if Sri Lanka had done nothing different except abolish food subsidies, the consequence would have been that a large share of the population would have been hungry, not that the economy would have grown faster". As South Asia embraces globalisation, at a time when the global economy itself faces challenges to its stability and continuing growth, it must address the underling causes of rising inequality that are amenable to public action.

The newly demonstrated capacity of the international private sector to provide the needed investments and services in a whole range of sectors critical to development, such as the information technology and telecommunications sectors, means that areas requiring public action can be narrowed down and scarce resources concentrated for optimum effect.

Development of Social Capital

There is no universally accepted definition of social capital. In the broadest sense, the term encompasses those social relationships that help people to get along with each other and act more effectively than they could as isolated individuals. In this view, patterns of social organization, especially trust, mutuality, and reciprocity, are seen as important resources, which can result in benefits to individuals, groups, and society. It is in the last-mentioned category, the public-good nature of social capital, that the term has recently engendered a lively discourse in international development circles.

In a narrower, but commonly accepted sense, mutually beneficial cooperative behaviour is the essence of the social capital concept. Social capital is the cumulative capacity of social groups to cooperate and work together for the common good.

Social capital is the trust, reciprocity and mutuality that inheres to social relationships. It accumulates to the extent that members of different social groups can maintain respect for differences and learn to cooperate, especially beyond the family and clan. Trust and mutuality in the sociological sense are often identified as a "moral resource."

Social capital is best understood as the institutional dimension of transactions, markets and contracts. It determines the ways in which reliable, stable relationships and shared information among actors can enhance the effectiveness and efficiency of both collective and individual interests. It is especially relevant to market imperfections where public goods are involved. "Trust" is defined formally as expectation about the actions of others that have a bearing on one's own choice of action.

It is even claimed that social capital is the "missing link", partly because it adds a new focus to what has become known as "people-centered development", and partly because it can be seen as a complement to the more established capital categories (physical, financial, and human) to explain how development can occur in some situations and not in others.

While social capital is not a tangible resource, it is thought to supplement or catalyze the other types of capitals to produce better outcomes. While some of the current literature evidently applies new terminology to older concepts (community development, social cohesion, cooperatives, local participation), the new importance given to it is considered salutary by bringing social and cultural issues back into the development repertory with a fresh perspective.

It is also useful for bringing economists and other social scientists together for dealing with common or overlapping issues. There are different types and dimensions of social capital and that a single term is inadequate to explain the range of theoretical and empirical situations. One way to classify the conceptual literature is by focusing on the "ownership" or the beneficiaries of social capital.

A well-connected person, especially one of high status, is seen as having more of it, by converting these relationships to value to himself/ herself. The importance of "networking" is recognized by organization theory scholars as a way to get ahead in politics and corporations. A crucial component of this form of social capital is access to information and hence the importance of education and communication to marshal knowledge as a personal resource.

As currently used, social capital is the trust, reciprocity, and norms and networks of civic engagement in a society that facilitate coordinated action to achieve desired goals. Obviously, social capital is rooted in history, tradition, and culture. Unlike human capital or physical capital, social capital is relational and embedded in social structure. If we live in a community with an active neighbourhood watch in which neighbours patrol and trust one another, we benefit irrespective of our individual trustworthiness and participation in the neighbourhood watch patrols.

Because of this public-good characteristic, social capital is said to be undervalued, does not attract private investment and is often a by-product of other activities. When people in groups or communities have repeated interactions, feel solidarity, and trust one another, the costs of completing a transaction are lower than when people are afraid that their trust will be violated and rights trod upon.

It is trust that leads to voluntary collaboration to overcome collective action dilemmas. The worldwide success of indigenous rotating-credit societies, collaboration to manage common pool resources, and various arrangements among poor farmers and small firms to share labour and tools, are manifestations of social capital as a productive asset.

Social trust, norms of reciprocity networks of civic engagement and successful cooperation are mutually reinforcing. Effective collaboration institutions require interpersonal skills and trust, but those skills and that trust are also inculcated and reinforced by organized collaborations. While the measure of multiple associations has been accepted by many scholars as an indication of social capital, he has been criticized for uncertain causality, for not sufficiently distinguishing the negative as well as positive uses to which associations can be put, and for underestimating the role of the larger political setting for the presence or absence of local "civicness."

Social capital can be understood in terms of two distinguishable but interrelated categories: structural and cognitive. This separation is as fundamental for social capital as the distinction between renewable and nonrenewable resources is for natural capital. The structural category, broadly speaking, is associated with social organization of various kinds and particularly with roles and rules, while the cognitive category is based on mental processes and psychology in the domain of ideas and includes particularly norms, values, attitudes, and beliefs.

The first domain is more visible and external, and the second is more invisible and interior. But both concurrently affect the behaviour of persons, individually and in smaller or larger groups. Socially agreed and enforceable roles and rules within various social structures are the mechanisms by which social capital is built up and accumulated- stored, modified, expressed, and perpetuated. These two categories of social capital are highly interdependent.

Each contributes to the other, with both affecting behaviour through the mechanism of expectations. Operationally, the major difference is that cognitive social capital is very hard to change by deliberate interventions, since it represents an historic accumulation through cultural norms while some of the structural aspects manifest in different kinds of specific organizations, such as users' associations, can be influenced by investment incentives and policies in the medium run.

While all groups require some degree of social capital to operate, some groups build bonds of trust outside of their membership, thereby creating positive externalities. Whether the impetus has come via structural or cognitive causes, social capital evolves into the shared knowledge, understandings, and patterns of interactions that a group of individuals adopts in dealing with each other. They can be far more productive with whatever physical and human capital they draw on, if they can agree on a broad form of coordination and commit themselves credibly to a sequence of future actions. This agreement can be based on mutual learning about how to work better together.

Another useful distinction is to separate social relations within communities and groups of similar cultural background and status from extra-community ties between dissimilar individuals and groups. Much of the literature and the empirical evidence on social capital focuses on the community or "grassroots" level, where the social relationships among people with common neighbourhood, ethnic, religious, or family ties can constitute important sources of security, mutual help, and conviviality.

Traditional rural communities, while very poor, are often well endowed with this type of social capital, either in the whole community or within certain social subgroups. The worst cases of the absence of even minimal social capital are identified as "amoral individualism". It exists where there is neither familial nor generalized trust, and where self-interest literally permeates all activity. .

Economic groups in poor communities need to forge extra-group linkages so that (i) the economic and noneconomic claims of community members can be resisted when they threaten to undermine the group's economic viability and expansion; (ii) entry to more sophisticated factor and product markets can be secured; and (iii) individuals of superior ability and ambition within the group itself are able to leave and insert themselves into new and more complex social networks.

One of the problems seems to lie in an unquestioned acceptance of the public-good nature of social capital. But in the real world there are enormous asymmetries in access to power, leading to monopolies, oppressions, and exclusions by highly organized groups that in terms of their own membership, can be characterized as possessing a strong social capital stock, but which have negative utility for the broader society. However, empowering poor people by promoting their membership organizations can be seen as a strongly positive social capital accumulation.

An important implication of these concerns for development practitioners is that the social value of associations is not static but can shift over time. The ethnic entrepreneurship literature is a good example of these dynamics. Entry into a given community gives an immigrant access to financial and personal support so that a small business can be started. Lacking material assets (physical capital) and language skills (human capital), the immigrant is able to call upon his social capital to launch a new life.

Social capital in this sense is based on ethnic solidarity. If the business is successful, however, there will come a time when the ethnic community is neither large enough nor heterogeneous enough to provide the product and factor markets necessary for more complex economic exchange. Access to new networks extending beyond the original community is therefore required. In this sense, social capital will expand to extra-ethnic networks. In many Asian countries, ethnic immigrants become so successful that their networks are a source of serious social tensions and conflicts in the society at large, into which there has been inadequate social integration.

This is also evidence that "positive" and "negative" aspects of social capital can coexist. All of this suggests that social capital is open to differing perceptions. Just as with other types of capital, social capital can be put to negative or positive social uses; it has benefits and costs for both the participants and for society at large, and one must carefully consider its externalities when the values to the "insiders" and to the general public welfare diverge.

Economists tend to approach the concept of social capital through the analysis of contracts and transactions. Individuals in neoclassical theory are considered as motivated by self-interest. Economists have problems incorporating into their theories motivations such as friendship, loyalty, and empathy. Political sociologists and anthropologists approach the concept of social capital through analysis of norms, networks within and between social groups, and organizations.

There is emphasis on how these networks and organizations help people gain access to power, decision-making processes, resolve conflicts, and generate a workable system of governance. Individual motivations in the sociological view are not exclusively dominated by self-interest but influenced by social ties and loyalties that exist within a particular social structure.

Sociologists have also related socially determined motivations to human capital. In some cases, the link between social capital and development outcomes is indirect or uncertain. Schools can be built by contractors or by communal self-help. Marketing can be performed by competing private traders or by cooperatives. The success of a large credit union depends as much on professional management as on face-to-face cooperation of members.

While the board is elected by members, the running of the jointly owned enterprise does not require hands-on cooperation by the membership. Policies and the rules governing an organization require member approval, but day-to-day decision making is delegated to management. Unless there is an active volunteer corps, members do not increase their capacity for learning to solve problems jointly.

There are, however, situations where there is a more direct relationship between some forms of social capital and observable outcomes. This is the case in dealing with common property management. If, in an irrigation system, the farmers do not continually cooperate, agree on and enforce rules of mutuality, the water will not flow to all the irrigators; the systems break down due to lack of maintenance and cannot be sustained.

In ecologically fragile environments, if stakeholders cannot agree and accommodate their behaviour, the results are likely to be disastrous to all. In the case of the low-caste flayers in Uttar Pradesh, there is a direct relationship between their organizational efforts and their income. Inputs and observable results in these cases are thought of as tightly coupled. This phenomenon is related to what is referred to in the literature as "path dependency", that is, how culturally learned characteristics influence future cooperative possibilities.

Many analysts stress that the interpersonal and intergroup linkages need to be horizontal rather than vertical in order to result in socially desirable benefits. Hierarchical social capital is seen as quite different. While it is also built on norms of reciprocity and mutual trust, those networks are vertical. Traditional patron-client relationships, expressed in feudal tenancy, money lending, political patronage, or mafia protection are of this nature.

Horizontal relations outside those of the influence of the patron are actively discouraged. Dependency and mistrust of outsiders or "others" are generated. The greater the stratification of a society along class, status, and income, the more vertical ties prevail. The pervasive existence and importance of patronclient relations (vertical ties) have been almost unanimously deplored by development planners as an obstacle to more democratic political and economic evolution. But there are also dissenting voices.

For the concept of social capital to be useful analytically and empirically, one can distinguish different breadth and levels of this type of capital. There are six types:

1. Family and kinship connections, relating to the single household, the extended family, and the clan, based on strong ties of blood or ethnicity. Such connections can extend to the village or neighbourhood, in cases of relative homogeneity of culture.

2. Social networks, or associational life, related to groups and organizations that link individuals belonging to different families or kinship groups in common activities for different purposes (economic, social/cultural, political). These probably constitute the form of social capital closest to its more common definition of "networks of civic engagement", linked to the concept of "local or community-level or local interest associations."

3. Cross-sectoral linkages, or "contacts spanning differences in sector and power." These may be

termed "networks of networks" that link together organizations belonging to different sectors of society in the search for solutions to complex problems.

4. Sociopolitical capital, representing relations between civil society and the State, giving a society the capability to mediate conflict by hearing, channelling, and composing multiple citizen demands. Political capital relates to the informal institutional arrangements that may lead, on one hand, to clientelism, rent-seeking, and exclusion, and on the other to effective representation, accountability, and participation.

5. Institutional and policy framework, or the set of formal rules and norms (constitutions, laws, regulations, policies) that regulate public life in a society. This form of social capital has a somewhat double nature, because it can influence the formation of other forms of social capital, and at the same time be a resource that facilitates coordinated action by citizens.

6. Social norms and values, defined by a social group or a nation's shared cultural beliefs (common convictions) and the effects these have on the functioning of society as a whole. These norms and values bear on all other forms of social capital.

Roughly, the first three types can be characterized as operating at the micro level, while the second three can be thought of as macro types of social capital. This kind of typology is also useful to clarify not only the coexistence of different kinds of social capital but also possible substitutions in a dynamic developmental context.

Tribal communities in India, for example, had organized themselves for centuries to derive their food, fodder, tools, and building materials in a sustainable manner from forest lands that they governed and managed as common property. The British government did not recognize community ownership and, in fact, passed legislation during the 1860s to create a Forestry Department and to exert monopoly power over ever-greater territories.

By the time of independence, the Government of India exerted full control over more than 40 percent of the total forested area of India. Similar stripping away of the legitimacy of local institutions occurred throughout Asia, Latin America, and Africa. Work in India has shown that such social capital enhanced the ability of the poor to allocate resources efficiently and increased their resilience to hazards. In exploring the roots and determinants of Hindu and Muslim riots in India, Varshney focused on intercommunal networks. He studied associational forms of engagement and everyday forms of engagement.

It is important to note that the positive relationships between social capital and developmental outcomes are not only the results of social capital by itself, but of its complementarity with other capital investments such as infrastructure or credit. While the term "social capital" has only recently entered the development discourse, there are other terms and concepts already in use that have similar or related meanings.

The closest affinity is with the notion of participation. Both deal with interpersonal and interinstitutional relationships, and both stress the instrumental and intrinsic value of cooperation, mutual accommodation, trust building, and problem resolution. In development practice, beneficiary participation has acquired a wide acceptance as an important strategy to improve project performance and sustainability.

Informal as well as formally constituted user groups promoted through participatory interventions represent both existing and potential endowments of social capital. At the same time, achieving devolution or ownership of development resources and management to beneficiary groups is seen as one of the ultimate goals of participatory strategies. Investing in participation, just as in building and enhancing social capital, has costs and benefits.

Dynamically, participatory processes can lead to accumulation of social capital while social capital builds up and is maintained by participatory activities. In ADB practice and documents, participatory structures or organizations or strong community involvement in project activities convey the existence of social capital. Social capital is also relevant to the concept of civil society, insofar as the latter term refers primarily to relationships between private individuals and to the way private cooperation and associations function, especially in what has come to be called the voluntary sector. The boundaries of civil society are not clear.

Some include all interest groups such as political parties; others restrict the term to civic nonprofit groups. NGOs, when performing public-good functions, can generate social capital (philanthropy, advocacy of social inclusion, or rights of deprived groups). By assisting to mitigate poverty, NGOs can also become key "bridging" institutions in coalitions or part of coproduction partnerships.

Some NGOs are also able to assist in capacity building among the poor, not only enhancing human capital in terms of personal skills but also in building "organizational capacity" among the poorer groups, which is an important form of structural social capital. A vigorous and "dense" civil society is often identified with the existence of high social capital. However, this is not necessarily true.

The State can restrict or facilitate civic associational life. The degree of corruption, the treatment of human rights, and the justice systems all have powerful consequences on the ways social and economic transactions are conducted; they influence the potential level of generalized social capital in a country. Legal institutions and administration of justice have important bearings on generalized trust and social capital.

Some social exclusion theorists even propose that exclusion and negative social capital go together: poverty and social exclusion reflect the success of collective action by rent-seeking groups in a competitive economic and political environment. Some older concepts are now less often heard, but are related to social capital.

A social contract is normally defined as an unwritten political-economic agreement, determining social participation, property rights, and above all, the distribution of wealth and power. If people can forge and sustain a social contract among different, it is said that society's stock of social capital increases. Not unlike other terms in the behavioural sciences, social capital has quickly become embroiled in lively debates over meaning, interpretation, and utility.

The social interactions that result in social capital are reciprocal and regularized in norms of behaviour. Social capital can accumulate as a result of cooperation within a group or as a result of intergroup cooperation. It is believed that intra- and extra-community linkages are mutually reinforcing. The cooperative behavioural characteristics (norms, rules, and values) must be durable or persistent to qualify as a form of capital, as economists use the term.

Social capital is thought to enhance the effect of other types of capital, by making investments more effective; it may induce investments in physical capital or be stored in human capital. How these different "capitals" interrelate is still not clear. Social capital is generally interpreted as referring to social interactions within civil society and between civil society and other agents. Optimality is thought to require certain congruence between micro and macro linkages.

While social capital is often identified as a public good, it can be put to socially positive or negative uses. This makes the social valuation process normative. The tendency is to apply the term to processes and institutions in which the sum of gains and losses to society are positive and where the resulting power and income distributions are more equitable.

In many settings such expectations are unrealistic; hence, efforts at connection and synergy may simply reinforce patronage and clientelism. This balancing is also necessary where positive and negative features coexist in a given setting. While the cognitive forms of social capital (values, culture, beliefs) are historically constructed, and hard as well as slow to change, some of the key structural forms embedded in networks and organizations resulting in collective action may be influenced by development interventions and policy changes over the medium run.

ADB is already dealing with social capital problems under other concepts and titles, especially as a part of "participation." It remains to be seen if adding social capital to the existing terminology would lead to greater understanding and to practical utility for the development profession.

Social Impacts of Environmental Development

South Asia is rich in natural resources. The forests, rivers, lakes, wetlands, coral reefs, and other ecosystems in the region are biological powerhouses. The region includes the second largest rain forest complex, more than half of the world's coral reefs, and about 17 percent of the most important wetland areas in the world. This rich habitat is home to much of the planet's biological diversity. Rivers, coastal and marine fisheries, mangroves, and coral reefs are among the most diverse and productive in the world. Southeast Asia is also the hub of diversity for wild and domestic cereal and fruit species.

The tropical moist forests in Southeast Asia host 20-25 percent of the earth's plant species and the greatest variety of animals. The true value of this biological diversity defies conventional methods of quantification. The region's ecosystems provide services that range from the maintenance of global biogeochemical cycles, to sources of export revenue, and sources of food and income for the poor.

Over the past four decades, the region's rich resources have undergone dramatic changes resulting from accelerated economic and social transformation. Large increases in population, agricultural output, industrial production and capital, and advances in science and technology have transformed the economic foundations of most countries within the region.

Economic change has been supported in part by the region's natural resource base, both as a source of material inputs and a sink for pollution, and other negative outputs from economic activity. Now these processes of development have put the region's unrivaled natural resources at great risk. Environmental degradation in the region is pervasive, accelerating, and unabated. At risk are people's health and livelihoods, the survival of species, and ecosystem services that are the basis for long-term economic development.

Economic development and poverty reduction are increasingly constrained by environmental concerns, including degradation of fisheries and forests, scarcity of freshwater, and poor human health and premature death as a result of air and water pollution. During the 1960s, the economies of most South and Southeast Asia underwent a remarkable transformation that boosted agricultural production and fundamentally changed rural Asia.

Diversification, commercialization, and advances in crop production technology fueled agricultural growth in many of the Asian Development Bank (ADB) developing member countries (DMCs) and were instrumental in reducing poverty in the area. The Green Revolution that began in the late 1960s was a welcome remedy to food shortages and the startling population growth in Asia, Latin America, and Northern Africa.

The remarkable efforts of international agricultural research and extension organizations resulted in new, high-yielding crop varieties and new water and soil conservation techniques. These efforts were followed by investments in rural infrastructure and irrigation, increased inputs such as fertilizers and pesticides, and resulted in the implementation of policies that regulated agricultural trade, commerce, and credit.

Agricultural intensification was just one aspect of an overall economic transformation of developing economies within the region. Even with substantial increases in agricultural productivity, the relative contribution of agriculture to gross domestic product (GDP) actually declined in many DMCs. Industrialization and urbanization also became the dominant forces behind economic growth in the DMCs in Southeast Asia and India.

By the mid-1980s, the flow of international capital and intensified export-oriented trade helped create large urban centers that were commercial, financial, and industrial giants. The region now has nine cities with populations each exceeding 10 million people. The economic transformation has been accompanied by a significant decline in poverty, especially in the high-growth economies of East Asia.

Poverty rates in most East and South Asian countries that benefited from the Green Revolution dropped significantly as a result of higher agricultural productivity and greater urban employment opportunities. In many cases, these changes resulted in higher living standards. Government policies also promoted inappropriate irrigation processes and inadequate drainage systems that resulted in large-scale salinization, water logging, and eutrophication in agro-ecosystems.

Fisheries, the other major food source in the region, are also under tremendous pressure, particularly in rivers, lakes, and coastal areas affected by pollution from land-based activities. Fisheries face serious decline in catch, and poorly conceived aquaculture systems provide examples of some of the region's most spectacular economic and ecological debacles. In most cases, rapid industrialization and urbanization took place without adequate attention to environmental concerns, resulting in massive industrial pollution of the region's air and waterways and escalating demands for energy and other material and resource inputs.

Megacity Management in Asia provides a detailed account of rapid, large-scale urbanization and its environmental consequences. Although cities offer many residents considerable opportunities, for a higher quality of life than rural areas, they are also becoming increasingly unhealthy places because of air and water pollution. Cities are also major consumers of energy and materials. In cities lacking adequate urban infrastructure, major environmental problems emerged in sanitation, water supply, transportation, and waste disposal.

Failure to provide economic opportunity and basic environmental services to urban and rural poor could have destabilizing environmental, political, and economic consequences of global proportions. Environmental degradation especially impacted the poor and undermined to some degree the broad-based social welfare benefits of economic growth. Typically, it is the poor who are most immediately dependent on threatened fisheries, forests, and other natural resource systems for their livelihoods.

The health effects of declining air and water quality especially impact the urban poor who lack access to clean water and adequate sanitation. Also, the poor are often the most vulnerable to natural disasters. Over the past 15 years, and in response to mounting environmental problems, many countries in the Asia strengthened environmental regulatory institutions.

In a few countries in Asia, strong and well-financed environmental regulatory institutions were in place and demonstrated considerable success in reducing air and water pollution and addressing other environmental problems. In most cases, however, the pace of policy and institutional reform has been desperately slow and lacked the financial resources and political will necessary to address environmental problems. Modest gains from incremental policy reform have been overwhelmed by intensive economic growth and rapid urbanization and industrialization.

Collectively, this environmental degradation constitutes a substantial constraint on future economic development within the region and a major obstacle to efforts to eradicate severe poverty in the DMCs. Asia is not alone in facing these environmental pressures. But of all the regions of the world, it is within this region that the dynamics of economic growth and environmental degradation interact most forcefully, presenting an urgent challenge for policy makers to shift the trajectory of development to pathways that result in improved social welfare and restore rather than degrade the region's life support systems.

The state of the environment in the region includes problems such as soil degradation, scarcity of freshwater, climate change, loss of forest cover, loss of biodiversity, and declining urban air and water quality. By 1985, countries in the region had already lost 70-90 percent of their original wildlife habitat to agriculture, infrastructure development, deforestation, and land degradation. The most severe losses have been in Bangladesh, India, and Sri Lanka.

Tropical forests are of particular concern because of high rates of species richness and endemism. Pressure on the land in Asia is the most severe in the world. Particularly affected are the region's rural poor who are dependent on agriculture and its ancillary activities. Many countries in the region already face an acute shortage of productive land resources that can support its growing population. According to the United Nations Environmental Programme (UNEP), in 1990, approximately 850 million hectare (ha) had some degree of land degradation, representing more than 28 percent of the region's land area.

There are 350 million ha of degraded land in India, Pakistan, and PRC, most of which are grasslands (UNEP 1999). About 1,320 million people or 39 percent of the region's population, live in areas prone to drought and desertification. Under current development conditions, safe supplies of freshwater are at risk in many countries of the region. The explosive growth in populations and economies has had the greatest impact on the region's freshwater resources.

Freshwater with-drawals increased more in Asia during the past century than in any other part of the world, and these withdrawals have resulted in supply and water quality problems. Lack of an adequate supply of clean water is the most severe environmental problem in many parts of the region, and the lack of clean water impacts human health and slows the development of economies. Water utilization rates will increase further in many other parts of the region in the next quarter century as populations and economies grow.

Irrigation in Asia accounts for 80-85 percent of total freshwater withdrawals. The large-scale irrigation schemes implemented during the Green Revolution are extremely inefficient, delivering as little as 40 percent of the water to crops. Subsidies exacerbate the problem by encouraging the expansion of inefficient supply systems and by discouraging demand-side behavior that would improve water delivery services. Expansion of the total land area under irrigation is continuing, albeit at a slower rate than in prior decades. The development of water resources has disrupted the full spectrum of freshwater ecosystem services.

Dams and reservoirs coupled with extensive deforestation in some watersheds have reduced stream water levels, lowered water tables, degraded riparian wetlands, diminished freshwater aquatic diversity, and increased flood damage. Water quality has been steadily fouled by sewage, industrial effluent, urban and agricultural runoff, and saline intrusion. Levels of suspended solids in Asia's rivers almost quadrupled since the late 1970s. In Asia's rivers, the median fecal coliform level, an indicator of the health risk from human waste, is three times the world average and 50 times higher than the level recommended by the World Health Organization (WHO).

Access to safe drinking water is worst in South and Southeast Asia, where almost one in two Asians has no access to sanitation services and only 10 percent of sewage is treated at a primary level. In many parts of the region, economic development is most active in coastal zones, putting enormous pressures on coastal ecosystems and fisheries. Problems within coastal areas include widespread poverty; declining fisheries' productivity from over-harvesting, destructive fishing, and loss of habitat; increasing environmental damage through shoreline development, land reclamation, and pollution; reduced access of traditional users to fishing grounds; and damage to tropical marine ecosystems from global climate change and rising sea levels.

Air pollution levels in the region's most populated cities are among the highest in the world and climbing, causing serious human health impacts. Unlike the effects of water pollution, which are borne mainly by the poor, no resident of any major city in the region is safe from the effects of air pollution. However, the poor are dispropor-tionately exposed to air pollution, living along roads and in industrial areas, thus suffering the highest concentration of air pollutants almost constantly. The combustion of fossil fuels is the largest source of air pollution in urban areas.

In the vast majority of Asian cities, transportation is the major source of pollution. The number of cars in Asia is growing exponentially. Wood fuels and low quality coal pose a number of environmental and human health problems. Indoor air pollution from the smoke of burning wood fuels is one of the largest environmental risk factors for ill health of any kind. Developing countries consume about 77 percent of the world's supply of wood fuels.

Although, wood fuels account for 7 percent of the world's energy supply, Asia is by far the biggest consumer of wood fuels, accounting for nearly 44 percent of global consumption. WHO estimates that 1.5 billion people live in unhealthy air. Four million to five million child deaths are attributed to acute respiratory infection each year. The urban population in Asia is growing significantly. By the year 2020, an additional 1.5 billion people will be added to Asia's urban centers. Such a massive number of people will need adequate infrastructure and services, prominent among them being water supply, housing, and sanitation facilities.

An adequate facility for solid waste disposal is required to ensure an urban environment conducive to the well-being and productivity of residents. Declining urban environmental quality has occurred despite considerable efforts in urban planning during the last three decades. Urban development master plans for most cities have been prepared for wastewater collection and treatment, drainage, solid waste management, land use, and (in a few cases) air quality management. Few of these plans have been implemented, mainly because of the lack of management, control, and financial resources.

Many South Asian cities have dramatically improved solid waste collection but at the turn of the century many found that they had no place to dispose of the wastes. Waste minimization efforts would reduce capital investments required for wastewater and solid waste conveyance and treatment, but the capital requirements are still huge. For most large cities in the region, sustaining an adequate and safe supply of water for domestic and industrial uses is a major problem. Virtually all surface waters in the region have become severely degraded upon entering urban waterways.

Industrial growth and urban expansion have greatly contributed to and increased the generation and accumulation of solid and hazardous wastes in many DMCs, outrunning the collection efficiency and disposal capacity of many municipalities. Some cities have significantly improved solid waste management. For example, Kolkata, which generates about 2,500 metric tons of waste per day, has developed effective collection and disposal systems that capture 95 percent of the waste stream.

Air pollution in South Asian cities causes nearly 100,000 premature deaths per year and over 1 billion work days of lost or reduced productivity. Smoke and dust in large cities and in the region are a major cause of respiratory diseases. Environmental degradation has economic as well as noneconomic costs. These costs manifest in several forms: adverse impacts on human health, loss of productivity, and lower overall well-being. In Asia, estimates of economic costs of environmental degradation range from 1-9 percent of a country's gross national product (GNP), depending on thecountry and the impacts included in the estimates.

3

Information Revolution and Social Changes

IT's current status will be viewed from two major perspectives:

— Use and adoption of advanced information technology, and

— Production and creation of information technology.

To understand the factors driving and shaping the future of both IT use and production trends, we examine the history and development of models that exist today and key environmental factors, such as government policies and funding. Asia includes both the world's most advanced IT users and producers and also some of the least advanced.

The most basic measure of a population's use of IT is its use of the Internet. Common measures used in the past, such as telephone or television use, do not capture the essence of today's information technology, which goes well beyond simply receiving locally broadcast information or holding one-on-one conversations.

Internet use measures the extent to which a country's people are proactively accessing, exchanging, and providing information on a global basis.

By this measure, Asia is home to markets with both the most IT use and the least in the world. Even in 2000, South Korea, Hong Kong, Japan, and Australia significantly exceeded the United States in the extent of Internet use, and Singapore has surpassed the United States since then. Japan, South Korea, Hong Kong, and Taiwan all had greater mobile phone use than the United States at the end of 2002 as well. However, Asia is highly polarized; Internet use falls off by one or two orders of magnitude after the top ten.

A corollary to IT penetration is the absolute size of IT markets. For example, Hong Kong society is one of the most "connected" and IT-fluent in the world with 383 users per 1,000 population. However, the total number of Internet users in 2000 was only 2.6 million, whereas China, a country with much lower IT penetration, had 22.5 million users. So although China is not an IT-fluent society as a whole, its influence on the global IT world is significantly greater. IT producers customize products and services for the China market, and global investment dollars are attracted to its sheer size.

Underscoring just how influential and attractive China's IT market is, we note that its Internet user base exceeded 60 million in 2002, almost triple the level in 2000. The markets that "matter" are not only large, they also have high growth rates. Australia, Taiwan, and Hong Kong have already slowed to mature growth rates, as have Singapore and New Zealand among the medium-size markets. It is also important to note that although the Asia IT market is relatively fast-growing, its absolute size is well below its 55 percent share of world population.

In the first quarter of 2002, Asia accounted for 23.5 percent of personal computers (PCs) sold globally. Asia's mobile phone use is a more substantial market on the global scale. For example, China alone had over 200 million mobile subscribers at the end of 2002, making it the largest mobile market in the world, larger even than that of the United States. However, 99 percent of China's mobile use is basic telephony (voice calls), which is the most basic IT application.

Asia is also home to some of the world's most sophisticated mobile markets, but they are smaller in comparison: Japan had 70.2 million mobile users in mid-2002, of which over 75 percent subscribe to data services and the Internet on their mobile phones. Asia's role in the global IT industry as a producer or manufacturer. From this perspective, Asia contributes well more than its proportionate share and is a dominant and critical global IT player.

Remarkably, Asia accounts for more than 80 percent of the total world output of the following IT products: desktop PCs, notebook PCs, cathode ray tube (CRT) monitors, flat panel displays, modems, network interface cards, modems, hard disk drives, computer mouse devices, keyboards, televisions, game boxes, mobile phones, personal digital assistants (PDAs), entry-level servers, hubs, and switches.

Asia is equally dominant in its output share of critical components and materials used in the IT industry. For the world's semiconductor industry, Asia produces over 70 percent of all bare silicon material, over 90 percent of epoxy resin for integrated circuit (IC) packaging, over 80 percent of memory semiconductors (dynamic access random memory (DRAM), static random access memory (SRAM), and flash memory), and over 75 percent of outsource manufactured semiconductors.

Other critical IT parts made primarily in Asia include a wide range of passive components (resistors, diodes, and capacitors), connectors, sockets, switched power supplies, liquid crystal display (LCD) panels, printed circuit boards, and casings. Asia's share of global IT hardware output is not only large, it is still on a steep upward climb, as a growing number of ever-higher-value parts and products get outsourced to the region for production.

Applied Materials, the leading world maker of semiconductor manufacturing equipment, notes that in the first quarter of 2002, 71 percent of its equipment was sold to Asia, compared to 41 percent in 1996. This is a leading indicator that Asia's semiconductor output will as much as double in the years to come. Asia's leading IT producers in absolute terms and also in terms of how critical IT exports are to economic performance. In particular, IT exports are a top component of the economy in Singapore, Taiwan, Malaysia, Thailand, and the Philippines.

Without a doubt, the Internet has penetrated all segments of virtually every country in the world, but the degrees vary considerably in Asia. In advanced IT use markets with high Internet user penetration, such as the United States, Japan, and Korea, the primary point of access is the home or other points of private use, such as PC arcades, Internet cafes, or personal mobile devices. This is a significant indication that IT use in advanced markets has become integrated into the users' way of life and daily living, and personal investment has been made in purchasing or renting an Internet access device.

Advanced IT use markets correlate well with both wealth and early literacy. Another reason for high rates of home or private access to IT in these markets is use by children and young adults, who are IT literate at an early age. The key IT applications that account for the greatest amount of time spent on home or private Internet access include communication (e-mail, instant messaging), entertainment (gaming, music, film, photo-sharing), e-commerce (shopping, gambling), and education (news, information-gathering).

The majority of Asia, however, lacks either the wealth or the IT literacy required for personal IT or Internet usage, or both, which leaves access limited to only those with a computer at work in either a private company or a government office. Schools in virtually all countries are also access points for IT but mainly in higher education institutions and with tens or hundreds of users per machine.

With such limited access, primarily through businesses, it is not surprising that Internet use falls off by one or two orders of magnitude after only a handful of advanced IT use countries. It is estimated that although the home or other private access point accounts for approximately 50 percent of primary Internet use in the advanced markets of the United States, Japan, and Korea, the home accounts for less than 10 percent of Internet use access in Thailand and the Philippines and less than 5 percent in Indonesia.

China and Vietnam are notable for their high proportions (over one-third) of primary Internet access through schools, reflecting a young IT user population and government policies that support IT infrastructure in universities. Although businesses are the leading mode of access to the Internet for Asia, uses are not highly sophisticated. Aside from basic e-mail and office automation, the primary use is supply chain management, resulting from Asia's significant export manufacturing industry.

On-line supply chain transactions were the largest category of Internet commerce in Asia, accounting for 27.3 percent of the total $7.25 billion e-commerce market in 2000. Another customer-oriented import/export Internet application that Asia has taken up readily is customer relationship management (CRM) software. CRM consists of multimillion-dollar software and systems enterprise applications for identifying, tracking, fulfilling, and servicing a business' customer requests and communications.

CRM systems also tie into a company's back office for invoicing, billing, and credit. In 2001, the global CRM market was $16.35 billion; Japan accounted for $2.9 billion or 17.7 percent, with the rest of Asia totalling $1.8 billion, or 11 percent. Aside from Japan, leading adopter countries of note are Australia, South Korea, and Singapore. From a global economic perspective, Japan accounted for 15.4 percent of world gross domestic product (GDP) in 2000, and Asia, minus Japan, accounted for 8.4 percent of world GDP.

Aside from the basic use of e-mail and supply and customer management, only an estimated 15 percent of all networked businesses had Internet protocol-based (IP-based) virtual private networks (VPNs) in 2000. Having an IP VPN is the minimum requirement to move into higher value-added services or applications such as mobile workforce deployment with real-time connectivity, remote dial-up access, firewall and authentication services needed to complete secure financial transactions, IP telephony, unified messaging, application software outsourcing, web or content hosting, and collocation.

Indeed, only a further 9 percent of networked companies that did not have an IP VPN said they had plans to implement one in the coming year. Considering the global IT market slowdown, which worsened through 2000 and 2001, it is safe to assume that only a fraction of that 9 percent has actually since implemented one. Businesses are leading the initial Internet and IT charge in Asia, and the clear driver is the need to be tied into the global economy and trade. Exports are a key component of most Asian businesses, and the Internet is a "must" for maintaining contact with overseas customers.

Indeed, most Asian businesses of any size will have a web presence and a basic network for e-mail. However, beyond that, we do find numerous inhibitors to greater use of advanced applications aside from simply e-mail and supply and customer management. The most stubborn inhibitor to greater IT or Internet use by businesses is the current lack of good profitable business models. However, there are examples of solidly run businesses that have faltered on greater use of or reliance on IT.

By 1995, Global Sources was far and away the best-known and largest provider of business-to-business trade information from Asia. It catalogued over 100,000 suppliers in Asia into industry sectors for over 300,000 active buyers globally and processed millions of requests for information annually. One imagines that the Internet would be ideal for a company like Global Sources. Indeed, in 1995, it launched an online business division, which management envisioned would eventually replace all of its traditional print and CD-ROM-based businesses.

Since 1995, although global trade and sourcing from Asia reach new peak levels every year, Global Sources' revenue has stagnated and profitability has fallen. A key issue cited by Global Sources management in interviews is that although people expect to pay for magazine subscriptions, web content is perceived to be either free or very cheap. Online advertising also does not command as high a price as print advertising, even though the viewership and content is the same in either medium.

Commercial use of the web has not only reduced value and profitability for Global Sources; it will inevitably put the company out of business if some new business model is not devised. For many reasons, Asia does not have IT businesses. One reason is the geographically and linguistically fractured nature of Asia; the U.S. market, in contrast, constitutes a sizable single market. Asia has also arguably not yet achieved the minimum Internet user penetration and per capita wealth needed to make its IT businesses a success. However, the more stubborn underlying reason has to do with Asia's approach to traditional media itself.

Until very recently, the large majority of all media companies in Asia were either directly state-owned, or quasi state-owned and were sold to the public at highly subsidized rates as a public service. Even the few privately owned media companies tended to be subsidized by tycoons or conglomerates who fancied being newspaper owners. Advertising rates in Asian media are a fraction of those in the United States. The tradition of paying fair market value for media and respecting the copyrights of their content is weak, to say the least.

The initial perception of the Internet as free or low cost did not help, accounting for the inability of Global Sources to get its subscribers to pay similar rates for content online that was identical to what they paid for in magazines or on CDs. The media industry, in general, is in transition in Asia, and IT businesses face unique challenges finding solid footing in the meantime.

Although e-tailing has grown in Asia, its scale remains small and fragmented, and it is challenged by the ubiquitous low-cost nature of traditional retailing. For example, Americans are increasingly booking their own travel online through Expedia or Travelocity; Expedia's second quarter 2002 revenue of $145 million represents fees on $1.33 billion in travel bookings. The most notable success in retail Internet use thus far in Asia has been gaming and gambling.

WebEx-type businesses may do well in Asia, but establishing them will take time as businesses upgrade their IT infrastructure. The bottom line is that every business cost must have a clear return or ultimate financial benefit. Basic networking and a web presence is a must for Asian businesses to communicate internally and with customers, but beyond that, there is no proven body of cases of solid financial return for greater IT investment. As long as reasonable return on investment remains elusive, many in the private sector will remain on the sidelines of advanced IT use.

Some technology and financial infrastructure barriers also remain in the way of greater or more sophisticated business and commercial use of IT. These issues will be increasingly addressed by the rapid pace of technology advances. Although there are many advantages to having a web-based, remotely accessible network, corporate IT managers, and even governments, are clearly concerned that it makes them more vulnerable to cyber-crime and hacking. This is primarily a technology issue, where much private and public sector effort is being expended to find robust and easy-to-implement solutions.

Asian businesses face the same IT security challenges, using the same network infrastructure as any other global business, but the high incidence of local disregard for copyright and intellectual property protection in traditional businesses probably makes an Asian business leader more sensitive to this concern than his or her western counterpart. Inability to monitor and manage a network effectively is a related concern to security and to the SLA issue of network reliability.

Remotely managed or globally distributed IP VPN networks are prone to transmission congestion, bottlenecks, or system crashes. Already, significant advances even in the last year have been made to improving the quality and reliability of IP networks. Reliability, accountability, and geographic reach of network providers (SLAs) are ongoing areas of improvement in this steadily maturing business.

The financial infrastructure issue is related to e-commerce or e-tailing; how does an Asian Internet user complete a transaction online? Credit cards are overwhelmingly the payment method of choice. Not surprisingly, countries with high rates of online transaction completion have mature banking systems and widespread use of credit. Markets where over 60 percent of e-commerce transactions are actually completed online are Japan, Korea, Australia, New Zealand, Hong Kong, Singapore, and Taiwan Countries where only 8 to 14 percent of e-commerce transactions are completed online include Malaysia, China, Thailand, the Philippines, Indonesia, India, and Vietnam.

In these cases, e-commerce represents buying decisions made online but actually completed offline in some other physical way. Lack of a credit card system is an inhibitor to e-commerce in these countries, but the hurdle is one that can be overcome and has been in some countries. Alternative, and equally effective, payment systems being adopted include debit cards, prepaid cards, and direct account transfers (commonly used for stock transactions). A more cumbersome payment method popular in China is fund transfers made through post offices.

Development of IT Industry

In Asia, the driving forces to high IT use and high IT production are surprisingly distinct from each other. Being a major user does not necessarily lead to major production, nor vice versa. Of the countries that are both major IT users and producers, only Japan and Korea have gained some synergistic advantages between the two, and even that is only very recently, and with limited degrees of success. We will therefore consider the development models of the users and producers separately.

High IT penetration in the markets came about from some combination of the following factors:

1. Wealth (affordability of services and devices),
2. Business imperative (office automation, supply chain, and e-mail),
3. Relative quality of content and applications (compared to existing traditional media/ communications),
4. Availability of local language content and applications,
5. Government policies, and
6. Existing infrastructure.

The remaining high-IT-use markets rely on factors 1 (wealth) and 6 (existing infrastructure). Australia, New Zealand, Hong Kong, and Singapore are wealthy markets, and all homes and offices are wired anyway. Custom localized applications have developed in all four but were not requisites, since English comprehension is widespread. Inhibitors and Lurking Concerns. There is no distinct set of factors inhibiting IT use in Asia-the countries that lag are faced with the negative version of the driving factors.

Some emerging IT use markets, such as Thailand and Malaysia, are actively addressing the issues listed above although, ultimately, the key is the overall level of economic development. The compelling hurdles are affordability and content/application quality. Infrastructure is not an issue, since technology is available to install on any existing level of platform. Even in the United States, for example, over 90 percent of homes have access to high-speed Internet service via phone lines, cable TV, or satellite, but only 7 percent subscribe.

Other countries such as China, India, and Vietnam are becoming highly bifurcated IT markets. All three countries have urban centres that are highly IT penetrated, whereas their rural and remote areas remain untouched. Shanghai's mobile phone penetration is 46 percent of households, compared to 16 percent for the country. This divide is likely to widen before narrowing, with driving factors applying in cities and inhibiting factors prevailing in rural areas.

One lurking concern that faces all Asian countries is the possibility of an IT backlash or slowdown in the future. Natural business forces may lead to a slowdown because some of the key drivers of consumer IT use in Asia are the same factors that inhibit greater IT use in businesses. For example, excessive competition, which makes it difficult for businesses to sustain profits from IT, is providing consumers with more extensive, better quality, and cheaper communications access than ever before, and richer, cheaper, and more diverse content and applications.

The next major phase comes after the local industry has accumulated some wealth and industrial expertise. Not content to simply make cheap souvenirs and household products, or to assemble portions of complex products, the regional industries reinvest to gain the know-how to produce more complex products. In the case of Japan and Korea, they moved on to making cameras, watches, televisions, radios, and electronic toys. Basic industries also matured, such as chemicals, plastics, steel, and advanced materials, leading to increased local content.

Although still considered low-value in the global IT world, these local companies began to make a name for themselves as consumer electronics manufacturers: Sony, Panasonic, Mitsubishi, Samsung, Lucky Goldstar (LG), and Acer. In Southeast Asia, control of IT remained in foreign hands, but the value-added expanded from simply assembling disk-drive boards to assembling head stacks, ICs, and final products such as monitors, printers, and mobile phones. In all areas, automation was increasingly used to ensure better uniform quality and to handle more complex precision components such as semiconductors.

A key reason is that the IT industry in these countries is controlled by foreign companies who have no particular interest in transferring knowledge or developing talent. In fact, disk-drive companies such as Seagate and Maxtor move from country to country in search of the lowest-cost labour. And although workers and line managers are locally hired, senior management is invariably foreign. Southeast Asia has also suffered from the rapid rise of China.

China offers similar access to a low-cost labour pool and with the added attraction of a potentially vast local market in the long term. Additionally, Taiwan manufacturers, which used to rely heavily on Malaysia and the Philippines, have largely shifted to China for the common language convenience. Finally, political and economic instability have proved deadly to the fledgling IT industries in the Philippines and Indonesia.

Given that global IT hardware demand is not sufficient to support large factories in all of these countries, it is not surprising that in the last five years, IT production has migrated toward the lower-cost centre of

China. Hence, total GDP has fallen significantly since 1997 in Indonesia, Malaysia, the Philippines, and Thailand, whereas it has risen in China. China's population is 3.4 times larger than all four Southeast Asian countries combined. These basic numbers sum up the overwhelming challenge that such countries as Malaysia and Thailand face.

Being a low-cost producer is no longer possible (unless standards of income and living are dialed back to 1980s level, which is undesirable and politically untenable), and they have pitiable market sizes with which to attract global IT industrial interests. Niche, locally owned, value-added industries are needed to stem the erosion of the IT industries in Southeast Asia, although it appears that the path to this future will be left to the next generation of leaders to find.

Within Southeast Asia, a possible break-out country is Singapore, although key conditions are not ripe. Singapore's IT industry has been dominated by foreign companies. As contract manufacturers,. they are second tier to U.S. and Taiwanese counterparts and are not used for leading-edge products or semiconductors. Past attempts to improve quality or to engage in original design have not been successful. The key issues holding Singapore back are lack of local entrepreneurialism, a very small local market in which to try out new ideas, limited labour availability, and high operating costs.

In India, the environment simply does not seem ripe yet; software created there has negligible copyright protection, services are hard to scale, the domestic market is tiny, and manufacturing has not taken root. Political instability and a discouraging venture formation environment are added hurdles. As a result, India faces a similar problem of "brain drain" as Taiwan.

Noteworthy Indian entrepreneurs are numerous in the United States and many have known corporate success. In 2001, 60 percent of all H-1 visa holders (residence in the United States based on employment of a skill in shortage in the United States) in Silicon Valley were software engineers, with Indian citizens constituting 43 percent of the total.

Asia has thus far entirely bypassed the enterprise solutions business, currently dominated by U.S. and European companies such as IBM, BEA Systems, Computer Sciences Corp., Oracle, Siebel Systems, People Soft, SAP, Sun Microsystems, Hewlett-Packard, Cisco Systems, Lucent, EDS, Siemens, or even smaller companies such as Micromuse, Veritas, i2 Technologies, Tibco, EMC, and many others.

Asia's IT involvement up to now is primarily focused on making stand-alone, standardized. or easy-to-use products. Essentially, Asia lacks entirely the IT services, software, and value-added consulting businesses. Although Asia's tourism industry is world-renowned for the excellence of its service, its IT industry is not.

The hardware product is no worse than comparable U.S. brands, but its service network, support, and value-added offerings are very weak. This hurdle is likely a complex one involving many factors such as corporate culture, language, usage patterns, and value perception. The early exceptions to this rule are, yet again, found in Japan, although they are not likely to start an Asia-wide trend anytime soon.

Asia's IT industry is likely to stick to low-cost advantages and manufacturing for the foreseeable future. Mobile Internet and broadband are two advances pioneered in Asia, which, however, have not been successfully exported yet despite some considerable effort.

Government policies play a major role in the establishment and ongoing development of Asia's IT industry (and, indeed, all aspects of industry). Government policies are unanimously favourable in their intentions toward the IT industry and almost as unanimously favourable toward promoting IT use. Since the IT industry is such a critical part of most Asian economies, the governments are even somewhat competitive about offering the best investment conditions and providing the most assistance to domestic IT companies.

As governments decide they want to foster the development of a local IT industry, banks and finance companies are directed to lend to companies in the industry, without consideration of the borrower's stand-alone creditworthiness, and often at below-market interest rates. This has been used aggressively in Japan and Korea. Taiwan, Thailand, and Malaysia have practiced policy lending as well, but to much smaller extents, and in more limited circumstances.

China has as well, but as part of the broader context of the communist state-owned enterprise system. Although policy lending had a clear beneficial effect in the early growth and establishment of the keiretsus and chaebols, it is now viewed as one of the major underlying causes of the Asian financial crisis in 1997 and of Japan's ongoing recession.

In China, Malaysia, and Thailand, qualifying high-tech companies are allowed a certain number of tax-free years, followed by some reduced tax years, before having to pay the regular statutory corporate tax rates. Typically, tax-free years do not start counting until after the company reaches profitability. To attract export manufacturers, most Asian countries have established free trade zones, typically near ports or airports.

Locating an assembly factory in such a zone means that a company does not need to officially import materials and components, which will only end up being immediately exported after assembly. Significant bureaucratic hassle is avoided and time as well as cash flow saved, since import duties do not need to be paid for the duration of the manufacturing process.

Most countries have created industrial parks to attract IT companies. The government takes over a large acreage, clears it, builds roads, brings in all utilities, including reliable power supplies and quality data communications, and sometimes even builds standard factories. All an IT company has to do is literally move in. Rent is usually subsidized as well. Sometimes, the industrial parks are also free trade zones or can automatically confer tax-free status on their tenants.

Industrial parks are numerous throughout Asia and are considered an ideal way to generate high-quality jobs and long-term economic benefits. Business and Trade Development. Aside from undertaking research, some governments also take an active role in pushing the wares of its companies. Japan's JETRO (Japan External Trade Organization) is a model example. Established in 1951, it provides Japanese companies with international market intelligence, assistance with international communications, trade shows, promotion, etc.

One of the most controversial policies used in Asia is domestic market protection in favour of local IT companies. This policy has taken many forms, such as import duties on competitive foreign offerings, local content requirements on sales of foreign equipment, onerous registration processes for imported equipment or software, and outright import bans. In Japan and Korea, there are few formal legal obstacles to foreign equipment sales, but domestic brands still constitute the overwhelming local market share.

Trade suits and treaties such as the World Trade Organization (WTO) have helped to address some of the most egregious market inequities, but most Asian IT companies can still count on being heavily favoured in their home markets. Government IT Spending. Finally, governments in Asia are themselves leading purchasers of IT. As we will discuss in the next section, Australia, China, Hong Kong, Korea, and Singapore are known for their sizable e-government initiatives to modernize both internal government operations and to provide improved delivery of public services.

Government IT purchases are, not surprisingly, often used as a showcase for local suppliers or to promote government policies. The most noted example is China, which has a political agenda for most major purchase agreements it signs. China has been vocal in denouncing the use of Microsoft and is using its e-government initiative to demonstrate the effective use of the openly available Linux operating system.

Despite the best of intentions, some of the policies listed above have had unintended negative consequences. Broadly speaking, government assistance is extended as a springboard to future success, but the initiatives that are meant to be transitional have occasionally become a crutch that stunted future development or competitiveness, as evidenced to varying extents in Malaysia, China, and Japan and Korea.

As already highlighted, policy lending and subsidies have almost always backfired. Policy lending did enable the IT industries' rapid growth to a large size, but it made them ultimately less competitive overall. Firms that should have gone bankrupt were propped up, thereby reducing the country's overall efficiency and return on capital. The financial burden has also pushed the Japanese and Korean economies to their limits. China, of course, has also been addressing the same issue: state-owned and state-funded companies have been increasingly pushed to either sink or swim on their own merits.

Domestic market protection has also proved to be a double-edged sword: It created a much needed market foundation for fledgling IT companies but, with some exceptions, ill-equipped the same companies to compete globally. It also led to a higher economic cost, with consumers having to pay more, or to limited product and service options. Another major unintended negative consequence has been corruption. When there is little or no engagement between the government and industry, as in the United States, there is little room for official corruption, since every company must apply for funds on its own merits and compete for business or die.

In Asia, governments are intimately connected with IT companies, serving many roles, some of which create conflicts of interest. Considering all the various policies used by governments to promote IT, officials have been acting as lenders, investors, shareholders, regulators, suppliers, customers, and partners for trade and R&D. Historically, in the telecommunications industry in Asia, there was only one type of service-fixed line voice, and typically one operator-which was usually state-owned by the tele-com regulator or ministry. The last decade has brought major changes.

First, the service types expanded to include pager service, wireless phone service, and data service, which can be further divided into business data, broadband, and Internet service. Second, Asian governments have jumped on the deregulation bandwagon to speed up penetration and enhance service quality. The coincidence of the two trends has left many countries with a confusing array of operators, alliances, and tariff schedules, while governments try to walk the fine line between making affordable services widely available and ensuring reasonable, healthy rates of return for operators.

All governments have made considerable progress toward achieving a deregulated telecommunications market, with the greatest strides made in the wireless business, where there were no complicating legacy franchises or infrastructures. The relative success of the deregulation efforts can be seen in the surge of user bases and the growth of the new operators. Regulating ministries, which used to own the operator, have moved to sell their stakes to avoid conflicts of interest. Rates have gone through periods of intense competition in some countries but are beginning to stabilize.

Markets that are considered to have reached a competitive equilibrium are Korea, Taiwan, Japan, and Hong Kong, whereas China and Thailand are still considered to be in the deregulating and market adjustment process. The final element of government policies to consider is some governments' alternating attraction to, and yet apprehension about, the power of

IT. The most conflicted government on this front is China.

China's government has been aggressive in its deregulation of key IT industries, has steadily liberalized foreign investment policies, is itself a leading IT and Internet user, and is a keen promoter of a domestic IT industry. However, factions within the political hierarchy are clearly uncomfortable with the unparalleled global information access and dissemination possible through the Internet.

In 2002, over 2,400 of the highly popular Internet cafes were shut down temporarily in Beijing and Tianjin because of a fatal fire in one cafe. Government officials are supposedly checking that all cafes comply with safety standards and are registered before reopening them. The government is concerned with the growing use of "subversive" content such as pornography and content from the foreign media, dissidents, and such outlawed groups as Falun Gong.

Internet cafes and universities are the most common Internet access points in China and the closures allow the government to enforce the installation of tracking software to monitor usage, as well as to collect licensing fees, which are not regularly paid. In recent months, China's government has sporadically employed more technically sophisticated methods of censorship as well. Similar unevenly enforced restrictions have also been applied in the past to the use of satellite TV dishes.

The funding of IT companies in Asia comes primarily from corporate wealth or individual wealth (these amount to the same thing in countries where companies are primarily owned by individual tycoons). The majority of all IT companies in Asia today were spun off established companies (not necessarily IT companies), or are still part of larger conglomerates, or evolved from traditional businesses.

Very few were actually founded and are still controlled by entrepreneurial engineers or IT visionaries. Venture capital basically does not exist in Asia, in the true Silicon Valley sense of independent funding of innovative concepts at an early stage. Private equity exists and is primarily invested in mid-and late-stage private companies. This could be one major reason for the lack of innovation in Asia's IT industry.

In fact, many innovative and entrepreneurial Asian professionals can be found in the United States, where the financing environment is more open to new ideas. Every major economy in Asia has a main stock market, which is often referred as the Main Board or the country's primary stock market. In most countries, there is only the primary stock market. In Asia, the primary stock markets all require a minimum of three recent years of profitable operating history as a minimum listing eligibility.

4

Gender Development in South Asia

Gender disparity can be narrowly defined as the purely descriptive observation of different outcomes between males and females. However, to move beyond the descriptive level to ask what might cause gender disparities reaches into the complex interplay of the possible sources. Discrimination (the differential treatment of individuals because of their gender), biological differences, individual and societal beliefs and attitudes about appropriate gender-specific roles, and the choices of individuals and households based on all of these factors all play a role in determining gender disparities.

These factors are causally interrelated and it is very difficult to disentangle what are the underlying causes and what are merely proximate indicators or symptoms. India is enormous, with a population of over 900 million which is twice as large as all countries in Africa combined, or all countries in Latin America combined. The state of Uttar Pradesh has a population of over 140 million, which would make it the world's sixth largest country. But size alone is not the right criterion for determining the value of cross-country (versus within-country) comparisons, as it depends on the empirical characteristics of the phenomena to be examined.

Since countries, almost by definition, share a common currency and have free internal trade, one might expect economic phenomenon like inflation to be similar in all parts of the same country. Some gender disparities, like differential participation in the paid labour force or the gender division of labour, are the result of a joint, voluntary, and optimal decision-making on the part of a couple as a household unit, it would be very difficult to argue that female children voluntarily assume higher mortality risks.

As an indicator of gender disparity, the ratio of female to male child mortality, defined as the chance of a child dying after turning one but before turning five, is preferable to other mortality indicators. There are two reasons to believe that 4q1 is a better indicator of gender disparity, especially of the type that reveals behavioural differences, than mortality at other ages.

First, there is very little correlation between the gender ratios of neonatal and child mortality; in the sample outside of South Asia, the correlation is even mildly negative. It is reasonable to believe that, aside from outright infanticide, neonatal deaths are unlikely to be influenced by gender, because they are partly genetically determined and partly determined by prenatal care, when few mothers know the sex of the child.

Second, the disparities in the mortality ratios by gender grow with age. The median gender ratios in the non-South Asian countries, Indian states, and Pakistani provinces are nearly the same for neonatal mortality, somewhat different for post-neonatal mortality. Similarly, the variance of outcomes is much larger at later ages. The levels of many socio-economic indicators are strongly associated with per-capita income, like infant or under-five mortality, male and female educational attainment and enrolment levels, malnutrition, and the fraction of population in poverty.

Indicators of gender disparity also do not appear to be at all correlated with the general standard of living, as proxied by per-capita GDP, either across countries or within countries in South Asia. There is no particular pattern to the coefficients, either across indicators or regions. This lack of a relationship has several implications. First, if one is seeking to understand and explain the high levels of gender disparity in South Asia, low income is not one of the answers.

In the sample, poorer countries do not, on average, have worse gender disparity than high-income countries. Therefore, rising income levels that do not worsen the gender disparity will tend to reduce both female and male mortality, and the disparity itself, the ratio of girls to boys that die, will not improve. An overall strategy for improving female health status might then involve actions both to improve overall standards of living together with measures aimed at the disparity.

Trafficking

India and Bangladesh also serve as transit countries for traffickers moving people to other destinations. Trafficked persons may also be regular migrants from

Bangladesh or Nepal to India, who are then trafficked either to further destinations in India or elsewhere. In South Asia, Bangladesh and Nepal are the main countries of origin for trafficking, while India and Pakistan are considered countries of destination or transit to other regions, commonly the Gulf States or Southeast Asia.

Kolkata in India, for example is regarded as a major transit point for other destinations. However, large-scale trafficking in persons also takes place within these countries. Various studies have revealed that the traffickers from Bangladesh and Nepal function through several networks operating both within and outside the countries. In some instances there is evidence that organized criminal groups and other influential players back these networks.

The traffickers in most cases take the victims to their destination via circuitous and ever-changing routes, making retracing and apprehension of perpetrators practically impossible. Although the chief actors of trafficking are men, women also play vital roles in luring girls by displaying their lavish lifestyle in their visits to villages, befriending local girls, promising them jobs, and helping them run away from their homes.

It is estimated that 35% of the total number of girls and women trafficked from Nepal to India have been abducted under the pretext of false marriage or good jobs. Though the traffickers play a major role in the entire trafficking process, many other people directly or indirectly also contribute. Family members, community leaders, and teachers influence motivations and decisions for a person to leave their community and then become caught up in trafficking.

Those who benefit from trafficking are also implicated, including various labour agents, promoters, brokers, border police, hoteliers, transport agents, brothel owners and clients, factory owners, and household members who use these trafficked women and children as domestic workers. The modus operandi of traffickers include luring their victims by means of attractive promises such as high-paying jobs, glamorous employment options, prosperity, and sometimes fraudulent marriages.

Parents and other family members are fooled or otherwise blinded by false promises and deception. It has been widely perceived that in many cases family members and other relatives play an important role in recruitment by colluding with the traffickers for which they may receive payment. In Nepal this is particularly prevalent in regions where girls have traditionally been sent knowingly by families as entertainers or CSWs, which is perceived as an important source of income for the families.

Along the borders between Bangladesh and India ,and Nepal and India, the enforcement officers and checkpoints are few in numbers and widely dispersed. Thus it is hard to maintain strict vigilance of who is crossing the border. Border security forces are well aware of the problems of illegal/irregular migrants and trafficking, but do not have facilities or resources to quickly distinguish between different types of migrants.

Trafficked persons are usually afraid to admit to their circumstances or are confused, and interviewers may require skillful questioning that takes time to uncover the extent of coercion or deceit involved in each individual circumstance. Enforcement officers sometimes resort to pushing back at night irregular or illegal migrants picked up during the day without distinguishing between trafficked persons and illegal migrants. Although the State is aware of loopholes in the border, systems are unable to adequately address the problem due to institutional, political, and international influences. Those who have been trafficked remain at risk of being found again by the traffickers and sent back across the border, and are generally unable to return home anyway.

In some instances, traffickers cross the border on fixed days of the week at fixed hours. It is said that this is common knowledge in surrounding communities, and NGOs working in areas where this happens have found it difficult to believe that State enforcement agencies are unaware of such activities. It is the common perception of communities living in villages and districts along the border that the network of smugglers/agents are organized and protected.

Prosecutions are rare and fraught with difficulties, and using official crime statistics to ascertain the scope of trafficking presents a very low estimate of its incidence. Reports by UN agencies and NGOs indicate that the smuggling of migrants and trafficking in women and children are on the increase. The UN assesses that globally at least 4 million persons (men, women, and children) are trafficked every year.

Most statistics quoted concern the number of trafficked women and children from Bangladesh and Nepal and few identify the number of Indian women and children trafficked out of the country or internally. Individuals generally do not identify themselves readily as victims of trafficking, as they are afraid of their captors or concerned that they will be treated as illegal immigrants.

Numbers of trafficked persons might be generated from estimates based on visual or linguistic differences among commercial sex workers in general in brothels. It is difficult, however, to identify Bangladeshis from Bengalis in India, and their numbers may be greatly underestimated. Nepalis on the other hand are more physically distinguishable and estimates of their numbers may be more accurate.

The number of prosecutions against traffickers is low compared to the estimated amount of illegal activity, and so does not provide a good indication of the extent of criminal activity. This results from a combination of factors including limited resources for the police and other law enforcers, who, in the case of Nepal, are increasingly preoccupied with the now almost endemic civil unrest. Cases are hard to prove and lengthy to take through thc court system requiring resources from the plaintiffs and witnesses.

A special court has been established in Nepal to try and expedite cases of trafficking and other serious charges using judges and lawyers familiar with the appropriate legislation. This court has its limitations, however, as it only sits in Kathmandu, so all those involved have to travel there to appear before the court. There is no law on repatriation in India ,no National Crime Records Bureau (NCRB) category under which to record it, and therefore there is almost no accurate data available. The only data currently available is from NGOs active in rescue and rehabilitation programming for victims of crossborder trafficking.

Micro studies are generally unavailable around the border, and government statistics from the three countries do not provide a comprehensive picture of operations. According to most reports, Bangladesh and Nepal provide the highest number of trafficked girl children to other countries in South Asia. The Bangladesh National Women Lawyers Association (BNWLA), in a study undertaken in 1997, cited the numbers of children being trafficked from Bangladesh as follows:

— 300,000 Bangladesh children work in the brothels of India 4,700 children were rescued from traffickers in the past 5 years;

— 4,500 women and children are trafficked to Pakistan yearly (SAARC and United Nations Children's Fund [UNICEF]);

— 1,000 child trafficking cases were documented in the Bangladeshi media press during the year 1990 to 1992; and 69 children were reported being rescued at the border during a 3-month study in 1995.

In an attempt to determine the magnitude and trend of the problem, a mapping exercise of missing, kidnapped, and trafficked children and women from Bangladesh was undertaken based on 10 years of media coverage from 1990 to 1999 by the Centre for Women and Child Studies (CWCS). It revealed that in 1990, the number of trafficked children was 37. The trend increased until 1997, when the total was 927, with a downward trend since then.

In source areas in Nepal, some micro studies have been carried out in small areas. For example, the Centre for Legal Research and Resource Development (CeLRRD) in 1998 carried out a field-based study that compared the number of girls under 18 years who were out of the district at known and unknown destinations. The proportions whose destinations were unknown were high: in 24 village development committees (VDCs) of Sindhupalchowk 1,713 were out of the district, but the whereabouts of 1,168 were unknown.

Several studies in Bangladesh have identified that large numbers of children are brought to urban areas as domestic workers, often by their families or trafficking rings. Even middle-class families condone exploitation of these children in their communities. Those children who escape often end up as street children vulnerable once more to being trafficked for CSW.

There are no studies on the extent of use of trafficked labour in the industrial sectors, but anecdotal evidence suggests that in the garment sector, for example, many young girls are brought from rural areas under false promises of high wages, and kept in conditions where labour brokers and supervisors demand sexual services in return for finding employment. As the current economic recession hits the garment sector, many thousands of young women are losing their jobs, and many of them are lured or coerced into CSW.

Many of these young women also feel they cannot return to their communities to their old life with few income opportunities and restricted mobility, so they are looking increasingly for migration opportunities outside Bangladesh, again putting themselves in high-risk situations for exploitation and trafficking. There is no data collected anywhere in Bangladesh on internal trafficking flows. Rural-to-urban migration has been increasing rapidly in the past 10 years.

New arrivals in urban areas are vulnerable to being coerced and exploited by those already settled or by organized traffickers who can easily identify a newly arrived and vulnerable woman or child. Bangladesh shares a 4,156-kilometer (km) border with India that has 20 official checkpoints and out of its 32 districts, 30 districts are on the Indo-Bangladesh border.

In Bangladesh, the collection points for trafficked women are usually far from border points. Women rescued in Dinajpur (north) were from Cox's Bazaar (south). Girls from the southern part of Bangladesh are usually trafficked across northern borders. One study estimates that almost half of the trafficking from Bangladesh to India takes place through Benapole in Jessore District. Points like Thakurbairi Chandurila, Kaiba Sultanpur, Chodarpur, Chapainaababgunj, Hili Akhwara, Chuadanga, and Poladanga are other commonly used entry points to India.

West Bengal has nine districts adjoining the border that are mostly different from one another socio-economically and culturally. Some are more prosperous and developed agriculturally, e.g., Nadia, where farmers primarily grow jute and betel leaves, is a prosperous area. The Sundarbans area of south/north 24 Parganas is very weak agriculturally, and thus trafficking is a much more common economic activity for communities. Crossing between Bangladesh and West Bengal becomes a daily routine for many people as they may live in either of the countries and earn their living in the other.

Thus, keeping a check of those being trafficked, married off, infiltrating, and immigrating illegally or irregularly is an uphill task and has to be achieved through innovative methods and day-to-day vigilance. Crossing the border takes not more than Rs. 50 per person. Having crossed the border, the trafficked victims are mainly kept in West Bengal, and in some cases also in the state of Orissa. They are sorted and graded and sent to different destinations such as Middle East, Delhi, Mumbai, and Agra.

Often, they are sold to pimps who then sell them to brothel keepers in red-light areas of Kolkata such as Sonagachi, Kalighat, and Bowbazar. Some are sent to Bashirghat in the neighbouring district of 24 Paraganas. Under the 1950 Treaty with India, citizens of each country are guaranteed equal treatment. This means in practice that there is no immigration control for Nepalese travelling or migrating to India, and hence no records maintained. Maiti Nepal, an NGO working in the field of combating trafficking, is vigorously involved in interception of possible trafficked persons at the border crossings.

The organization stated in an interview with the RETA team that three to four girls are intercepted in eight exit points daily-suggesting an estimate of over 1,200 per year. There is no data maintained of how many of these girls are truly in the process of being trafficked and how many might be running away from their families or migrating for other reasons. Various cases have been noted where Nepalese girls have been trafficked either directly or after spending time in India to places such as Hong Kong, China; Thailand; and Gulf countries.

As the patterns of trafficking of girls from Nepal to India have become established, the incidence of internal trafficking has also increased. Many rural girls are trafficked to urban areas like Kathmandu, Pokhara, Dharan, Nepalgunj, and Birgunj. Girls from rural areas migrate to cities in search of jobs, and a better future but end up in dance restaurants, massage parlours, bus stands, and wayside dhabas (fast food and tea shops) and bars where they are forced to provide sexual services to the customers.

CSWs are found all over Nepal especially in large cities, border towns, and marketplaces, but it is unknown what proportion are under .age and/or working under coercive circumstances. In Nepal there are estimated to be 26,000 children of the street, i.e., those who both work and live in the street and an additional 3,700 children, who live with their parents but spend most of their time playing and working in the street.

There is a far greater proportion of boys than girls among the street children. The major cause of this imbalance is that many girls are duped into sexual exploitation. The border exit points identified above are located in the southern districts that stretch along the border from east to west of Nepal. Out of 26 official exit points, have been used traditionally for human trafficking. Since monitoring has been stepped up in the recent years of some of the most frequently used crossing points by NGOs, traffickers appear to be detouring these points.

Surveillance of all crossing points is not possible by either NGOs or the government enforcement services. India is both a destination and transit area for trafficking of women and children. There is no data or discussion regarding India as a sending country. This is an area that needs additional attention, as it would seem implausible that Indians are never trafficked out of India. However, it is estimated that cross-border trafficking represents about 10% of the coerced migrants, with approximately 2.17% from Bangladesh and 2.6% from Nepal.

Interstate trafficking, therefore, could make up as much as 89% of trafficked victims. Given this, addressing internal as well as crossborder trafficking issues is essential to any strategic approach at the national level. The 1999 NCRB report notes that its data on crime rates should be viewed with caution, as a sizeable number of crimes against women in India go unreported, largely due to the social stigma attached with reporting.

For example, NCRB data indicates that, in 1999, there were 9,368 trafficked women and children. This is significantly less than 1991 data, which reports that 16,000 women were trafficked. Enforcement officials also noted that little priority is given to reporting trafficking activities, as they face many pressures and little available time to investigate and follow up on specific cases.

Under the Indian Penal Code, crime at the national level has increased by 15.3% over the last decade. Factors that influence crime rates, such as growing urbanization, unemployment, and income disparity, must be taken into account on a region-by-region basis. Offences under the Immoral Trafficking (Prevention) Act, which contributed 50% of the national share of crimes against women, were only reported from 23 cities, and no aggregation was made between rural and urban crime data.

Incidence of trafficking under the Immoral Trafficking (Prevention) Act has shown a steady increase since 1997, with an increase of 7.7% over the 1998 rate. Reported crimes against women were highest in Tamilnadu State (10.5%). The incidence of kidnapping and abduction of women and girls recorded an increase of 6.4 %over the 1994-1998 average. Information on kidnapping and abduction cases broken down by purpose (i.e., adoption, begging, camel racing, prostitution, illicit intercourse, selling body parts, sale, slavery, and unlawful activities), gender, and location have only been collected since 1998.

For example, the total number of cases of kidnapping and abduction registered in 1999 was 15,956. Among the total female victims, 1,960 females were reported kidnapped or abducted for marriage and 9,159 for prostitution purposes.

It has been argued that the traditional practice of ruling classes in Nepal of keeping Tamang girls from the areas surrounding Kathmandu as servants and entertainers gave impetus to the practice of taking Nepalese girls into the Indian brothels. This practice has continued to the extent that 'it is now estimated that more than 300,000 Nepalese women and girls were sold off to the sex market globally."

According to a regional map drawn in 1997 by the United Nations Children's Fund (UNICEF) there were 5,000 sex workers in Kathmandu alone, of whom 1,000 were children. Studies of brothels in India can also provide an indication of the number of Nepali girls working there, and hence an estimate of the numbers trafficked. These estimates, however, do not account for those women who may have migrated voluntarily or are willingly remaining in this sector. The most commonly cited estimates are that 5,000-12,000 Nepali girls, aged 12-20 years old, are trafficked out of Nepal to other countries for prostitution each year and that an estimated 100,000 to 200,000 Nepali girls and women are currently working in the Indian sex industry.

5

Dimensions of Trafficking

For women, the casualization of female labour increases vulnerability to trafficking. Landlessness is also increasing in some countries for varied reasons-pressure from increasing population density, environmental erosion, natural disasters-without corresponding increases in employment opportunities in other sectors. There have been substantial livelihood losses in areas where the demand for traditional skills is declining.

These conditions lead to increasing numbers of women and men moving in order to seek alternative livelihood options-and hence become more vulnerable to being trafficked. Despite these complexities, some generalizations are useful to assist in identifying those who are most vulnerable to being trafficked and strategies to overcome these vulnerabilities; and to assist in interception, rescue, and effective integration of survivors back into communities of their choice with improved life options. Links between trafficking and migration are clearly evident in most accounts of trafficked persons.

Some argue that, while trafficking involves human rights abuses, it fundamentally involves movement of people and should perhaps be better understood by using migration theory. The fact that a vast majority of trafficking episodes start after migration or movement from one place to another has already begun validates the need to look at what causes people to move, and why they are vulnerable to being trafficked during movement. This is a starting point to understanding the factors contributing to human trafficking.

In Bangladesh, a stakeholder-led Thematic Group on Counter-Trafficking (coordinated through the International Organization for Migration [IOM]) has been meeting regularly, seeking to clarify various aspects of human trafficking. This group identified the following needs or motivations that compel a person or an agent of a person to move them from one situation to another, i.e., migrate. These factors do not apply only to Bangladesh, but to migration in general:

— To meet basic needs, e.g., food, shelter, clothing, health;

— To increase security to ensure sustainability of basic needs over time;

— To increase status and/or income;

— To escape stigmatization from incidents such as incest, rape, former sex worker, divorce, widowed;

— To respond to or avoid social considerations, e.g., marriage without dowry, elements of society that limit women's personal development, political oppression, etc.;

— To take up adventure based on a desire to experience life and explore the world; and

— To obtain emotional stability for many reasons such as dysfunctional family situation or need for emotional support system.

These motivations and/or needs are influenced by a series of agents, including other family members, recruiters, smugglers, traffickers, returnees or other migrants, community leaders, and neighbours. A series of factors also hinder or facilitate a person through a migratory process that can result in either a positive outcome (where needs are met or motivations achieved) or a negative outcome.

Examining the needs and motivations that initiate the migratory process and the factors that influence the outcomes can help to identify activities to reduce the vulnerability of those most at risk to being trafficked.

The most commonly identified push factor that starts the trafficking process is poverty. The necessity to meet basic needs, in combination with other factors (as identified above) is the most commonly identified motivation to migrate or to encourage a family member to leave. Those most vulnerable to trafficking generally come from the poorest and marginalized segments of communities. However, a simplistic view of poverty based on low-income levels or livelihood options does not assist in understanding why it is that women and children appear to be the most vulnerable to negative outcomes from migration, such as trafficking.

An understanding of the noneconomic elements of poverty-lack of human and social capital, gender discrimination-also helps identify the most vulnerable to marginalization from the development process and, simultaneously, to trafficking. Governance issues also play a role in allocating resources and services in a community; those living in poverty tend to have limited access to these development opportunities, further reinforcing their vulnerability to trafficking.

Despite Bangladesh's low human development index, which is lower than most South Asian countries, there has been a decline in those living below the poverty line from 47% in 1996 to current levels of 45%. Some key social development indicators have improved, for example the education gap between male and female primary school enrolment, which stood at 22% in 1985, declined to 3% over the past 15 years.

Health indicators, however, remain poor, especially for women, reflecting the limited services available and general conditions of poverty for such a large proportion of the population that result in malnutrition and the many associated health conditions. While women in Bangladesh have much lower skill levels than men, their contribution to the economy is largely unrecognized. Women are still primarily involved in the nonmonetized sector and subsistence activities, and hence tend not to be reported in macro statistics.

Women make up a disproportionately high percentage of unpaid family workers in agriculture and informal manufacturing sectors, and as such are the most underemployed. When women do receive wages in the informal sector, there are wide gender differences. Women's participation in the formal work force has increased, as the demand for low-cost, unskilled labour has grown in the urban areas, particularly in the garment sector.

India invests far less in its women workers than in its working men. Women also receive a smaller share of what society produces: they are less endowed than men with health care, education, and productive assets that could increase their return to labour. Women's nutritional levels are lower than men's; more women than men die before the age of 35.

Three-fourths of Indian women are illiterate. Some 90% of rural and 70% of urban women workers are unskilled. While women are vital and productive workers in India's economy and make up one third of the labour force, there is a statistical purdah imposed by existing methods of measuring labour that renders much of their work invisible.

When work such as collecting fuel and fodder or working in dairy, poultry, or kitchen-gardening is added to the numbers of those who work in the conventional labour force, women's participation rate in the economy totals 51%, only 13 percentage points below the rate for men. Macro-economic reforms have resulted in an increasing commercialization of agriculture throughout India. This has resulted in:

— Labour-intensive cropping patterns replaced by capital-intensive systems, particularly in the coastal districts;

— A shift from paddy production to cash crops. As a result, many women have been forced to work as day labourers on farms where wage differentials between male and female workers are high; and

Increasing need and demand for occupational skills, leading to an institutionalization of gender bias in agricultural and natural resource industries. There is little opportunity for unskilled labour. The impact of structural-economic change in the agricultural sector in

India seems to have increased the proportion of casual workers, thereby demanding flexibility and mobility from the labour force.

For women, the casualization of female labour increases vulnerability to trafficking. Livelihood loss is directly linked to vulnerability to trafficking. There has been substantial livelihood loss in the fishing, weaving, tobacco, and cotton sectors in India, which has contributed to increased vulnerability. In the fishing sector, for example, the depletion of resources and nonimplementation of the Marine Fishing Regulation Act and Aquaculture Bill have facilitated conglomerate takeovers in the industry, forcing many men to seek wage labour on the roads and women to seek income from whatever means available.

An examination of the highest source for trafficking of women and children in Southern India reveals that trafficking is more common in areas that are prone to drought or other natural disasters, situated in less-productive agro-climatic zones and where large numbers of families live below the poverty line. Those who make low wages, if any, are functionally landless; one third of women and girls in CSW in metropolitan cities were from drought prone-areas, clearly supporting the link between poverty, powerlessness, and vulnerability to trafficking.

Nepal ranks as one of the world's poorest countries with a per capita gross national product of $220 a year. Gross domestic product (GDP) grew by 6.4% in 2000 compared to 4.4% in the previous year. About 42% of the population lives below the national poverty line of Nepalese rupees (NRs) 4,400 ($77) per capita per annum, which is based on minimum caloric intake, housing, and other nonfood standards.

ADB's recent poverty analysis for Nepal shows that poverty incidence, intensity, and severity have not improved over the past quarter century, a finding mirrored in the country's human development indicator scores. The poverty analysis confirmed that poverty is much more prevalent, intense, and severe in rural areas, where poverty incidence is almost double that of the urban areas. The incidence of poverty in the mid-and far-western development regions and in the mountain districts greatly exceeds the national average.

Women's contribution to the economy in Nepal is significant but continues to be largely unrecognized. Only recently some policies and programs have been developed that target women as entrepreneurs or economic growth agents or that increase women's access to economic resources, paid employment, training and promotion, as well as laws guaranteeing healthy and safe working conditions.

Women are still primarily engaged in the low-productivity, low-wage, and high-underemployment agriculture sector. Work participation starts at an early age, especially in this sector. Women are simultaneously engaged in reproduction, household work, and income generation. For example, 70% of labour and 26% of farm-level decision making in livestock raising is made by women.

There remains in South Asia extensive persistent poverty and the evidence that women are disproportionately excluded from development opportunities through deeply rooted gender-based discrimination. The following table provides some basic indicators drawn from the Gender-Related Development Index in the United Nations Development Programme

(UNDP) Human Development Report 2001 for the three RETA countries as compared to the Philippines, demonstrating the greater gaps in development achievements between women and men in South Asia.

Women's poverty is more severe than men's poverty because of lack of access to resources and very low rates of human capital among women (education, health etc.)- as illustrated by comparisons between adult literacy rates; enrolment rates in primary, secondary, and tertiary education; and significantly higher maternal mortality rates than achieved in other Southeast Asian countries

In 2000 UNIFEM published a biennial report - Progress of the World's Women that demonstrates that women's share of employment in industry and services in India and Pakistan has hardly increased between 1980 and 1997 and remains the lowest for Asia. All three RETA countries invest less in their women workers than in their working men despite women's economic contributions. Although the causal factors vary from country to country, certain generalizations can be drawn:

— Women's flexibility and cheap labour are sought in both the formal and informal sectors where they are forced to use simple technologies and limited resources;

— Systemic gender-related inequities, for example unequal access to land, productive resources, information, and skills and education, in addition to continuing inequity in the labour market and harassment at work, enhance women's vulnerability to economic change;

— Women also maintain primary responsibility across South Asia for domestic tasks and shoulder these multiple tasks even under conditions of economic and social stress; and

— Women's low status is most dramatically reflected in the fact that in all seven countries in South Asia there are fewer women than there are men. The negative sex ratio can be attributed to excess mortality of women and girls resulting from both direct and indirect discrimination in the provision of food, care, medical treatment, education, and above all physical and sexual violence.

It can also be argued that the feminization of poverty in South Asia is accompanied by the feminization of survival strategies. In hard times, women are more likely than men to exploit every possibility for work or income, including precarious activities and poorly paid work at home or in the informal sector (including provision of sexual services).

More women in South Asia are now moving to take up employment opportunities in urban centers, seasonal agricultural work, or unskilled work in foreign countries. These decisions are hard for women to take compared to men, as they might have to find alternative child care, and they face harassment and discrimination in public spaces and the workplace.

Women are also more vulnerable to the negative social effects of economic restructuring and recession as they are generally unskilled. Programs and services developed by the government to address unemployment are less accessible to women and investments in women's skills and opportunities (that would increase overall family status) are rarely made. According to ADB's study in 1999, Women in Nepal, the incidence of poverty among female-headed households is not comparatively higher than among male-headed households.

Discriminatory practices such as gender-based wage differences and harassment by employers and other men seeking to deny women equal access to the marketplace have not been addressed. Government agencies have also rarely delivered economic development programs directly to women to improve productivity and incomes in the informal sector. NGOs have had more success with microfinance projects that also build skills and introduce new technologies and trades.

However, few of these are targeting urban areas, where so many women are now seeking survival strategies. To tackle these obstacles, a more gender-sensitive approach is required in the formulation of economic and social development policies and programs to ensure that women benefit from development and are offered opportunities for empowerment.

At the same time it is vital to recognize that many poverty reduction programs for women will encourage greater mobility and migration of women. Even as poverty is reduced, exposure to the risk of trafficking will increase for these women, unless there are accompanying programs to provide safe and secure transportation, access to food and shelter in destination areas, and services such as help lines, effective protection from criminals by law enforcers, etc. Women need long-term (i.e., not project-dependent) livelihood opportunities that provide competitive earnings and working conditions.

Causes of Trafficking

A range of policies and environmental circumstances also

influence the incidence of poverty and vulnerability to risks for migrants to being trafficked. For example: Impacts of globalization have included the spread of modernization with greater access to transport, media etc., but also for many, the disappearance of traditional income sources and rural employment, pushing the poor and unskilled to migrate to survive.

Asia has also become a center for low-cost, labour-intensive manufacturing operations. Competition among countries in South Asia has driven the cost of labour down further, encouraging some employers to use illegal practices (such as bonded labour) to access cheaper labour sources. Conflicts and natural disasters that force communities to move, often en masse to meet their basic needs. When individuals within those communities have no skills or education, and are exposed to health risks, their capacity to secure sustainable livelihoods is limited, and their risk to trafficking heightened.

External migration policies that exclude many unskilled people, particularly women, from legal migration and are therefore forced to seek alternative livelihood options through illegal means. Human smugglers offer forged documents or transportation to other countries where they promise to link migrants with job opportunities. These are often the same smugglers who traffic labour. Those working in illegal situations are more susceptible to coercion by traffickers.

It is anticipated that migration policies will continue to discourage migration of unskilled labour, or that labour movements will be confined within South Asia and to certain Southeast Asian countries and that this situation will continue. These countries have poor records of protecting the rights of irregular and illegal migrants or trafficked persons, which perpetuate conditions that offer profits to opportunistic traffickers. For example, there is currently no migration policy in place in Bangladesh to address the impacts of these trends, or to promote development benefits from safe migration.

An examination of the highest source areas for trafficking of women and children in Bangladesh points towards a need for those living in poverty to seek to meet their basic needs, through whatever means available. For those at risk of (or already living in) conditions of poverty, underemployment and unemployment remain high, and levels of functional landlessness are increasing because of population density, environmental erosion, or natural disasters without corresponding increases in employment opportunities in other sectors.

In the industrialized sectors, the proportion of casual workers has increased, and structural change in many sectors is leading to dislocation and unemployment for thousands. These conditions lead to increasing numbers of women and men moving in order to seek alternative livelihood options -and hence becoming more vulnerable to being trafficked.

Poverty drives many to take "unthinkable "decisions and commit "undoable "acts that might include the handing over of a child to either another family member or even a stranger on the promise of offering a better life for them. These promises may also include the prospect of sending back remittances to help other family members.

There are many cases in Bangladesh of families of young girls being trafficked to brothels in India openly acknowledging that their daughters are living under difficult and harmful circumstances, but seeing no other option for their survival.

Internally Displaced Persons (IDPs) are also highly vulnerable to being trafficked. The term IDP does not share a universally agreed definition by the international community. Conditions such as violence, human rights violations, environmental disaster, natural calamities, political unrest, and loss of land and property all displace families forcing them to search for places of refuge.

As IDPs are generally without resources and without official residence or government recognition, their status makes them more susceptible to adverse situations such as trafficking. In Nepal the escalating insurgency by the Maoists in the past 6 years has forced many thousands of women and children to leave their communities. Social disintegration and overall economic decline is intensifying the numbers of de facto IDPs.

It is estimated by some that nearly one third of the total male labour force has emigrated to India or other countries for menial jobs and mercenary services. The armed conflict is interrupting basic services, restricting development assistance, and breaking down family and community networks as men either join the conflict or migrate to seek employment elsewhere to support their families. This has left many women in the affected districts looking after their children alone and scraping together an income under increasingly difficult circumstances.

Women are also vulnerable to rape and sexual exploitation that are common features, if not actual weapons, of conflict. This type of suffering is leaving deep psychological wounds, which can severely undermine the capacity of both women and their communities to recover; and women are crucial to the recovery process of both their families and the wider community. Many thousands of women and children are moving to Kathmandu in particular.

Social exclusion based on gender can be seen as a major contributing factor to the risks of being trafficked, as identified above. Gender-based discrimination, as suffered by individual girls and women, is perpetuated and institutionalized in the family and community. Gender stereotypes are used to reinforce women's low status. Women are not encouraged to challenge control by men and are expected to accept their position in life without complaint. These stereotypes also reinforce in young women a sense of helplessness and of being unprotected without a man.

All these factors play into the hands of opportunistic traffickers who can more easily control young women and break their spirit. Rural society in South Asia is especially resistant to educating girls and women. Rural women tend to have more children, be poorer, and, in their struggle to survive, have little or no time and energy to spare on adult literacy programs if they are available. Children of female-headed households in rural areas are often put to work in order to ensure the survival of the family rather than continue in school.

In Nepal even though over 50% of rural children are enrolled in primary school, only 23% of girls attend secondary school. Education is also considered as a hindrance to marriage prospects for girls in many communities, as an educated woman is viewed as a potential threat to her husband and may upset the status quo within the family.

In India ,girl children are commonly seen as overwhelming burdens to their families. The unholy alliance between tradition (son complex) and technology (ultrasound) has created havoc in Indian society: some families see it as more desirable to spend a few thousand rupees on pre-natal sex determination tests and sex selective abortions, than to spend hundreds of thousands of rupees on dowry later on.

Lack of education condemns girls and women to low-skilled labour, and limits options for alternative income-generating opportunities. Lack of status within the family and community, coupled with little or no education, means that women are generally unaware of their rights or entitlements to protection from the law, even when threatened by traffickers. Despite official efforts to discourage payment of dowry upon marriage, the practice that requires a girl's parents to make payment of property, goods, or money upon a daughter's marriage remains strong in many areas of South Asia.

This practice is part of the complex web of ways that gender disparities are maintained as girls are considered a liability to their families, accentuating the preference for sons who will bring dowry payment into the family. The impacts of these practices on women are many -the inability to give dowry by the girls 'parents has resulted in a number of violent measures against new brides including physical and mental abuse.

The demand for dowry can also make it easier for traffickers to persuade parents to hand their daughters over to their control, with the false prospects of "dowryless "marriage. Some women are moving into decision-making positions in business and government in several South Asian countries. The quotas reserved for women in all levels of political office in Bangladesh and India, and to a lesser extent in Nepal ,are leading to more and more women running for openly contested seats.

Many efforts are being made through government and NGOs to build the capacity of these elected women to fulfill their mandates more effectively and take on greater leadership, especially concerning the empowerment of other women. In practice, however, it is taking some time for these elected women to take leadership in their communities to promote women's issues and gender equality. This growing political empowerment of women has come about partly from women's struggle from within their societies, but also due to external pressures and changes on traditional social practices from economic demands.

Gender-based discrimination is reinforced through traditional social practices and builds on ethnicity and caste. In India ,this can be well illustrated by the traditional Devadasi practices in Karnataka, Andhra Pradesh, and Maharashtra, the Jogin in Andhra Pradesh, and the Bhedias or Sansui in Madhya Pradesh. Parents from certain scheduled tribes marry girls to a deity or a temple.

The marriage usually occurs before the girl reaches puberty and requires the girl to provide sexual services for upper-caste community members from the temple. Such girls are known as jogini. They are forbidden to enter into a real marriage. A study for the National Commission for Women (NCW) indicated that 62% of women CSWs belong to the scheduled castes, and 30% to scheduled tribe groups. In many instances, traffickers recruit and send Devadasis to states or districts where there is less strict enforcement of the caste system.

In western Nepal where the trafficking of girls into sexual slavery has a long history, traditional customs like Deuki, Badi, Jari, and Jhuma all have become synonymous with prostitution. According to the Deuki system, girl children were dedicated to deities. Since these girls were neither educated nor had any resources or skills, prostitution was the only alternative for survival open to them. Where these practices continue, they represent a highly exploited and socially ostracized class.

Some "untouchable "Hindu castes, such as the Badi in western Nepal, are also designated as sex workers. The Badi people originally were a musician caste and have long been entertainers, doing sex work occasionally as a peripheral income source. During the past 50 years, modern media and technology have eliminated the demand for their singing and dancing, and hence these girls and women rely now entirely on CSW as caste exclusion has denied them education or access to other forms of employment.

Ironically this opportunity to earn income, even though through sex work, has meant that girl children are valued among the Badi -"He's very rich -he has many daughters. "Their families also now routinely sell these girls to traffickers for work elsewhere in Nepal or India without consideration of the harm this may cause them. The overwhelming majority of children vulnerable to trafficking are those belonging to poor families with few or no skills or assets, often working as seasonal labourers or in factories or construction sites. Those most at risk are:

— children separated from their families or with disrupted family backgrounds (e.g., orphans, victims of abuse, unaccompanied children, children from single-parent families, or from families headed by children);

— economically and socially deprived children (unemployed, poor, rural, and those without access to education, vocational training, or a reasonable standard of living);

— children from other marginalized groups (e.g., certain minorities, internally displaced persons); and

— children from the conflict areas themselves.

Some stakeholders also argue that the demand for child labour is increasing. Employers prefer children because they are naïve, uncomplaining, easily controlled, vulnerable, desperate, and dispensable. The children's ages range from 5 to 16 years with 13 years being the average age. Most of these children find jobs as porters, domestic servants, carpet weavers, transportation helpers, rag pickers, and shoe shiners.

Some of these children are trafficked into CSW, some are used for organ transplanting, and some find jobs in the circus. In all of these cases, the traffickers and employers are violating these children's basic rights. Among street children in urban settings these vulnerabilities intensify other power relationships. For example, from the very beginning of street life, girl children are considered as "fallen", putting them at extreme risk of sexual abuse/assault from other boys and men.

Children are also reluctant to leave abusive relationships that nonetheless provide them with some stability. Traffickers play upon this type of dependence and vulnerability in order to maintain control over children. A recent International Labour Organization

(ILO) study on Trafficking and Sexual Abuse Among Street Children in Kathmandu also identifies the complex series of reasons children end up on the streets in the first place, which provides indications for types of programming required to address these reasons.

While domestic violence and familial problems are identified by the majority, peer pressure and hopes for a good life combined with economic reasons are also very significant. Many children are moving around alone in the most vulnerable conditions to being trafficked. Even when children arrive with their parent(s), the pressure of urban life on new migrants can overcome their tenuous family ties and these children end up on the street alone. There have been few studies of those children most at risk in Bangladesh.

Research and Services NGO in Bangladesh (INCIDIN) has carried out two recent studies: one in 1997 for Red Barnet/Danish Save the Children; and, a second in 2001 for ILO and the International Programme for the Elimination of Child Labor (IPEC), Rapid Assessment on Child Trafficking in Children for Exploitative Employment in Bangladesh. There are few facilities available that can serve as shelters or temporary homes for street children. There are persistent problems with the quality of care provided in those that exist, especially in long-term homes where many children might end up being institutionalized for years.

Alternatives to this kind of care need to be urgently tested and funded, and professional standards for caregivers need to be established. While there are only limited and often substandard facilities available, many trafficked adults and children will prefer the option of remaining in exploitative or abusive living conditions under the control of traffickers, or returning to life on the streets. Children without birth certificates are especially vulnerable to trafficking.

According to UNICEF, a birth certificate not only represents recognition of a child's existence (and hence his or status under the law) but also ensures access to vaccination, treatment in health centers, and enrolment in schools. Traffickers find many of their victims in remote villages where poverty is high and registration rates are low, knowing that girls without papers are less likely to run away from their perpetrators.

Trafficking of children could be for sex or cheap labour. Helpless in the stifling environment, young boys end up working 14 hours in sweatshops, in hazardous occupations like tanning leather, or making explosives, firecrackers, carpets, or garments.

Governance is the system of government policies and programs necessary to perform a number of vital functions:

— make decisions and coordinate policies;

— establish an enabling environment for private-sector growth;

— deliver certain critical sets of goods and services; and

— promote equity.

The poor are more vulnerable to weak governance and increased risks of being trafficked. Contributing factors in this respect include absence of effective legislation, policies, and institutional structures in addressing human trafficking; poor law enforcement combined with corruption (e.g., police, border officials, politicians being bribed by traffickers); and exclusion of poor and vulnerable groups from basic social and economic services (e.g., women, indigenous peoples/low castes).

Good governance for poverty reduction requires public policies and practices that encourage the inclusion of the poor and other vulnerable groups in the development process. This involves pro-poor public expenditures; social services that are nearer to the users and have more relevance for the poor; and policies that generate equity, access to socioeconomic assets ,and enhanced social relations -including gender equity and the improved status of women.

To improve governance, it is necessary to empower communities, individuals, and groups so that they can participate in decisions that affect their lives. Recent efforts at government decentralization of decision making aim to improve planning and delivery of services to the district and village levels, so that communities can ensure that services are more responsive to their needs.

Quotas or reserved seats for women elected officials are now in place on decision-making bodies at many levels in all South Asian countries. Extensive efforts are underway to empower these women to respond to the needs of other marginalized women in their communities.

However, empowering women to seize these opportunities is a long-term process, and as identified earlier, those women most vulnerable to trafficking are the least likely to participate in social mobilization and remain unable to access services and programs that would build their resistance. Good governance also ensures the capacity to extend protection from criminal acts such as trafficking.

Migration and Trafficking

Migration is linked with trafficking in several ways. People may voluntarily choose to migrate but may be deceived about the kind of work they are subsequently expected to do. In this case, what started as migration has become trafficking. Or, a person may willingly migrate for employment but may be trafficked on from the initial employment site (e.g., a carpet or garment factory).

The initial process was not trafficking and no crime was committed until the second phase of migration occurred. Hence, while trafficking normally involves migration, migration does not always involve trafficking. This distinction is significant for potential antitrafficking interventions. Given that trafficking may occur either in a person's original home base (often a rural community) or in a subsequent work site (often an urban area), interventions to combat trafficking should cover both locations.

Interventions should also recognize that for each individual case, the factors that create the need or desire to migrate and the vulnerability to being exploited by traffickers during migration might be quite different. Likewise, it is important that antitrafficking interventions consider the direct or indirect impact on a person's right to mobility. Antitrafficking interventions can easily become antimigration interventions. Yet it is difficult to distinguish voluntary migration from trafficking at the departure point since the deception, if present, has not yet become apparent.

It is only after arrival at an unexpected and exploitative outcome that the crime of trafficking is apparent. In the early 1970s after independence, the Bangladesh Government did not allow professionals and highly skilled people to migrate to stop a "brain-drain. "The embargo was lifted in mid-1970s. But there was is no comprehensive policy either to encourage or discourage female migration.

In early 1981, through a presidential order, semi-skilled and unskilled female workers were barred from migrating overseas for employment. However, they continued to leave the country. In 1988, the Government reviewed the policy and withdrew the ban, replacing it with a restriction that allowed the Government to consider migration of semi-skilled and unskilled women on a case-by-case basis.

Then in 1997, following wider ministerial consultations, the Government re-imposed a complete ban on women migration except for those who were highly qualified professionals such as doctors, engineers, and teachers. This was the first time that a ban was imposed even on professionals such as nurses, secretarial assistance, and garment/factories workers, along with other categories of semiskilled and unskilled workers. Many argued this was necessary in the face of several highly publicized cases of abuse suffered by women outside Bangladesh.

Conservative elements in politics and Bangladesh society still feel that women should be protected. Facing criticism from the Bangladesh Association of International Recruiting Agencies and civil society, the Government revised the order allowing a few categories of women to work as domestic help if the employer belonged to any of the following three groups:

— Bangladesh embassy staff, financially solvent Bangladeshis such as doctors and engineers, and

— foreign passport holders of Bangladeshi origin or descent.

This ban has now been modified under a 1998 Circular to apply only to domestic workers for non-Bangladeshis, but the potential for more restrictive revisions to be reinstated remains.

The demand for trafficked labor comes from a wide range of sectors, including commercial sex work, where trafficked persons are required to provide sexual services in their own country, but some distance from their homes, or are transported to India or other destinations such as Pakistan, the Gulf States, etc. There is also a demand for CSWs in South Asia in sites other than brothels or dance bars, such as along highways, in small communities, and in temporary construction worker camps.

There is a growing demand for trafficked labor in factories where trafficked persons become debt-bonded to factory owners or coerced into work under slave-like conditions. Asia has become a centre for low-cost, labor-intensive, manufacturing operations. Competition between countries in South Asia has driven down the cost of labor even further, encouraging some employers to use illegal practices such as bonded labor to access cheaper and cheaper labor sources.

There are anecdotal accounts of trafficked child labor used as domestic workers, but this sector is poorly understood as a locus of child and trafficked labor abuses. There is resistance in many Asian countries to address the issue, as middle-class professionals are strongly implicated in hiring child labor in their homes, whether trafficked or not. Children are also trafficked into the control of begging syndicates, camel jockeying in the Gulf States, and other sectors of entertainment.

According to many reports (e.g., United States Agency for International Development [USAID],ILO) India has the largest number of child labourers in the world. Government of India estimates range from 17.5 million to 11 million, many of whom are highly vulnerable to being trafficked. Furthermore, persistent acceptance of the use of child labor in some sectors of work creates demand for trafficked children. Many studies have identified that high proportions of children involved in the worst forms of child labor have been trafficked.

It should not be assumed, however, that all these children are working under conditions of forced labor or are trafficked, and the Indian Government is actively seeking to eliminate all forms of exploitation of children. There has been some effort made to improve labor standards in Nepal, which are most successful when involving private-sector partnerships and increased corporate responsibility.

The demand for CSWs can also be tackled, for example through links with HIV/AIDS programming and awareness-raising among contractors and in construction camps in infrastructure projects. During the RETA's National Consultation, WOREC recounted that in a region where a cement factory was being built, their enquiries uncovered that the CSWs operating inside the camp were all women who clearly chose to remain in this sector.

However, some distance from the construction site, at least one VDC distant, traffickers had set up operations coercing adolescents and young women into providing sexual services for construction workers, but at sufficient distance from the camp so as to avoid detection. This implies that any efforts undertaken to address demand conditions, such as those presented by temporary construction camps, need to be carefully monitored and impacts assessed beyond the immediate confines of the camp.

There is remarkably little research on the demand conditions for trafficked labour. As governments and international agencies are starting to pay more attention to illegal and irregular migration patterns, the demand conditions that create profits for human smugglers and traffickers should be examined and understood more carefully. There is potential for ADB to play a role in these efforts, as labor-market conditions form a key area in poverty analysis and policy dialogue at regional and country levels.

Increased awareness among local-level governance structures can also play a role in shaming those using trafficked labor into changing their practices. Governance projects could take up these issues as areas where rule of law and respect for labor practices has the potential for longer-term outcomes of reducing the demand for trafficked labor.

Economic losses to communities and governments are enormous if considered in terms of lost returns on human or social-capital investments. The cost of countering criminal trafficking activities puts additional strain on already limited government resources for law enforcement. Vast amounts of potential income from trafficked labor is lost in "hidden " sectors such as CSW or is expropriated by criminal traffickers and diverted out of the formal economy.

There are many sectors of the Asian and Middle Eastern economies that rely upon low-cost and often trafficked migrant labour, but -if reasonable returns could be made on this labor by the migrants themselves and mechanisms put in place that facilitate remittance and reinvestment of such savings to improve livelihoods in a sustainable manner -poverty conditions could be alleviated and the vulnerability to trafficking (as an outcome from risky migration) could be reduced. As sending, transit, and receiving countries seek to stem trafficking and human smuggling activities, the economic benefits of safe migration should not be ignored.

Trafficked persons have often faced extreme psychological stress that in turn leads to trauma, depression and, in some cases, suicide. A trafficked woman or child may have been exposed to isolation, fear, sexual abuse, rape, and other forms of physical and mental violence. Emotional stress is usually compounded by constant fear of arrest and public stigmatization, making the thought of returning home fearful. These harms are both short term and long term.

Mental health experts understand more about the enormous impact of posttraumatic stress over many years that might influence the capacity of a woman to care for her family or negotiate through future emotional challenges once the original harm has stopped. Women and children located in the commercial sex sector, either trafficked or otherwise, face higher risk of contracting sexually transmitted diseases (STDs), HIV/AIDS, tuberculosis, and other diseases.

Mobile populations in general face greater risks of contracting STDs as their family and community lives are disrupted. Many of the children most at risk of being trafficked, particularly urban street children, are also considered to be high-risk groups for contracting HIV/AIDS through drug use, sexual contacts, and other behaviours. Stakeholders seeking to combat trafficking and to address HIV/AIDS are therefore working with similar risk groups and there are many examples of combined programming or collaborative approaches that have ensured women and girls are empowered to protect themselves from HIV infection and resist trafficking experiences.

Increased incidence of HIV/AIDS is also believed to have led to an increasing demand for younger commercial sex workers, who have higher probability of being free of disease. There remains strong resistance among many men to recognize they are HIV carriers. There have also been reports of myths circulating that having sex with a virgin will actually cure STDs. Tragically these false notions are creating a market demand for younger girls even below 12 years of age.

There are many highly innovative programs already in place in South Asia seeking to change high-risk behaviour, particularly among mobile male populations, that can curb demand for some of the most exploited commercial sex workers. However, links between trafficking and HIV/AIDS have to be explored with caution. Many trafficking awareness-raising campaigns have inadvertently conveyed the message to fearful communities that all trafficked persons are infected with the disease, leading to further stigmatization of all women returning to their communities.

There is also often tension between the public health objectives of HIV/AIDS programming and attempts to combat trafficking. In some cases, the delivery of public health messages concerning HIV/AIDS risks among CSWs has been carried out by co-opting the support of pimps or brothel owners, who are also abusing and exploiting child labour.

Approaches to Trafficking

Stakeholders are involved in programs and activities to address trafficking concerns in Bangladesh, India, and Nepal, including civil society organizations, government departments, international nongovernment organizations (INGOs), and donors implementing and funding programming to combat trafficking. In order to improve collaboration and cooperation between stakeholders and to ensure that there is no overlapping or replication of programming, several attempts have been made in Bangladesh and Nepal to identify who is doing what and where.

For example, in Nepal , MWCSW in 1998 published a Directory of Organizations Working Against Trafficking based on requests for information sent to as wide a group as possible. The National Network Against Girl Trafficking (NNAGT) prepared a map that identified the districts where each NGO was working in 1999. The Institute for Integral Development Studies has been preparing an updated list that will not only identify NGOs working from the Kathmandu Valley but also smaller community-based organizations (CBOs) in more remote areas.

In Bangladesh, Action Against Trafficking and Sexual Exploitation of Children (ATSEC) has sought to maintain a central list of member agencies and to provide an informal registry of stakeholders across the country.

India, as a much larger country, with a three-tiered system of government (national, state, and local levels) has a vast range of stakeholders from government and civil society involved in combating trafficking, and no formal process is in place to track the whole range.

The national government focal point remains in close contact with state- level focal points, and meets some on a regular basis. Several networks of NGOs exist, some of which also link with networks in other South Asian countries. However, it remains challenging for experiences to be exchanged and collaborative relationships to be maintained across such a large and diverse country.

The national focal point for addressing trafficking of women and children in Bangladesh is MWCA, but several other ministries share mandates associated with addressing trafficking concerns. Most current activities are being undertaken under the auspices of a 3-year pilot project, Child Development: Coordinated Program to Combat Child Trafficking (CPCCT) supported by NORAD. The project has a Steering Committee (under the chair of the MWCA Secretary) and has established a National Task Force on Trafficking chaired by the Minister of Home Affairs. The Task Force is mandated to review actions undertaken by the project including rescue of trafficked children and punishment of child traffickers.

NGOs are also involved in the implementation of the project, particularly rescue, repatriation, reintegration, and creating social awareness. A special antichild trafficking cell has been established in the Ministry of Home Affairs. Two other cells, one in Bangladesh Defence Rifles and the other one in Police (CID) have been formed under the supervision of Ministry of Home Affairs.

The functions of the cells are to identify those involved in trafficking, arrest them, and promptly rescue any trafficked persons. Current and planned initiatives to train the police, magistrates, and judges on child rights are expected to improve the enforcement of existing legislation. Initiatives will provide orientation to government and NGO workers on the consequences of trafficking, so that they can create awareness among the communities where they work.

Expected outcomes include dissemination of information about trafficking to law enforcement officials and increased efforts to take strict action against law enforcement officials themselves involved in trafficking. In recent years, the police have been more active in apprehending cases of border as well as internal trafficking, and have arrested some traffickers.

The Department of Social Services, under the Ministry of Social Welfare, has been implementing two projects with target groups highly vulnerable to trafficking: children of street-based sex workers and street children generally. However, these projects only target vulnerable street children, not women or other vulnerable children living under difficult circumstances. This Ministry was established in 2002 with the mandate to promote orderly migration and protect the interest of migrant workers in their country of origin and country of destination.

The Government, with technical assistance from IOM, is developing a policy and an NPA on Migration Management, including implementation of the UN Convention on the Protection of the Rights of All Migrant Workers and Members of Their Families 1990. Many stakeholders in Bangladesh argue that improved migration management and the dissemination of safe migration messages will assist considerably in the prevention of trafficking.

As a support to the Government in preparation for these policy-level initiatives, IOM commissioned several studies in relation to migration process, use of remittances, migration management system, and situation of migrant workers and their families. The Bangladesh Institute of Development Studies and the Refugee Migratory Movement and Research Unit of Dhaka 148 University helped IOM to conduct these studies. A consultation will be held under the leadership of the Ministry for Expatriate Welfare and Overseas Employment.

The national focal point for combating trafficking in women and children in India at the national level is DWCD under the Ministry of Human Resource Development. DWCD has counterpart focal points in each state government. As a result of Supreme Court directives of 1990, the Government of India constituted a Central Advisory Committee on Child Prostitution in 1994 to examine policy and program interventions. A desk was set up in DWCD to implement the recommendations of the central advisory committee.

In 1997, under a directive of the Supreme Court, the Committee on Prostitution, Child Prostitution, and Children of Prostitutes was established, headed by the secretary of DWCD. This committee looks into the problems of prostitution and trafficking of women and children in order to develop suitable programs. DWCD has also been mandated to implement an NPA to suppress trafficking in the country that incorporates the findings from the report of the Central Advisory

Committee on Child Prostitution, the recommendations of the National Commission for Women, the directions of the Supreme Court of India, and the experiences of various NGOs working in the area.

Government and NGO representatives also agree that this NPA is both comprehensive and innovative. However, there remain constraints to its implementation, which include lack of resources and inadequate accurate data on which to base policy formulation and advocacy to combat trafficking across other government departments. DWCD is working toward synergizing the multiple but isolated initiatives of international agencies to combat trafficking by collecting data on the spheres of activity and interest of UN and bilateral agencies.

DWCD and the UNICEF Country Office are organizing regional workshops on prevention of trafficking of women and children to review the situation of trafficking and sexual abuse in women and children in different regions and develop a plan of action. At the regional level, India has pledged to coordinate the implementation of the SAARC Convention on Combating the Crime of Trafficking in Women and Children for Prostitution, which was ratified by the SAARC countries at the Eleventh SAARC Summit held at Kathmandu in January 2002.

The Ministry has an internal focal point for combating trafficking activities. It is felt that an agency having all-India jurisdiction would be in a position to overcome interstate jurisdiction delays that hinder effective enforcement of the ITPA across the whole country. A proposal is currently under discussion with the state governments for setting up a nodal investigating agency under the aegis of this Ministry.

The state governments have women's cells at police headquarters and women in the police force. Efforts are being undertaken for sensitization on gender issues, under the overall coordination of the division dealing with the issue in the Ministry. National Human Rights Commission (NHRC) is a statutory body that performs the functions assigned to it under the Protection of the Human Rights Act.

The issue of child prostitution has been a major concern of the Commission; it has been working with DWCD, the National Commission for Women, and UNICEF. In order to better coordinate efforts, NHRC constituted a core group on child prostitution in 1998. At the request of United Nations High Commissioner for Refugees, a focal point was set up in NHRC in 2001 to address the human rights of women, including matters relating to trafficking.

National Commission for Women (NCW)'s mandate is to safeguard the rights and interests of women by running legal awareness programs, looking into complaints regarding the violation of women's rights, examining the non-implementation of laws and non-compliance with policy guidelines, providing relief to women by taking up their concerns with the appropriate authorities, conducting research, undertaking investigations, etc.

NCW has the powers of a civil court when investigating any case provided for by the NCW Act 1990. Combating the trafficking of women is one of its main areas of priority. National AIDS Control Organization (NACO) was launched in 1987 and the first National AIDS Control Project in 1992. The second phase of the National Project has begun for the period 1999-

2004 (with a total funding of approximately US$331 million). The emphasis is on a comprehensive, multisectoral approach.

The key components are targeted interventions with vulnerable (CSWs, street children, migrant labourers, etc.) and general populations, care and support for people living with HIV/AIDS, voluntary testing and counselling, hospital infection control, and STD programming. Interestingly, NACO's state-level mechanisms include the state AIDS control societies that are run by NGOs/technical professionals.

One such state-level mechanism, Aids Prevention and Control (APAC) in Tamilnadu, run by voluntary health services (VHS), has an intervention called Women in Prostitution. Twelve NGOs working in community-based mobilization, self-help groups (SHGs) and microfinance, advocacy, and accessing government schemes are involved with APAC. States are affected by trafficking in different ways, either as high-supply areas, transit points, or destination points.

The focal point for addressing human trafficking issues in the Government is the MWCSW. An NPA to guide the Government's response to the trafficking of women and children in particular was developed and approved in 1998 in consultation with local and international NGOs and multilateral and bilateral donor agencies and was reviewed and revised during 2001 in preparation for reporting on progress at the Second World Congress Against Commercial Sexual Exploitation of Children, held in Yokohama in December 2001.

The NPA has six areas of implementation: policies and strategies, enactment of appropriate legislation, raising awareness among the general population, health impacts, education, and rescue and rehabilitation. Other ministries and departments are also involved in antitrafficking activities. The police have been actively increasing their capacities to combat trafficking through law enforcement. The Ministry of Law and Justice has been involved in legislative reforms, and the Ministry of Foreign Affairs is implicated in efforts to improve bilateral and international agreements, especially concerning rescue and repatriation of survivors.

The Ministry of Labor has been less directly involved, but also sits on the 16-member National Coordinating Committee set up under the NPA to encourage crossministerial responses to combat trafficking. A task force was established under the NPA to act as the supreme coordinating body responsible for executing the plan and policies in combating trafficking. At the institutional level, the Task Force is designed to acquire political support from the local self-governance level and is also mandated to accumulate support from all stakeholders, including the civil society organizations. However, several factors have mitigated against its effective operation:

— high rate of turnover among staff within government agencies (increased skills and awareness are lost);

— lack of resources available for programming, and this situation has worsened with the reallocation of resources within government to address security needs;

— uneven commitment among members, particularly between national and local-level layers of the committee structures (for example, at local levels, meetings are ad hoc and regularization is hampered by civil unrest);

— the intended district plans of action have not been formulated;

— information gaps regarding respective roles and responsibilities.

However, it is important to recognize the formation of this Task Force as an important step forward to a more coordinated approach to addressing trafficking concerns. It provides a common platform and is a legitimate body that has the capacity to facilitate smoother and more effective implementation of the wide range of programming currently taking place in Nepal.

NGOs provide a wide range of services and are highly active in advocating to limit trafficking and resolve some of the bottlenecks in the current programming. These NGOs tend to be specialized in addressing trafficking (with only a few broader-based NGOs mainstreaming these concerns into their ongoing poverty reduction or community mobilization programming).

Their activities include awareness-raising (through mass information campaigns, rallies, street theater, workshops, seminars, education and communication materials, peer education in the workplace, education during other social mobilization activities in the village); community empowerment to prevent vulnerability to being trafficked; social mobilization through group formation with capacity building and community support systems for people in difficult circumstances; improvement of livelihood opportunities through income generation, vocational training, microcredit, cooperatives;

and safe migration initiatives through information, support, and health assistance for migrants.

Other programs focus on rescue and repatriation of trafficked persons, followed by reintegration (either into their original community or other locations). Networks of NGOs have developed within each country and collaborate on specific issues, particularly concerning advocacy for policy and legislative change. These include ATSEC (active in India, Bangladesh, and Nepal), Network Against Commercial Exploitation and Trafficking (NACSET)(started in India), South Asia Federation Against Human Trafficking (SAFAHT) (supported through the UNIFEM regional project), and SAARC People's Forum .

The National Network Against Girl Trafficking (NNAGT) (in Nepal) and ATSEC (in Bangladesh) have also developed a resource centre with reports, data, and other materials available to any stakeholder. There are several constraints on networking effectively including disparate and insular functioning; lack of coordinated activity and duplication of work; ideological divisions; ad hoc programming; limited strategic interventions; and a lack of conceptual clarity, particularly between trafficking and migration.

However, the crossborder nature of trafficking requires collaboration among civil society organizations from different countries, and the signing of the SAARC Convention should foster an environment more conducive to networking rather than competition for scarce government and donor resources. Within each country there are also many organizations working on issues such as gender equality and women's empowerment that have made contributions to combating trafficking even though they do not identify themselves as undertaking specific anti-trafficking initiatives.

Similarly, community-based organizations involved in social mobilization and legal and human rights awareness make contributions to combating trafficking. Many of these organizations are involved in social mobilization as a component of larger poverty reduction programs or infrastructure development, and indirectly make it easier for antitrafficking NGOs to work in the same districts. Any assessment of activities that have contributed to combating trafficking in a specific district or village would have to take into account this whole of range of programming.

As in many areas of development work, there are differing responses to the circumstances trafficked persons find themselves in from organizations working from diverse ideological foundations. For example, some organizations working on rescue and rehabilitation activities consider that CSW of any kind is harmful and at any cost women should be removed and protected from returning to work of this kind. In some cases this has meant they have restricted the movement of rescued trafficked persons within the shelters, and they are treated as children whose opinions and behaviour needs to be "changed." Others take a rights-based approach that recognizes that any adult has the right to choose to be a CSW.

This does not mean that these organizations condone the harm that is done to many survivors, or deny that prostitution represents an extreme form of exploitation of women as sexual objects. These different approaches are obviously reflected in the types of programming used for rehabilitation and integration.

Growing numbers of international NGOs and bilateral and multilateral donors are responding to the increased attention given to trafficking issues both within and from outside South Asia. Generally, the scope of programs currently in place is relatively limited (with a few exceptions such as USAID, ILO/IPEC, NORAD in Bangladesh) as most funders are supporting small initiatives and have yet to mainstream trafficking into related activities.

However, Oxfam GB and UK Government DFID are examples of exceptions as they integrate trafficking concerns into other programming. Institutions have been providing both technical and financial support to governments and NGOs to address the problem. These organizations include Redd Barna, Plan International, ActionAid, Asia Foundation, Oxfam, Save the Children Alliance, ILO/IPEC, UNICEF, UNIFEM, USAID, World Bank, IOM, NORAD, CIDA, etc.

The programs undertaken by these agencies range from awareness raising, rescue and rehabilitation, and developing training packages on human and child rights to convening workshops for judges, public prosecutors, and lawyers in enforcement of legislation. Key elements include protection and prevention of children at risk, dissemination of information on CRC and CEDAW, and support for government and nongovernment organizations to step up antitrafficking initiatives.

In Nepal an Informal International Agency Group is increasing the flow of information between these stakeholders and improving coordination of activities. For example, it has developed a list of activities funded by funding agencies and international NGOs. The Group provides a regular opportunity to discuss issues and inform people of upcoming events and activities. However, similar loosely based networking groups CARE-Bangladesh is currently undertaking an in-depth ethnographic study focusing on a sample of 50 sex workers from both sides of the border.

Antitrafficking Programs

Antitrafficking programs can be roughly categorized into three areas: prevention, interception/rescue, and reintegration. Community-based poverty reduction programming plays an important role in trafficking prevention, particularly if those already identified as at risk are included. Increasing the livelihood options for those with few resources (particularly women) is vital to ensure those most vulnerable withstand shocks such as natural disasters, forced resettlement, etc.

However, addressing economic issues alone is not sufficient to prevent trafficking. It is also important to strengthen social capital and build social protection and resistance to withstand the temptations offered by traffickers and "easy" income from commercial sexual exploitation. Many women's thrift and credit groups established under the thousands of poverty reduction programs in India not only build resistance but also provide savings to cope with crises, and minimize overheads/risks and transition costs for both microfinance institutions and poor women. Social capital formation is also facilitated by linkages with other institutions, and agencies or networks among themselves.

Awareness-raising programs are aimed at vulnerable groups, parents, teachers, community leaders, employers, lawyers, police, public officials, law enforcement agencies, and the general public on issues of trafficking, gender discrimination, women and child rights, victim's support, and impunity. Many programs include support for formal schooling or enrolment in special non-formal education classes, as well as vocational training or skill building, microcredit, income-generation programs, etc.

Some of the common activities include credit to buy cattle, chicken, or sewing machines, training on sewing/ tailoring, and bee keeping, etc. This holistic approach (taken by larger NGOs with greater resources) attempts to address the multiple factors causing trafficking. For example, efforts to collaborate among NGOs and coordinate activities led NNAGT to prepare a tentative mapping of NGOs working in different districts and disciplines.

The number of NGOs and their scope, mandate, and activities dramatically increased and diversified after the mapping was exercise was carried out. Initially several Dhaka-based NGOs implemented preventative activities (rallies, consultation meetings, village-level meetings,workshops, brochures and posters, roadside dramas, songs, and advertisements through radio and TV, etc.). Gradually they expanded their activities as their understanding of community needs evolved. They started working in the border and trafficking-prone areas through networks of NGOs and grassroots-level organizations.

The preventative approach concentrated on raising the awareness of different stakeholders (both government and civil society) about the existence and harms of trafficking of humans and the scope of the problem in Bangladesh. Until the Government had recognized trafficking as a problem, it was very difficult for NGOs to work on this issue under the umbrella supervision of NGO Affairs Bureau of the Government of Bangladesh.

Pro-women schemes have seen enhanced financial support from Rs13,036 crores in 2002/03, an increase over 2001/02 of 23% and specific increases are noted for girls 'elementary education. Women and children participation in the Integrated Child Development Services (ICDS) program has increased. In spite of the significant pronouncements on gender in the Union Budget for the first time in India, coupled with the priority already set in the Ninth Five-Year Plan, by and large this year's budget shows no change from the usual procedure of monitoring input rather than outcome and proliferation of too many programs with too little money.

ICDS is the largest poverty reduction scheme available from the Government of India that can build upon prevention of trafficking. It has been implemented widely in several states in red-light areas or source areas, and is the principal means of organizing children, adolescents, and mothers from below-poverty line families. Several innovations are tied to the ICDS at the state level, and it is a crucial program for identifying beneficiaries for schemes related to trafficking. The ICDS program is to be universalized by the first year of the Tenth Five-Year Plan.

DWCD aims to extend the ICDS to 5,000 administrative blocks from the present 4,388 blocks by the end of the next year. Recommendations have also been made for mobilizing community support and participation in the ICDS program, over and above ensuring availability of quality infrastructure. The Swarn Jayanthi Swa Rozgar Yojana is another major poverty reduction program in the Government of India (the prologue to the Integrated Rural Development Program (IRDP), Department of Women and Child Rural Agency (DWACRA), and other rural development programmes for self-employment) and is a vital scheme for development of trafficking source areas.

It provides an opportunity for NGOs/self-help groups/women's groups to support local-level livelihood activities linked to decentralized government structures. For example, in Madhya Pradesh and Kerala states these schemes have been well converged with Panchayati Raj Institution (PRI). Other DWCD programmes include the Support to Training and Employment Programme (STEP), setting up of training-cum-production centers (supported by NORAD), and the Socio-Economic Programme.

6

State of Fundamentalism, Women and Child Trends

Today, the growth of state sponsored religious fundamentalism has been one of the crucial issues affecting women in South Asia. This is occuring in the context of increasing evidence of violence against women—dowry murders, sexual harrassment, rape often by the police and army, and the throwing of acid on women in the streets. As a result of campaigns and agitations by women's movements, these incidents have been highlighted and the governements have passed some preventive laws, albeit with many loopholes and limitations.

However what is significant is that in recent years there has been a shift away from even the liberal rhetoric of equal rights for women and laws have been passed to withdraw the legal and political rights which women already had won. These developments are linked with the broader process of economic and political changes which have laid the basis for religious fundamentalist groups to grow, as well as for the support to these tendencies by the governments in these countries.

The emergence of fundamentalist groups is not specific to South Asia alone. Fundamentalist forces, often with state support have emerged in Sudan, Nigeria, Egypt, and Malaysia, with Iran offering the best example of what implications this phenomenon has for women. Iranian women took an active part in the anti-imperialist struggle against the Shah, making the veil into a symbol of resistance only to find themselves pushed afterwards into the restricted roles of mothers and wives. The "chador" became a legally binding requirement, the age of marriage was reduced to 13 years and divorce became nearly impossible.

These trends with very specific injunctions for women can be seen also in developed capitalist countries, thus belying any link of this phenomenon with backwardness and underdevelopment. In fact manu of these movements use the latest and most sophisticated technology in modern communications.

In South Asia in recent years a number of developments show the increasing hold of religious fundamentalist forces in the region. In 1986 the Indian Parliament passed a bill called the Muslim Women's Protection of the right of Divorce Bill, which withdrew a right from muslim women to appeal for maintainance under a special provision in the Criminal Procedure Code.

In Pakistan, the Hadood Ordinance of 1979 sanctioned flogging for adultery and rape, with little to distinguish the two, a Law of Evidence reduced a woman's evidence to half that of a man, and a proposed Shariat Bill, now seeks to deprive women of even more political and social rights, including their participation in politics.

In Bangladesh, while there have not been specific changes in the law as yet, attempts are being made to assert "Islamic" codes of dress and conduct for women. Women announcers on television were told not to cover their heads and not to wear "bindis" on their foreheads. At the moment there is a bill being debated on making Islam the state religion. These attempts to reverse the status of women and withdraw the rights which earlier generations of women had won, all in the name of preserving traditions and the fundamental tensest of a religion needs to be understood in relation to the role of the state.

While this is clear in countries where a religion is the state religion, even in countries which purport to be secular, there seems to be support if not outright sponsorship of fundamentalism. Interestingly these trends go alongside government policies and programmes to integrate women into development. These are not just part of the rhetoric of the International Womens Decade which most governments have to project as part of their "modern and progressive image".

The apparent contradiction between special programmes for women's employment and skill training and the passing of restrictive laws which raise images of medievalism in the 20th Century, can be seen as two sides of the same imperative to control and direct women's labour, fertility and sexuality to suit both capitalist and patriarchal interests.

Although significant work has been done on the implications of capitalist development on women's work and the fact that the needs of capital and the needs of patriarchy can either coincide or conflict with each other, more work need to be done at a theoretical and empirical level on the relation between the state and women's subordination. The basis for the emergence of fundamentalism, the connection of this with the increasing attempts to reassert control over women, and the implications of such a state ideology for the women's movements in the region are discussed.

It is argued that religious fundamentalism as a state ideology could provide a coincidence of patriarchal and capitalist interests in the present context in South Asia. These preliminary reflections will, hope lay the basis for further theoretical understanding and more importantly, practical strategies to counteract such retrogressive trends.

Post colonial states in South Asia have followed a capitalist path of development, notwithstanding the rhetoric of socialism, whether of the Indian or Islamic variety. There exist differences in the nature of the state, for instance, the specific constellation of class forces, the degree of dependence or independence from foreign capital, or the degree of repression and the right to assert democratic rights.

However, development programmes in all these countries for agricultural and industrial growth, have resulted in structural changes in the ownership and control over productive assets, especially land which have furthered the process of class and sexual differentiation. One contribution the decade has made is the challenging of the notion that development policies are sex-neutral; today there is a wealth of empirical material which documents the differential effect of development policies on women and men.

Technological changes, legislation, etc, interact with a preexisting class and sexual division of labour, both within the community and within the household. This has resulted in a deepening of inequalities between women and men, in terms of their access and control over food, education, health care and productive resources. State intervention is today, explicitly restructuring not just the arena of the economic but also other arenas of civil society, those which concern the most "private" areas of religious beliefs, reproductive choices and man-woman relationships. Given this pattern of development, the continuous aggravation of inequalities of wealth, income distribution and uneven regional growth, have resulted in various formes of oppositional movements for land-rights, higher wages, regional autonomy and implementation of legal rights.

These movements have usually been repressed by governments and power wielding groups, resulting in a tremendous increase in class, caste, communal and sexual violence since the mid-sixties. The inability of the governments to tackle the roots of these problems has resulted in a crippling crisis of legitimacy. The ruling parties in all these countries are seeking to create an ideological unity through the sponsoring of religious fundamentalism. This is expressed openly in General Zia's Islamisation drives and in a more covert form in India and Bangladesh.

In 1977, the secular principles of the Bangladesh constitution were reversed and since then, the government has been supporting the growth of Islamic institutions and linking up with Islamic state. At the moment there is a bill introduced in parliament to make Islam into a state religion. In India , the complicity of the ruling party in the attacks on Sikh families in Delhi in November 1984, the succumbing to muslim and Hindu fundamentalist pressures and the total lack of political will to solve the increasing communal tension in the country, have shattered the illusions of the secular ideology of the Indian state.

The trend is towards a communal state ideology with majority Hindu fundamentalism as a dominant component. There are differences in the specific factors necessitating the use of religious fundamentalism to create an ideology unity. In Pakistan, the nationality question is the most important. The only way by which Punjabi domination in the economy, bureaucracy and military could be preserved by the ruling party was by stressing that there were muslims .

A homogenous "muslim" identity had to be stressed to avoid confrontation with the very real structural inequalities between the provinces, each with their own distintive culture and language. General Zia himself, is said to have stated that without Islam, Pakistan, would disintegrate overnight. In Bangladesh whose creation, in fact, is the best expression of the fragility of religion as the basis of national identity, the upsurge in Islamic activities is linked to other factors.

The dependence for foreign aid on the oil-rich-Middle East, and the co-option of right wing fundamentalist forces in the ruling party, are some of the factors pushing towards the Islaminsation of Bangladesh. In India, the situation is more complex since it continues theoretically at least, to be a secular state . Rather than a direct projection of religious fundamentalism as a state ideology, there is a more indirect sponsorship of fundamentalist forces.

The emergence of state sponsored religious fundamentalism has to be seen in the broader context of the communalisation of Indian Society "Communalism" as an ideology projects the "belief that because a group of people follow a particular religion, they have as a result, common social, political and economic interests." Analysis has shown that this assumption of a homogenous identity ignores the real divisions of caste and class and that in fact, a "communal identity" has no natural basis but has to be created.

Inspite of the production of historical and contemporary studies which provide evidence of the above mentioned processes, many commentators continue to see the South Asian region as one torn by inherently antagonistic religious communities, with the roots of this antagonism traced to the medieval past. Recent attempts to analyse the Punjab situation, see the conflicts as the outcome of a "Sikh" history and tradition. Such analysis not only ignores the very significant caste and class divisions amongst Sikhs, but also ignores the role of the ruling party in creating the present communal situation in that region.

The demands put forward by the regional opposition party in Punjab i.e. for water, territorial redivision with neighbouring states and Chandigarh as the state capital for Punjab, which were secular demands, were continuously ignored by the ruling party till they became linked with the communal demand for a separate nation i.e. Khalistan.

The emergence of communalism as an ideology which leads to violence between groups who coexisted peacefully before has to be situated historically and in relation to the specific socio-economic and political factors leading to such developments. Historians have established that communalism in the Indian subcontinent, was a product of colonial underdevelopment, located most specifically amongst the middle classes.

The breakdown of existing class identities and status systems, along with economic stagnation forced middle class Indians to compete with each other for the scarce resources. The ensuing frustration, combined with a sense of deprivation and fears of the loss of identity, created a volatile situation in which a religious issue could trigger off immediate violence and extreme brutality.

Given a crisis of identity, the protection of cows, or music before a mosque became crucial issues, issues of life and death, because these religious symbols came to represent symbolically, the preservation or destruction of these middle classes themselves. It is therefore, not accidental that communal struggles during the colonial period occurred mostly over government jobs, educational concessions and the political positions in the legislative councils and municipal bodies which enabled control over them.

Communal struggles were therefore over secular issues. In fact, the "purely religious or theological content of communalism has tended to be meagre" In addition, from the end of the 19th Century, communalism became an important instrument of colonial policy in the effort to thwart the rising national movement. Communalists, especially the Muslim League were encouraged through the ready acceptance of their demands, official patronage etc.

The Indian national movement itself, though secular in its objectives, also used communal consciousness. There was a distinct hindu tinge in the leadership's work and thought. Many nationalist identified nationalism with the revival of Hinduism. Modern literature in Bengali, Hindi and Urdu was partly communal in tone, portraying muslims as foreigners and oppressive lecherous tyrants, while hindus were portrayed as heroes struggling for positive values. Many leaders used hindu symbols, idioms and myths in their political speeches and writings.

India was often referred to as the Mother Goddess or compared to Durga, Kali, and other Hindu goddesses. Gandhi too, appealed to people in the language of religiosity, for e.g. his interpretation of independence as Ram Rajya. The same divisions affected women in the early women's movement and national movements. In their struggle for suffrage, education and legal rights, both hindu and muslim women attacked the system of seclusion.

However, as communal divisions intensified, hindu feminists began to see purdah (seclusion) as a custom bought to India by muslim invaders and a cause for the fall in women's high status in the Golden Age, and muslim women, fearing that they would be swamped as a minority in a India ruled by a hindu majority, began to defend passages in the Qur'an about female modesty. This Hindu tinge in the national movement and the susbsequent failure in fostering the development of a national consciousness in the post independence period, left the space for communalism and casteism to grow inspite of a secular Constitution. While communalism in the present period does not have the same causes as under colonialism, at level of ideology, it does find an echo in past memories of communal violence.

Contemporary Communalism in India

In the decade between 1950-1960 communal incidents were few but since the 1960's there has been a tremendous increase in communal violence involving many more communities and creating new divisions as for instance, between Hindus and Sikhs. These incidents occurred mainly in urban areas, though recently, communal violence has spread to rural hinterlands as well. Analysis of these incidents have shown that they were systematically planned with selective targets and were a disguised from of economic competition between the two communities.

In many cases, the targets were Muslim artisans and small entrepreneurs who had achieved a degree of relative prosperity and were cutting out the traders who happened, to be Hindus. This competition for scarce resources - markets or jobs has even led to the old caste conflicts being converted into communal struggles today. Another significant factor behind these incidents of violence was the evidence of the complicity of the ruling party in either engineering these riots or not acting swiftly to prevent their occurrence.

Fact after fact in Punjab, Delhi, Meerut, Bhiwandi, all point out the complicity of the ruling party and the state apparatus. Behind the specific "riot" however, is the much more disturbing growth of communal ideology amongst large sections of people. Over the years there has occurred a consolidation of Hindu sentiments, a process which escalated when some dalits converted to Islam in South India.

Hindu organisations held conferences, and went on all India pilgrimages carrying holy water from the Ganges. Organisations like the Hindu Manch, Vishwa Hindu Parishad, Hindu Ekta Manch, along the older Rashtriya Swayemsewak Sangh, have initiated militant programmes to counter what they perceive as a threat to Hinduism. These organisations are highly authoritarian in structure, have paramilitary wings and an ideology of Hindu expansionism.

For instance, the Vishwa Hindu Parishad has openly declared that Hindus are the only people who accept India as their motherland and that national integration is synonymous with Hindu consolidation. This includes the recovery of Pakistan, Bangladesh and Afghanistan as part of Greater India. Like fascist organisations elsewhere, these are all male dominated, if not exlusively male organisations. These organisations have been given state patronage, are allowed to function freely with members of the ruling party publicly supporting and attending their conferences and meetings. This phase of communalism in India is significant in that it emerges in a context of rising religious fundamentalism.

Communal tensions in earlier periods have not neccesarily been accompanied by fundamentalist movements. The other significant factor is the role of the ruling party in supporting these religious fundamentalist forces, especially Hindu fundamentalists. In sharp contrast to its positions in the late 1960's and 70's, the ruling Congress Party has now shifted from its earlier public condemnation of communalism and of hindu organisations and support to the victims of minority communities to a more generalised condemnation of communalism and the foreign hand in public pronouncements along with a series of concessions to communal demands, a refusal to indict individuals identified as being responsible for the violence, and a stifling of secular opinion, both, within, and outside the ruling party.

This shift in the stand of the ruling party on communalism was partly due to an electoral strategy to cash in on the "Hindu vote", especially in North India. When this strategy did not result in large scale support in the 1986 by elections, there was a shift back to and a succumbing to Muslim fundamentalist demands by pushing through the Muslim Womens Bill. The ruling party played one communalism off another in the electoral numbers game. However, it would be a mistake to see the consolidation of communalism today only as the backlash of a short sighted electoral strategy.

There are far deeper factors at work which need further research and exploitation, to enable us to understand the reasons for people's responses to communal propaganda and the increasing crisis of the ideological legitimacy of the Indian State and its need for a new hegemonizing ideology. An area for further exploration would be to see how far the attempt to forge a national identity after the collapse of anti-colonial nationalism would take the form of a projection of a Hindu nationalism.

Such an ideology has today ready recipients in the products of the peculiarly Indian pattern of industrialisation i.e. the sections of the population who live off rentier and trading profits, the bulk of whom come from the "intermediate" or backward castes which form the Hindu majority. It is these sections, along with the newly emerging rural kulaks, who today seem to be supporting the fundamentalist movements. Whether

India becomes a Hindu fundamentalist state or not is an open question but the fact is that it is today a communal state with government support and even sponsoring of religious fundamentalism.

These developments are occuring in the context of a growing authoritarian state structure. Over the years there has been increased investment in the police, paramilitary forces and the army, along with the passing of laws like the National Security Ordinance, Terrorist Affected Areas etc. which give wide powers to the police and the state apparatus over the lives of citizens. State sponsorship and the emergence of fundamentalist organisations among Hindus, Sikhs, Muslims, and Christians along with an increasingly authoritarian state structure, has serious implications for the future of democracy in India.

These trends in the South Asian region have also very specific and disturbing implications for women. Processes of class formation and the construction of nationhood are not seperate from the particular forms of women's subjugation in these countries. Religious fundamentalism as a crucial component of communalism provides a lethal combination to prop up or resurrect patriarchal controls over women.

The terms fundamentalism, revivalism, obscurantism, are often used interchangeably and loosely. There is considerable controversy over the use of these terms. Religious fundamentalism is used rather than revivalism. Revivalism implies a "renewed attention to" or "interest in" while fundamentalism implies an adherence - often a strict and literal adherence to a set of basic principles. Thus there could be movements of religious revivalism which could over time become fundamentalist i.e.

focusing on only one set of principles can vary, as studies on Islamic Fundamentalism have pointed out.

Movements inspired by religion - revivalist or fundamentalist have played a revolutionary anti-imperialist role in the national movements of the 19th and 20th centuries, and have also expressed the needs and aspirations of working people. Religious movements therefore are not necessarily conservative. Similarly, religious fundamentalism does not always refer to the past - in fact what is being asserted as a basic tenet is often a totally modern practise. This is why it is problematic to call the recent occurrence of sati as a revival. In addition, the meanings that people give to these principles can also vary.

Fundamentalism then, can only be understood in relation to a specific historical context. It is crucial to identify when it emerges, which are the social groups initiating as well as constituting the support base of this phenomenon and what exactly is being projected as the basic principles of adherence. One feature of fundamentalism is its selectivity in choosing what is the true and original teaching. In the sense fundamentalism constructs a particular version of Islam/Hinduism/ Sikhism/ Christianity as the only valid representation of that religion.

This construction makes little distinction between what is textual and what may be local specific cultural practices. Most significantly it abstracts from history and projects that particular amalgam of belief, ritual and practice with a transcendental validity. In Pakistan for instance, the islamisation process selects elements from 19 schools of jurisprudence as well as customs and practises which existed in the 8th and 9th centuries in what is Saudi Arabia, Iran and Syria of today.

Similarly, the "Hinduism" being projected by various Hindu organisations as the only true Hinduism denies the historical existence of two seperate and anatgonistic religious traditions amongst people designated as Hindus. One tradition was Brahmanism which was based on Vedic texts and the Dharmashastras, restricted to the upper castes, buttressed by royal patronage and the creation of a priestly caste.

The Shramanic tradition (the Bakthi movements were seen as inheritors of this tradition) was popular amongst lower castes, had a universalistic ethic and exhibited a wide diversity in ritual and belief. Historically one cannot speak of Hinduism as such but a variety of 'Hindu' religions. The Hinduism being claimed by fundamentalist organisations draws on the first tradition but here too it incorporates elements from caste customs, particularly Kshatriya notions of honour, as well. Social scientists have labelled this very modern Hinduism - "syndicated Hinduism".

That this contemporary construction of Hinduism (the same process could be seen in other religions) has no need of either textual or historical verification was brought out very clearly in an interview with Ramanand Sagar, the producer of a television serial on the Ramayan recently. When asked about the historical sources for the film, he mentioned how during that period women did not cover their torsos but it was impossible for him to allow that on the screen since the image of Sita as a pure, chaste and ideal wife was so strong and important that showing her without a blouse would violate the moral message of the serial!

Similarly when the Council of Islamic Ideology in Pakistan was discussing whether women should have the right to vote, whether blood money or compensation paid to a female victim should be half that of a male and whether women's evidence should be half that of a man's evidence in court, there was no discussion of "khula" which is the Quranic equivalent available to women, of men's right to the "talaq" form of divorce. Since then the Hadood Ordinance and the Law of Evidence have been passed and there is now the proposal for a Shariat Bill which will extend the jurisdiction of the Shariat Court to all areas of life.

However, even here there is the process of selectivity - while the Federal Shariat Court is seen as having only an advisory role regarding fiscal matters, in matters, of Muslim personal law, anu judgement passed by the court will be binding. Almost all the issues concerning women's rights fall under personal law. It seems that the criteriea for selection and implementation of true Islam is the crucial area of man-woman relations rather than more general theological issues.

A similar process of selectivity can be seen in the codification and implementation of personal laws in India. While a common criminal code exists for every Indian citizen, areas of marriage, inheritance, divorce etc. are governed by separate personal laws for Muslims, Christians, and Hindus. More studies need to be done one on the process by which these personal laws were codified involving not only a specific interpretation of each religion but also the incorporation of the assumptions of colonial administrators and native representatives.

Hindu personal law for instance, was interpreted initially in 1772 when Warren Hastings appointed ten Brahmin pandits from Bengal to compile a digest of

Hindu scriptural law in civil matters - marriage, divorce, inheritance, succession. These interpretations, however were only codified into one uniform law in 1941. Prior to this, there had been separate laws for different castes and communities i.e. separate customary laws existed for Nairs, Nambudris, Kulins, Jats etc. The Draft Hindu Code was thus based on specifically Brahmanical interpretations of Hinduism.

Changes were introduced into this as a result of the struggles of women and men in the early women's movement and hence contained some rights for Hindu women. It is significant, however, that the Hindu Code Bill was only passed after Independance after a great deal of opposition. A process of secular reform to abolish all personal laws for a uniform civil code prior to indenpendence was scuttled on the grounds of political expediency and although the ideal of a uniform civil code is enshrined in the Directive Principles of the Constitution, till today, seperate personal laws continue to operate.

It is not accidental that issues of religious identity are tied so closely with the regulation of relations between men and women . All personnal laws, including the reformed Hindu law have certain common features which reinforce the patriarchal, patrilineal and patrilocal family. This is the main family form in India, especially in the north, central and eastern parts of the country. Even where matrilineal forms have existed, as in the taravad of Kerala, economic changes and colonial policy have invested defacto rights over property in the hands of men.

Government intervention through changes for example, in laws on inheritance have tended to maintain this patriarchal authority. In situations of the breakdown and emergence of new class / caste / communal identities it is these elements of man - woman relations which become crucial markers of identity. It is significant that during the agitation in Punjab, a demand was put forward for a seperate personal law for Sikhs as well.

This customary law deprives women of the right to property, and to divorce and contains the provision for a widow to marry her husband's brother all these features link patriarchal control to newly emerging class interests particularly the need to maintain and keep control over landed property by sections of the Punjab peasantry. It is also not accidental that while the ruling party ignored the other secular demands for water, territory and Chandigarh as the capital city, this communal demand was being considered. It is this linkage which needs to be explored to understand why religious fundamentalism has very specific implications for women.

In India, since the 1960's agricultural development has been based on a technological package to increase agricultural productivity, marking a shift away from the earlier focus on land reforms. The effects of the Green Revolution have been extensively documented. Although there are regional differences, depending on prior patterns of landholding and landlessness, as well as technological constraints imposed by the kind of crop, there have been considerable changes in women's participation in wage labour and their position relative to men in the rural areas.

Capitalist development has resulted in many peasants and marginal farmers losing their landholdings at the same time as there has been the crystalisation of a new layer of rural kulaks (rich farmers) . There has been a dramatic increase in the number of agricultural workers, within which section the number of women is higher and increasing faster than the number of men. The 1981 Census showed that half of all rural female workers (as against a quarter of all women is more seasonal and as a result, most women are casual workers.

The numbers of female cultivators has declined relative to men, highlighting women's lack of independent access to land. In addition, in 15 states, surveys reveal an increase in the differential between male and female wages, with women's earnings being close to half or less than half of men's earnings. On other hand, the emergence of a rich peasant class had led to the withrawal of women of this section from work in the fields. However, this has not meant an improvement in the status of these women. Seclusion only serves to hide the labour women perform within the household, which sometimes increases as a result of hiring in wage labour.

In any case, this process does not result in any increase in women's economic control over resources and property or decision making. In Bangladesh, there has been an increasing trend of landlessness documented along with an increase in the number of poor female headed households. Female headed households are estimated to range from 6.4% to 16% of all rural households. Around 40% of all rural women are today seeking wage employment.

Studies done on rural areas in Pakistan especially in the Punjab point out the high degree of male out-migration and the importance of foreign remittances in changing the rural setting. Although men do return home for crucial production periods, women have begun to enter areas of work and take over decision making in spheres previously the prerogative of men.

One study notes the contradictory implications of these changes. While some women are wearing modern clothes and cosmetics, for many others there is now the introduction of seclusion as women are withdrawn from work in the fields. The same study also points out to the increase in social networking between women in different households and the issues which are discussed together range from marriage alliances, problems with family members to monetary matters.

There are also variations in the effects of industrialisation strategies, but certain broad trends can be identified. In India, women were mainly employed in textiles, mines and plantations. In all these sectors there has been a decline in women's employment, especially in textiles and coal mines. Of all non-agricultural jobs that women lost during the period of 1911 and 1961, only 8% were due to these jobs becoming obsolete and in the remaining cases women were simply replaced in their past occupations by men.

However it is important to note that women are still employed by these industries either as contract labour or through the decentralisation of production to sall sweatshops or home based units, especially in the textile industry. The decline in the relative and absolute employment of women in the traditional sectors is also a part of the general crisis of these sectors of the economy in modern sub-sectors like pharmaceuticals, electrical appliances, motor vehicles, machine production, heavy chemicals, which anyway have a low labour absorption, women are concentrated in certain industries like garments, food processing, electronics i.e. the new export oriented factories, many of which fragment production to household units, as well as in the unorganised sector.

Since womens employment in the organised sector is less than 33% of the urban female employment, this increase of registered employment seems to be in the unorganised hence low waged sector. In Bangladesh, given the low level of industrial development, women are only recently being employed in the new export industries set up in and around Dhaka. 80 to 90% of the garment workers are young, unmarried women, mainly from the urban areas.

In Pakistan, data based on the 1975/76 CMIU shows that the total non-farm employment for women was less than 3% of the total. In the manufacturing sector women again are concentrated in the food processing, textiles, cotton ginning, pharmaceuticals, garments and electronics factories. The CMI date clearly does not reflect the level of women's employment since it does not include the category of casual contract labour or subcontracted home based production.

Broadly then one can see that capitalist development, in agriculture and industry , has resulted in an increase in landlessness, increased dependence of women on wage work which is seasonal, low earnings and the increase as well as invisibilisation of their work in the unorganised sector. In broad terms then more women are being forced into looking for work and the work that is available is in the unorganised sector, with a large section engaged in subcontracted home based production.

The new export oriented industries are drawing in a new layer of younger women. Although studies of these industries show variations of age and marital status thus showing a deviation from the South East Asian model, many of these young girls are having to take over the traditional obligations of fathers and brothers for instance, to provide a dowry for their marriage and are now earning their own dowries.

Studies of young women workers in the garment and electronic factories show a sizeable number who come, from disintegrating middle class to lower middle class families, who hope to earn enough to have a large dowry which is seen as the passport to marriage and an escape from factory work. However the bulk of their earnings were in fact going towards household expenses, as the families struggled to maintain a increasingly threatened middle class status.

In these families, the traditional structure of male provisioning could be maintained in practice. The pressures of increasing poverty in the countryside as well is forcing a renegotiation of structures of authority. As women are moving out of the homestead in search of work and therefore away from the direct control of family patriarchs, they are entering "male space" in search of wage labour in addition there is the attempt to reassert control by regulating women's mobility and access to wage labour and product markets.

Religious fundamentalism as a state supported ideology in the given economic and cultural context of South Asia could provide a similar justification for controlling the mobility, fertility and sexuality of women. Already communal organisations have started issuing aggressive statements about the right place of women. In the communal violence recently in Ahmedabad, Hindu fundamentalists put forward what they called a "theory of truth", in which they condemned abortion as murder and advocated that women return to the home and give up their jobs in favour of unemployed men.

Apart from the changing structures of women's work, the other factor which could lay the basis for support to fundamentalist ideas is the growing strength of the women's movement and a generalised awareness about women's rights in the region. There has been a rich tradition of women's struggle against patriarchal structures in the history of South Asia. The nature of these struggles has depended on the specific historical circumstances and options available for women during these periods.

The early 20th century women's movement for example, did not question the sexual division of labour within the family, but did build independent organisations and fought militantly for equal rights, whether for the right to property which benefited few women, or for the vote, which benefited all women, as well as for higher wages, food and the right to organise which benefited working class and peasant women.

After independence there was a lull but in the late 1960's and early 1970's in India a new womens movement emerged. The economic crisis of the sixties led to numerous working class and peasant movements all over the country, and in the early seventies, women's issue began to be taken up in the context of these general struggles. In urban areas, small women's groups emerged, constituted by women who were or had been linked with radical left groups as well as activists involved in development work.

After the lifting of the Emergency in 1977, women's groups mushroomed in the larger cities of Bombay, Delhi, Hyderabad, Bangalore. What was new about these groups was the fact that they autonomous organisations, used different forms of organising based more on the consciousness raising model rather than the mass recruitment strategy followed by the party linked womens organisations, with a stress on non-hierachical internal organisation structures.

Since the seventies, the new women's movement has grown tremendously and has taken up the issues of dowry murders, police rape, domestic violence, reproductive rights and recently the issues of rights for Muslim women and sati. There are two levels at which the issues of patriarchal control are being challenged. The first, and the dominant trend is to expose and agiate around the most extreme manifestations of women's subordination in India - dowry murders, police rape, abortion of female foetuses after amniocentesis, sati etc.

This is done often within the terms of the argument of the early social reform and 20th century movements of condemning these as social evils and therefore mobilising a much wider layer of public support. The second level is the less publicised work that women's groups particularly the women's centres in Bombay, Delhi and Bangalore are doing in connecting these extreme forms to the structural violence against women within the existing patriarchal family system.

The issue of dowry murders is linked to the much more hidden and more widespread issue of violence within the family and the fact that women do not assert their right to property. Such issues provide a far greater challenge to patriarchal authority and as a result provoke a more violent reaction from conservative sections of society. Religious fundamentalism could provide a ready ideology specially since the preexisting structures of the patriarchal household with intra-household discrimination between male and female access to food, health care and other resources has often been justified in the name of religious traditions.

The preexisting culture of son-preference has already made the South Asian region significant in having a declining sex radio, i.e., the decline in the number of women relative to men in the population. While in most countries, developed and developing, women outnumber men, the populations of India, Bangladesh, Pakistan, and Nepal are exceptional in having an adverse sex ratio. In Bangladesh in 1981, there were 94 females of 100 males, in Pakistan there were 87 females to 100 males and in India there has been a long term decline in the proportion of women to men in the country's population. According to the 1901 census there were 972 females per 1000 males while in 1981 there were 935 females per 1000 males.

The recent rise in the latest census is restricted to certain regions and does not seem to project a reversal of the earlier trend. Although there are regional variations, studies have now established that this unusual sex radio is due to higher female death rates which are a result of unequal access to food and health care within the household. Numerous studies have by now established that son-preference is not linked to religion but has a close correlation with labour force participation of women.

The practise of dowry for instance has spread in the last 30 years in India to entire communities and castes who had no tradition of this form of marriage payment. Even in the predominantly Muslim countries of Pakistan and Bangladesh, the practise of dowry has increased and both countries have a Dowry Prohibition Law. While labour participation is an important variable, the increase in dowry practises do not always relate to the withdrawal of women from work outside the home.

The increase in dowry has to be seen in the context of rising consumerism (commodities and bank loans openly for dowry), the competition to get men with jobs in the organised sector (a new form of hypergamy), which is also a form by which certain men are accumulating seed capital to set up new businesses or investments. There have been quite a few cases of men marrying two or three times, each time collecting a dowry and murdering the wife.

The incidents of sati, where large crowds gathered to watch a woman being burned, and the subsequent defence of this in the vernacular press and by sections of the intelligentsia can only be understood by examining the ideological systems which legitimise this. Specific cultural practices can acquire a more widely embracing religious sanction and in a context of preexisting son preference, religious fundamentalists could find support for asserting 'traditional' roles for women.

It is significant that Hindu fundamentalists have not condemned the burning of Hindu brides though they have been vociferous over the issues of Muslim women's rights. The challenges to patriarchal structures of authority, arising from the demands of the capitalist labour market and as a result of the confrontations by the women's movement, leads to attempts to reassert control and reimpose systems of domination. It is in this context that religious fundamentalism with its emphasis on circumscribed roles for women can find ready support.

However, the significance of man-woman relations in understanding the emergence of fundamentalism also lie in the broader process of identity formation in the context of socio-economic changes. Communal identity and control over women In this section, some tentative links between notions of masculinity / feminity and the construction of communal identities are explored. This is an area which needs a lot of research as well as conceptual reflection since there is always the danger of a crude psychological reductionism.

Communal identities do not exist as fixed primordial essences but as we have seen emerge in particular socio-economic contexts and are created identities, which attempts to homogenise other differences within the community. In this process of identity creation women figure in crucial ways at a symbolic level they become symbols of culture and tradition, i.e. identity markers while at the material level their particularised feminine identity forms the complementary role to enhancing a particularised masculine identity.

In the commual image, a Muslim was/is a man of low morals and uncontrolled lust, who was/is never ready to seduce, abduct, and assault hindu women. The Hindus were seen as mild, docile and emasculated. These stereotypes have often been transferred to other communities without much change. The same stereotype as the Muslim now exists for the Sikh, or the adivasi or the dalits.

In fact, studies reveal that the fertility rate of muslims has been declining and anyway has no relation to polygamy. It is not too far fetched to imagine that population policy, in a context of state -supported fundamentalism, could be directed not just on a class basis, as it has been so far, but also on a community basis like other countries in South-East Asia. On the other hand, the fears of a minority community can mean additional pressure to produce more and more children.

In either case, women increasingly loose control over their own bodies. Control over woman and the exercise of patriarchal authority has to be differentiated across classes as well as decomposed to allow for the variations that emerge if the control is over women's labour, or sexuality or fertility. Given these differences , however, in south Asia today, this control is exercised by particular men i.e. it is fathers, brothers, maternal uncle or husbands who have rights over their daughters, sisters , nieces and wives.

What is significant about state sponsored religious fundamentalism is that it not only gives further legitimacy to this control but, more importantly, shifts the right of control to all men. The legitimacy given by the state to follow and enforce a particular interpretation of a religion means that any man on the street can stop any woman who does not conform to the "traditional" and "proper" role assigned to her. This can be seen clearly in the countries where the State is declared a mono-religious state.

At the moment such incidents are few in South Asia but continued state sponsorship of fundamentalism would intensify and sanction such acts of violence. Given the context and background sketched above, the emergence of state supported religious fundamentalism clearly has very serious implications for women. The contradictory tendencies at the level of government policies for women and development with the aim of drawing women into the labour market, and the attempts through legislation to restrict womens access to the public world are part of one process by which the interests of patriarchy and capital are ensured.

Religious fundamentalism as a state ideology thus provides the possibility of a coincidence of interests between patriarchy and the demands of the capitalist economy. This remains of course an uneasy coincidence but it would be a mistake to continue seeing the logic of the market as necessarily leading to a liberal ideology of womens work. An ideology of restriction even though large numbers of women are being drawn into work outside the home and therefore competing with men, can be a viable ideology of legitimation.

There are however, other countervailing tendencies within South Asia which could reverse these trends. One of these are the growing social movements which are challenging and questioning the overall paths of development as well as specific issues of patriarchal control. In India, for instance, feminists from the women's movement and the democratic rights movements have entered the arena of general politics.

Women's groups have been one of the first to condemn communalism, have been actively involved in supporting victims of communal violence, and held special investigations into the situation of women during communal clashes. Most significantly, feminists have taken initiatives in supporting proposals for political solutions for instance in Punjab and are engaged in a national discussion on the dangers of rising fundamentalism.

In Pakistan, women groups have been fighting on the terrain of religion itself and have argued for improving the conditions for women within the Islamic structure. In Bangladesh, there are strong representations being made by minority groups and women's groups against the proposed bill to make Islam the State religion. These developments have led womens groups to directly confront the ruling parties in their countries.

This is a significant development since inspite of militant struggles and anti-government and anti-patriarchal slogans, most of the campaigns were directed towards changes in the laws and often demanded more intervention by state authorities in implementing these laws. In practice, the movement has operated with the assumption of a liberal state. Today, it is clear that even demands for legal changes are not going to be granted easily. This implies that womens groups will have to develop a fuller understanding of the State and State ideologies and evolve strategies which go beyond reflex actions.

It would mean tackling the wider questions, not just of the relationship between patriarchal control and the socio-economic changes in the region, but also the problematic issue of cultural identity creation. Although the present constitution of communal identities is repressive for women, there are positive elements which lie behind the need for cultural identity in the present context. This has to do with the broader process of the failure of the creation of a national identity in post colonial states as well as the restrictions in a identity based on caste, community or the family, especially for women. Such a perspective is crucial since the link between the state and religious fundamentalism in each country is closely tied to the political dynamics of the South Asian region as a whole.

Child Labour in South Asia

Child labour is often perceived as a form of child abuse.

and popular opinion in high-income countries seems to believe that child labour stems from opportunistic businessmen seeking cheap labour and callous parents happy to live off the earnings of their children. Thus, economic growth and the economic gains from global integration either will not affect child labour or may increase it by expanding the earnings opportunities open to children. Consequently, lowering the demand for child labour in poor countries is a main focus of anti-child labour policies.

Moreover, governments in both the U.S. and Europe have committed to employing punitive, income-reducing measures such as trade sanctions to punish countries with high levels of child labour. This labour demand focused policy has been developed in an environment where surprisingly little is known about the determinants of child labour.

There is no consensus in the academic or public policy literature on what child labour is. In general, child labour is grouped into two types of categories. Market work includes work for wages as well as work in a household farm or enterprise. Household work includes work in the production of goods and services that are generally not traded outside of the household. This includes caretaking, food production, and other household chores.

In general, most studies of child labour supply ignore household work, but this omission can lead to very misleading conclusions. Many countries focus their official estimates of child labour on child work for wages (cash or in-kind). This narrow focus generates misleading conclusions. In 1999 and 2000, UNICEF interviewed children across 30 developing countries and discovered that factory work is rare Only 3% of children work outside of their household for pay.

Unpaid domestic work is more common than is work for pay. UNICEF found that 2% of boys and 5% of girls perform unpaid domestic work for households other than their own. However, most working children are employed in their own household, helping with household duties or the family's farm and business. In both Vietnam and Nepal, most working children participated in household agricultural work. In fact, 92% of working children in Nepal and 87% in Vietnam work in household agriculture. In both rural and urban areas, most working children work for their own household in agriculture. Both girls and boys participate in own-farm work.

The pervasiveness of agriculture in the developing world accounts for higher participation rates in agriculture. However, higher within household participation rates than outside of the child's household requires some additional explanation. Perhaps parents prefer their children to work within their household so that parents can better monitor the child's working conditions and treatment. Alternatively, children may be more productive within their own household, because parents are better at affecting child behaviour than are other adults.

Child porters and domestic workers are the two most common types of "worst forms" of child labour. Among child porters, there are two main types: short distance porters that work in urban markets and bus parks and long distance that work in the countryside. The ILO estimates that typically long distance porters stay and work with their families while short distance porters have often migrated to find work.

Domestic workers are endemic in high caste, urban households. The ILO estimates that 43% of employers of child domestics are government or non-government service holders. In Kathmandu, 1 out of 5 households employ children. Domestics are believed to be evenly split between paid (to parents) and unpaid (more correctly, paid in a lump sum) workers. Most domestics are thought to be from rural upper and middle castes. Some domestics (15%) attend school.

Three of the most vulnerable forms of child labour in Nepal are Ragpickers, bonded labourers, and trafficked children. Ragpickers (khate) pick rags and other rubbish out of garbage dumps for resale. One in four ragpickers in Nepal are in Kathmandu. They are mostly boys and often street children. Over 50% of ragpickers live away from their homes. Most bonded labours in Nepal are embedded in the Kamaiya system of bonded labour.

These worst forms of child labour are not only prevalent in Nepal. Children in both Pakistan and Vietnam may be vulnerable in similar ways. For example, like Nepal's Kamaiya system of bonded labour, Pakistan's Peshgi system of bonded labour appears to be prevalent. Under the Peshgi system, an employer takes a child from its parent in exchange for a payment that is spread out over the period of child servitude.

Bonded labour is believed to be acute in certain industries. The Bonded Labour Liberation Front works to end bonded labour in Pakistan. They highlight brick kilns, carpet industries, agriculture, fisheries, stone/brick crushing, shoe-making, power looms, and refuse sorting as industries where bonded labour is pervasive. They estimate that a half million children are allegedly bonded in the carpet industry alone. It is impossible to identify in the existing data how many of the 8.3 million children working for wages outside of their household in Pakistan are bonded. The Bonded Labour Liberation Front estimates that eight million children are bonded in Pakistan.

UNICEF estimates that 30% of all sex-workers in the Mekong sub-region are children. Estimates of the extent of the problem in Vietnam are hard to find. Bond and Hayter (1998) report that outside of 253 prosecuted cases of child trafficking between 1991 and 1999, there is no evidence of child trafficking in Vietnam. Nevertheless, because identification of trafficked children is so difficult, it is impossible to identify the true scale of the problem in Vietnam, but it may easily be on the scale observed in Nepal. Recent advances in rapid assessment and targeted surveys may hold promise for, in the future, building understanding of these worst forms of child labour. Gender may influence child labour in ways similar to age. The returns to education may vary with gender. This seems likely to be especially important in Nepal and Pakistan where adult men and women participate in different economic activities. Likewise, the returns to activities other than age may also vary across genders because of discrimination of the sex typing of tasks.

Moreover age and gender may interact in important ways. First, girls develop earlier than boys so they may be capable of more sophisticated tasks at certain age. As puberty onsets, boys may develop comparative advantage in more physical activities. Second, the sex typing of tasks may be more important in the types of activities performed by older children. Hence gender difference in household or market work may manifest itself both in the types of activities performed at a given age, and these gender differences may vary with age.

In early secondary school ages (12-14), boy-girl differences in school enrolment are greatest, and in these ages girls also experience slightly greater participation rates in market work than boys. However, the largest gender differences are in household production, and these gender differences are increasing in age. Gender differences in participation in all activities are substantially larger in Nepal.

Gender difference appears to extend to all forms of market work in Pakistan. However in Pakistan, beginning at age 7, boys work more in market work than do girls. The rate of growth in the gender difference begins to accelerate after age 8 and begins to stabilize by age 12. By age 14, female participation rates in market work are almost 45 percentage points lower than male participation rates. These age and gender differences illustrate the importance of country characteristics in the allocation of child time.

In Nepal, having a sibling working in household production raises the probability that a child works in household production by 18 percentage points. Having a sibling employed in market work raises the probability that a child works in market work by 38 percentage points. The role of parental attitudes in child labour supply is important, because if parents want children to work, then increases in income or efforts to help poor households may have little effect on labour supply. Then the only hope for addressing child labour is to direct efforts at labour demand.

In urban Pakistan, parents claim that supplementing household income is the main reason for sending a child to work. When asked why children work, households in Pakistan overwhelming responded to help with the household business. In fact, most children work within their own household. In both Nepal and Vietnam, approximately 95% of children work within their own household either for themselves, the household farm, or the household business.

Pakistan stands out with dramatically higher wage employment with 23% of children in market work working for wages. Nevertheless, even with this prevalence of wage work, still 77% of children work for themselves or their household. In Nepal, a household with home enterprises has higher levels of child labour in both household and market work than does a household with neither a home enterprise (non-farm) nor a farm. In general, child labour is highest in agricultural households. Agricultural households also have the highest participation rates in Vietnam.

The comparison between non-farm households with and without a home enterprise is less transparent. Non-farm households with a home enterprise have lower participation rates in household work, but higher participation rates in market work than non-farm households without home enterprises.

In urban areas, the association between enterprise ownership and child labour varies by country. In Nepal, home enterprises are associated with greater participation rates in house and market work, but the opposite is true in Vietnam. In the Vietnamese case, households with home enterprises are richer than households without, so this difference in living standards may explain the reverse association found in Vietnam.

Employment opportunities open to a child within the household may also depend on household composition. For example, in larger households, there may be more people undertaking economic activities in which children can help. Moreover, household composition may influence the household's labour demand for child labour.

Large households may have more tasks in which children are needed. Alternatively, with diminishing marginal products of labour in household production, more workers may lower the value of a child's marginal product in household production thereby forcing a decline in work and increase in schooling to maintain equilibrium within the household. Of course, another factor to consider is that larger households tend to be poorer. Thus, demand for child labour may be higher.

The gender gap in market work in Nepal appears to be increasing in household size. As household size increases, girls tend to be working more than boys in market work. Parental residency may also affect child labour supply. In the framework of Foster, co-residency differentially affects investment decisions because of the household's decision-making process. In the present case, having a parent present may influence how the household values investments in the child. Alternatively, there may be a relationship between the presence of the parent and the types of duties expected of a child.

Household living standards may be a key attribute in determining how much a child works. On the one hand, poverty may be a key cause of child labour. Poor households likely have higher marginal utilities of consumption. Thus, the value of an additional unit of child time in work is higher in a poor than a rich household. Hence, even if children in poor households value their child's well-being the same as in a rich household and even if poor children receive the same market opportunities and returns to education, child labour will be higher in a poor household.

Moreover, any factor that influences household income absent child labour (Y) can affect child labour supply. High non-child labour income lowers the marginal utility of consumption. The household equilibrium of equation (2) in Section III then implies a shift away from work towards education.

On the other hand, living standards improvements do not necessarily decrease child labour. Children in richer households may be better nourished and thereby better workers. Similarly, improvements in living standards may affect the technology the household uses for household production or there may be complementarities between purchased inputs and child labour in household production.

With diminishing returns to schooling, this increase in productivity in household production may reduce schooling. In addition, it is not necessarily the case that households care about the future well-being of their children. This is an implication of the parental callousness models that pervade the public policy perspective on child labour. Thus, the effect of living standards on child labour is an open, empirical question.

Much of the descriptive evidence on living standards and child labour in the three countries considered here suggests a strong link between poverty and child labour. For example, the Kamaiya system of bonded labour in Nepal allegedly exists because children are used as bonds on household loans. When a household is unable to repay its loan, children are taken.

Similarly, in Pakistan, households commit children to the Peshgi system of bonded labour for cash transfers.

Obviously, the existence of these two systems does not necessarily imply a causal role for poverty in child labour. In the Kamaiya system, perhaps callous parents are defaulting on loans, because they do not value the collateral. However, descriptive evidence from Vietnam argues that negative shocks are responsible for an inability to pay debts. This in turn forces children to work.

A recent World Bank study examines the link between living standards and school enrolment in Pakistan. There is no reason to believe that poor households observed at one point in time would have labour supply in anyway similar to rich households observed at the same point in time if the poor households had the rich household's income or expenditure.

As with child labour supply, the rate of increase in school attendance with living standards increases dramatically near the estimated cost of purchasing 2100 calories per day per person. However, the association between school attendance and living standards levels off in the neighbourhood of the poverty line.

In the poorest households, living standards improvements over-predict the observed increase in school attendance, but the predictive power of living standards for increases in school attendance is dramatic in the rest of the distribution. The household's problem in determining child labour supply is to weigh the marginal utility of the additional consumption stemming from having the child work against the marginal utility associated with improving the child's well-being from not-working.

Community characteristics may affect the household's marginal utility of consumption, because a household's wealth may be strongly correlated with its community's living standards. Community characteristics may also affect the returns to education. For example, Foster and Rosenzweig find that between community differences in schooling in India can be explained in part by differences in the returns to education associated with the timing of adoption of green revolution technologies.

Differences associated with geography in the economic activities of children are evident in a simple rural-urban comparison of what children do by age. In urban areas, children tend to be more involved in market based production activities. Moreover, the correlations are strongest in the same-type of activities. Community house work participation rates better predict a child's participation in house work than they do the child's participation in market work.

Much of the policy focus on child labour worries about how the demand for child labour in certain industries increases child labour. This obviously begs the question of whether the presence of certain industries in a community increases child labour. However, a precursor to answering this question is to understand the industry distribution of child labour. Hence, children employed in the industries other than agriculture that have been the target of much existing anti-child labour policy, are a tiny fraction of all working children.

Most children working in market work are employed in agriculture. The largest employer of children outside of agriculture is the private household. Manufacturing accounts only for 1% of child labour. Thus, all of the policy attention on manufacturing misses most child labour. Two industries have received a great deal of special attention in Nepal: carpets and small-scale mining. Concerning the first, based on inspections of 23 carpet factories, the Asian-American Free Labour Initiative claims that children are 9% of the carpet industry's workforce.

Child labour in small-scale mining of coal, quartz, and magnesite has also received substantial recent attention. Most of the child labourers observed in a joint UNICEF/ILO study were girls carrying coal. The government's definition of child labour is a child participating in activities that would violate ILO Convention 182. Operationally, this means that a child labourer is: a) a person below 10 years of age that participates in market work and does not attend school; b) a person 11 to 14 working more than 24 hours a week and not attending school; c) a person 15 to 17 working more than 42 hours a week and not having completed primary school; and, d) a person below age 18 working in dangerous work or being forced to work in exploitative or abusive work.

In Pakistan, the distribution of market working children across industries is not available, because the government focuses on wage work only. Hence, Pakistani official statistics should reveal substantially less employment in agriculture even if agriculture's importance matches that seen in both Vietnam and Nepal. The second largest industry after agriculture is manufacturing. Not surprisingly, agriculture is more prevalent in rural areas whereas manufacturing dominates urban employment. Also prominent in urban areas is the employment of boys in wholesale and retail trade as well as in transportation.

Wage working girls in urban areas also participate heavily in the service industry. Thus, the problem of child labour in manufacturing is primarily an urban phenomenon. Moreover, it is only one component of the type of industry that employed urban children work in. Within manufacturing, the carpet weaving industry probably draws the most public attention in Pakistan. Carpet weaving is largely in the Punjab and Sind provinces, and most carpet weaving is performed on looms in individual homes rather than in a factory with a large volume of looms. Of course, this means there is no way to reconcile estimates of 900 000 children working in carpet weaving with the Federal Bureau of Statistics official child labour numbers.

Many children could be working in carpet weaving within their own household without pay. These children would not be counted as labourers in official statistics. Because of the cottage nature of the carpet industry, regulation of child labour within the carpet weaving industry is very difficult. Even large manufacturers subcontract out weaving to "thekedars" that control looms set up in individual households.

The involvement of children in the production of sporting goods in Pakistan has recently garnered a great deal of attention. Approximately 70% of all soccer balls sold worldwide is produced in the Sialkot district of Punjab. As with carpet weaving, this soccer ball production is a cottage industry; children stitch soccer balls for export in family units. While most working children work in agriculture in all three countries, there may be scope for the presence of other types of industries in a community to affect child labour.

Children are less likely to work in household work in the presence of agriculture and aquatic industries. They are also slightly less likely to work in household work in the presence of handicrafts or trade and commerce. With manufacturing or services in the community, child labour in household work is slightly higher, but the data do not reject the hypothesis that there is no association between child labour in household work and the presence of manufacturing or service industries in the community.

As with household work, the presence of agriculture lowers the probability of market work and wage work. In fact, only manufacturing, aquatics, and services are positively correlated with wage work. Interpreting these regressions as causal effects is, of course, impossible. They merely measure the association between the presence of these industries and child labour in the community. All sorts of community characteristics are associated with the presence of industries in the community, and they may easily be correlated with child labour.

This may reflect children substituting for parents who participate in handicrafts. Children leave market work to fill in for parents who are occupied in local handicrafts industry. Similarly, the presence of manufacturing and trade and commerce increases child work in household production and lowers child participation in market work. Communities that gain aquatics industries observe large declines in household work as well as declines in market work. Hence, there is little evidence within the data of systematically higher levels of child labour in communities with certain types of industries. In fact, the addition of industries where child labour is often feared most (manufacturing, handicrafts) seems to be associated with declines in child labour.

Some child labour advocates might respond to the above results on manufacturing by arguing that the type of employer in the community affects how child labour is influenced by the presence of manufacturing. The presence of state operated or large private factories lowers the probability that a child works in household, market work, and wage work. Foreign operated firms are associated with less household work and no difference in market work. Collective operated factories are associated with increased household work and market work as are small private factories.

The location of factories presumable depends on community attributes such as its accessibility, the education and productive capacity of the local labour pool, among others. Nevertheless, the evidence from Vietnam is not suggestive of a strong link between the presence of foreign or large private factories and child labour. Aside from industry presence and the type of employers in manufacturing, community attributes such as infrastructure and accessibility may be important community determinants of child labour.

Household production declines more in communities with road accessibility and year round transportation access. However, communities with road improvements between 1993 and 1998 have smaller declines in household work. In contrast, communities with irrigation or electricity improvements experience larger declines in household work participation. Participation in market work declines by less in communities that are road accessible or that experience irrigation improvements.

However, declines in market work are larger for communities with year round transportation access, improvements in drinking water, and improvements in electrification. Wage work does not appear to bear a substantive (in magnitude) association with any of the observed infrastructure improvements or accessibility attributes. Interestingly, adult participation rates in wage work do not appear to have significant explanatory power for participation in household or market work.

With the household fixed effects, the coefficient on the adult participation variables are identified off changes in participation rates. Communities that increase their adult participation rates in wage work experience increases in household work and declines in market work. This is consistent with the view that some household work of children may be filling in for parents that increase their participation in market work. Higher levels of community participation in wage work, raises the probability that a child works for wages.

Employment opportunities available to children appear important as is the household's labour demand. Household living standards appear to affect how important these factors are. Community attributes seem relatively unimportant in determining child labour supply, especially relative to the importance of the household's needs. There is also some role for cultural factors in affecting child labour supply, especially with regards to gender differences.

Government policy in all countries focuses on prohibiting the employment of children. This focus on the prohibition of child labour appears misplaced given the empirical results above. Moreover, this emphasize on prohibiting child labour constrains governments and civil society workers from exploring ways to improve the working environments of children and to make work and schooling more compatible.

While poverty is a key determinant of child labour, policy largely attempts to curtail the demand for child labour. That is, poor children are forced to work for their survival, and policy aims to prevent them from doing so. When the type of work being performed by children is hazardous or horrible, this labour demand approach may be justified, but it does not appear to be complimented with efforts to help households avoid the need to send children to work.

In Nepal, international and civil society organizations have recognized the importance of this, more so than in the other two countries. Additional household income opportunities are coupled with payments for households that send their children to school. Outside of the limited work on education subsidies in Nepal, the other countries have done little to address why children work. Moreover, because of their focus on prohibiting child labour, policy has not focused on facilitating flexibility in employment so as to enable children attend school while they work.

Some non-governmental groups in Pakistan have experimented with this to great success, but there has been nothing in the way of formal policy initiatives. In fact, Vietnam appears posed to move towards longer school days, making work and schooling even less compatible. Moreover, policy aimed at labour demand tends to focus on specific industries that are geographically concentrated with a relatively small share of working children.

The establishment of command measures that restrict the types of activities in which children can work or that abolish child labour outright has been a priority for international organizations that work on child labour issues. The domestic legislation of all three countries considered here reflects this emphasis. There are two main international conventions on child labour supply advocated by the International Labour Organization (ILO).

First, Convention 138 establishes a minimum age for employment. Signatories on this 1973 convention agree to "to pursue a national policy designed to ensure the effective abolition of child labour and to raise progressively the minimum age for admission to employment or work to a level consistent with the fullest physical and mental development of young persons" (Article 1). Convention 138 specifies that the minimum age for employment should not be lessthan 15.

Second, Convention 182 attacks the worst forms of child labour. It defines a child as all persons under the age of eighteen. Signatories on this 1999 convention commit to "take immediate and effective measures to secure the prohibition and elimination of the worst forms of child labour as a matter of urgency" (Article 1). The convention defines what it means by worst forms of child labour: a) all forms of slavery or practices similar to slavery, such as the sale and trafficking of children, debt bondage and serfdom and forced or compulsory labour, including forced or compulsory recruitment of children for use in armed conflict; b) the use, procuring or offering of a child for prostitution, for the production of pornography or for pornographic performances; c) the use, procuring or offering of a child for illicit activities, in particular for the production and trafficking of drugs as defined in the relevant international treaties; d) work which, by its nature or the circumstances in which it is carried out, is likely to harm the health, safety or morals of children" (Article 3).

In addition to these two conventions, the ILO also encourages poor countries to sign a memorandum of understanding with the ILO to take active steps to participate in the ILO's International Programme for the Elimination of Child Labour (IPEC). Joining IPEC entails the creation of a national steering committee that develops a national plan of action for the elimination of child labour in the country. There is considerable international pressure for low-income countries to sign Convention 138 and especially Convention 182.

The 1990 Constitution of Nepal contains a provision to protect children and to guarantee them certain fundamental rights. It directs the state to establish and protect these rights and to make gradual arrangements for free education. The Nepal Labour Act 2048 (1991) is the first piece of post-constitution legislation directed at child labour. In the Act a 'child' is a person who has not attained the age of 14 years. The Act establishes that "no child shall be engaged in work of any Enterprise". The Children's Act of 1992 also addresses child labour.

While the National Labour Act made child work in an "enterprise" illegal, the Children's Act makes employment of children below the age of 14 as "labourers" illegal. The Children's Act has not been amended to conform to Convention 138 that specifies age 15 instead of age 14. Children 14-16 are not allowed to work at night. No child below the age of 16 can be made to work against his/her will. The Children's Act also prohibits the employment of children below age 16 in hazardous work or in "immoral professions". Efforts have not been made to reconcile this with Convention 182's prohibition of persons under 18 in hazardous work.

More recently, Nepal has passed several acts designed to target specific forms of child labour. The Bonded Labour Act prohibits the Kamaiya system and threatens sanctions against employers with bonded labourers. The Traffic in Human Beings Act prohibits trafficking in both children and adults. The general mismatch between Nepal's legislation and its signatures on international conventions is of relatively minor significance given the lack of enforcement of domestic laws on child labour. At present none of the child labour legislation described above contains rules, procedures, or substantive funding for enforcement.

In most cases, it is not clear what ministries are responsible for enforcing the legislation. Moreover, according to an ILO study, only a handful of sanctions have ever been attempted against employers and there is little awareness of the legislation at the ministerial or public level. Likewise, legal action through Nepal's court system is generally infeasible because of its notorious delays and difficulties.

In Pakistani law, a "child" is a person aged 14 or younger. The 1973 constitution of Pakistan establishes as the legal minimum age for employment in shops, commerce, industry, or at sea is the legal minimum for work in mines or in railways. In the early 1990s, the government began to take steps to address labour demand in some of the worst forms of child labour. Two main pieces of legislation in the early 1990s were designed to address some of the worst forms of child labour.

The Employment of Children Act of 1991 prohibits the use of child labour in hazardous occupations and environments. Children are not allowed to work overtime or at night. Moreover, the employment of children is prohibited in the following industries: carpet making; cement manufacturing; cigarette making; soap manufacture; cloth dyeing; garment manufacture; shoe-making; tanning and leather; printing, and weaving; manufacturing of matches, explosives, and fireworks; mica cutting and splitting; precious stones; paper; shellac manufacture; glass; tanning; metal and wood handicrafts; furniture; wood cleaning; and fishing.

Unlike the Nepali legislation, the Employment of Children Act specifies penalties for employers that violate the act. An employer using a child in a prohibited occupation may be imprisoned for up to one year and receive a 20 000 rupee fine. The second main piece of legislation is the Bonded Labour (Abolition) Act of 1992. It abolished and made illegal indentured servitude and the peshgi system of bonded labour in Pakistan. Moreover, the act cancelled all debt that bonded labourers owed their employers. Officially, the Department of Labour has labour inspectors that enforce these laws.

A US Department of Labor report (1994) found little evidence of monitoring or enforcing of either of these acts. More recently, the government of Pakistan has developed a national plan of action to eliminate child labour. The plan calls for making primary school education universal and for "rehabilitating" working children through education and job training. The concrete steps within the act seem to be largely directed towards helping facilitate many of the actions that international and non-governmental organizations have been undertaking to curtail child labour.

As with Nepal, enforcement of domestic legislation has historically been lacking in Pakistan. However, recently there appears to have been an increase of enforcement actions. Inspections in Punjab rose fivefold between 1998 and 1999. Out of 120 000 inspections, more than 3 000 employers were fined for violation of the Employment of Children Act. The average fine was 158 rupees.

Like Nepal, Pakistan has experimented with local level enforcement of child labour laws. The Bonded Labour Act empowered "Vigilance Committees" to inform the labour department of violations of the Bonded Labour Act. However, a Department of Labour Study from 2000 reports little activity or effort coming from these Vigilance Committees.

Compulsory schooling laws have two advantages relative to legislation against child labour. First, there is little ambiguity in school attendance. While it may difficult to establish if a child is working or how much it is working, it is relatively transparent if the child attends school. Second, one of the reasons to be concerned about child labour is because of its effect on schooling. By legislating schooling, it may be possible to attenuate the negative consequences of child labour without depriving households of the income that depend on from working children.

In Pakistan, two provinces have compulsory education laws. In December 1994, Punjab Province made primary education compulsory throughout the province. The North-West Frontier Province passed compulsory primary education in 1996. Unlike Vietnam and Nepal, there is no legislation in Pakistan requiring the primary education be free to all. In reality, legislation that requires primary school education to be free does not make schooling costless. Beyond tuition, households face uniform, supplies, books, and transportation costs.

Nepal has attempted to mitigate the ancillary costs by making books free through grade three. But in Vietnam, the evidence suggests that the real costs of primary school education have been increasing in the 1990s. Moreover, the opportunity cost of time spent in school may be the most important cost of schooling, and there is little scope for changes in tuition fees to influence this. Although violations of compulsory schooling laws may be more observable than violations of employment laws, enforcement may be even more difficult.

Policy towards child labour in all three countries focuses on these command measures against child labour. Thus far, there is little evidence of any effect of these command measures themselves on child labour. If anything, these laws prohibiting child labour may restrict discussion and debate of incentive measures to influence child labour. In much of Latin American, incentive based policies to encourage schooling and discourage child labour have recently become popular. However, the experience in Asia is more limited. Nevertheless, there are some promising signs for the future.

In Bangladesh, a Food-for-Education Programme provides monthly food rations to families that send their children to primary school. In Nepal, the World Food Programme recently launched the Girls Education Initiative. It provides a midday snack to primary school students and three litters of cooking oil per month for mothers that send their daughters to primary school. Unfortunately, financial incentive programmes are expensive and therefore relatively rare in most low-income countries. Moreover, donors and bureaucrats are often averse to transferring cash directly to recipients because of concerns about corruption or about how recipients spend the money.

In the Goat-to-School Programme in Brazil, children that attend school are given goats and training on how to tend and rear goats. Beneficiary households are directed to use the milk to feed their children and to repay the programme in goats without interest. Thus, this programme provides the household with an asset that yields an income flow, ameliorating the concerns about how cash transfers are spent. This particular Goat-to-School Programme is small in scale and has not been carefully evaluated in any easily identified research.

Nevertheless, it illustrates a potential way to create financial incentives for schooling that are relatively inexpensive and address some of the concerns about cash transfers. It also illustrates how a policy approach focused on banning child labour can constrain creative solutions to problems associated with child labour. In this case, far from eliminating child labour, the programme redirects it towards activities more compatible with schooling.

Schooling incentives may merely make children worse off, because their scarce leisure time now must be spent in school. However, targeting child labourers creates incentive problems. There is always the concern that targeting child labours may draw more children into child labour. Therefore, targeting based on a good (schooling) seems preferable to targeting based on a bad. Many international and non governmental organizations have focussed their anti-child labour efforts on specific types of employment. This is based on the perception that child labour is uniquely significant in a given industry or that certain kinds of work are unusually hazardous to child well-being.

Sector Specific Programmes

Sector specific programmes are the primary tool for addressing child labour in both Nepal and Pakistan. Sector specific programmes generally have two components. First, they aim to stop children from working in a specific sector. For example, the Rugmark Foundation certifies carpets produced in Nepal and (primarily) Pakistan as being "child free" if the manufacturer does not employ children. If consumers are willing to pay more for child labour free carpeting, or given equal prices, choose child labour free carpeting, then this type of labelling may induce companies to not hire children.

Second, sector specific programmes attempt to provide some retraining for displaced child labourers and occasionally replacement income support for the families of the children who have lost their job. For example, in 1998, the Pakistan Carpet Manufacturers and Exporters Association (PCMEA) and the ILO reached an agreement aimed at eliminating child labour in carpet-weaving. The agreement focuses on an area of Punjab Province where estimates suggest that approximately 8000 children work in carpet weaving. The project has two components. The project withdraws children (physically) from worksites then provides these working children and their families with formal and informal education.

In Nepal, the government has been substantially more supportive of efforts to liberate and assist bonded labours and their families. The Ministry of Land Reforms and Management has provided approximately USD 900 000 in fiscal years 2000 and 2001 for debt relief, housing, rehabilitation, and training of bonded labourers and their families.

Moreover, both Nepal and Pakistan are developing national retraining programmes geared towards rehabilitating displaced child workers. In Nepal, the Swiss Development Cooperation has been active in building a national skills development programme to improve retraining opportunities, and IPEC has been working with the SDC initiatives to both build awareness about child labour and to retrain children who lack skills.

In Pakistan, Bait-ul-Mal, the government welfare agency, has opened 33 centres around the country to retrain former worker children. The centres target children in hazardous forms of labour. They provide training and stipends to children and their families. Moreover, graduating students are guaranteed full assistance to continue higher education inside or outside of Pakistan.

There is little evidence on the efficacy of the retraining and income generation components of these sector specific programmes. Their main idea is to combine the command approach while either creating incentives for schooling or providing income support, thereby lowering the household's marginal utility of consumption today. Coercing employers to fire existing children appears to be relatively easy. Research is needed on whether this lowers child labour or improves the well-being of children and their families over the near, medium, and long-term.

In Nepal, inadequate schooling infrastructure appears to be a tremendous problem. Its schooling infrastructure is in disrepair. Only 43% of all teachers in Nepal have an education beyond secondary school, and a majority lacks any teacher training. Government, with the help of the Asian Development Bank, has recently begun a nine-year initiative called the Basic and Primary Education Project to recruit new teachers and to provide training to existing training to teachers.

In Pakistan, access to schooling seems to be a large problem with relatively few rural children living in proximity to a primary school. This problem is particularly acute for girls. Namely, UNICEF observed that a significant amount of the time of older girls is spent in household production, especially the care of younger siblings. Hence, UNICEF has been experimenting with establishing community based childcare centres so that older girls can attend school rather than watching siblings. This programme, like the Goats-to-School Programme acknowledges why children work and attempts to eliminate the household's need for child labour rather than simply trying to prevent children from working even if their household's subsistence depends on it.

Another policy option for eliminating child labour is to replace the technology that uses child labour. This could be accomplished through subsidizing mechanization or technology adoption. However, in the case of the three countries considered here, an easing of restrictions on imports of new technology might radically alter the structure of production.

A great deal of existing research suggests that the large declines in child labour experienced in Western economies at the end of the nineteenth century owes to changes in technology. In low-income countries, there is also substantial support for the role of technological change in ameliorating child labour. A casual comparison across countries suggests that child labour is lower in rich countries than in poor ones.

To help low-income families, the World Food Programme in Nepal is operating an anti-child labour programme, the "Rural Infrastructure Construction Works" project. It is a food for work programme that works through employing the parents of children by providing income to adults who work for three years in community infrastructure projects. Research by the ILO in Nepal suggests that the projects regular income mitigates the need for children to work.

Other income generating schemes may have similar effects. There is, however, the possibility that improvements in household income may lead to increased earnings opportunities for children. For example, micro-credit schemes are designed to create new household enterprises.

7

Social Action: The South Asian Strategy

The poor state of social development had been caused by problems which were common to all social sectors across the country. These included: weak planning and budgeting; low budgetary allocations, especially for inputs needed to maintain service quality; delayed release of funds and low budgetary utilization; inadequate and irregular supply of key inputs required for regular and quality service delivery; low utilization of existing services due to staff absenteeism, excessive staff transfers, and irrational staff allocation at both management and facility levels; lack of trained staff aggravated by recruitment bans; weak supervision, monitoring and accountability leading to poor governance; extensive gender biases, resulting in low coverage of female population; and absence of any involvement of clients in the design and management of services.

Underlying all these issues were lack of political commitment and inadequate focus on social services. It was in recognition of this disturbing state of affairs that the Government of Pakistan initiated the Social Action Programme (SAP) in 1992/93. The government approached international donors for support on this initiative, resulting in the introduction of the Social Action Programme Project (SAPP-I) in 1993-94. The main objectives of SAP (and also of SAPP) were to:

— improve the lagging social indicators;

— develop human resources; and

— alleviate poverty.

The Programme aimed at increasing access (particularly for women and poor), and improving quality and efficiency of services in the elementary education, primary health, rural water supply and sanitation, and population welfare sectors. This was to be achieved through an umbrella approach designed to address the above mentioned issues common to the social sectors. The key elements of this approach called for:

— increased funding to social sectors (particularly in the non-salary budget), and improved flow of funds;

— improved planning and monitoring, and capacity building of government agencies;

— initiatives to improve governance including staffing practices;

— increased decentralization of service delivery system;

— greater community participation and strengthening of public-private partnership; and

— increased focus on gender.

Social Action Programme is the largest initiative of its kind, not only in Pakistan but also in the region. The scale and complexity of the Programme can be gauged from its scope which spans four different sectors implemented in eight geographical areas. It is executed by 5 different departments (i.e., the Education, Health, Population Welfare, PHE, and LG&RD) in each province/area.

The Planning and Development and the Finance departments are also involved in SAP as they are coordinating and providing funds for the programme respectively in each province and area. In addition, at the federal level, the ministries of Planning and Development, Finance, Education, Health, and Population Welfare are also directly involved in SAP.

The Federal Bureau of Statistics and the Department of Auditor General are responsible for impact monitoring and auditing as well as for governance monitoring of SAP. In total, SAP consists of 27 sub-programmes spread over the entire country. The SAP Secretariats at the federal Planning and Development Division and at the provincial/area P&D Departments are responsible for coordination of SAP at their respective levels.

The Provincial SAP Steering Committee headed by Additional Chief Secretary (Development) of the P&D Department or Chairman P&D Board review the progress on quarterly basis while the National SAP Steering Committee chaired by the Deputy Chairman, Planning Commission reviews it on a six-monthly basis. The donor agencies supporting the Programme through the SAP Project (SAPP-I and SAPP-II) include the World Bank, the Asian Development Bank, the Netherlands Government, Department for International Development, the European Commission, and the Canadian International Development Association.

The first phase of the Project i.e., SAPP-I covered the period from 1993/94 to 1996/97, while the second phase (SAPP-II) began in 1997/98 with a planned duration of five years ending in the year 2001-02. The total financial outlay of SAPP-I was US$ 4.02 billion, of which about 76 percent was to be financed by the Government of Pakistan (GOP) while the remaining was to be provided through donor funding. The total outlay of SAPP-II is US$ 10.561 billion with a GOP share of close to 80 percent .

According to the SAPP agreements, the government was to increase the total expenditure in basic social services from its own sources from 1.6 percent of GDP in 1993/94 to 2.19 percent by 2001/02. The target for the last year of SAP was later revised downward to 1.95 percent of GDP. More than 90 percent of SAPP funds are spent in the four provinces, while the remaining goes to the four special areas (AJK, ICT, FATA and NA) and the federal ministries of Education, Health, and Population Welfare.

In terms of sectoral distribution, education accounts for about two-third of the total SAP spending while the share of health is close to one-fifth. The remaining portion goes to RWSS, Population welfare, and cross-sectoral activities such as monitoring, institutional development and Participatory Development Programme. The Social Action Programme Projects (SAPP-I and II) which are part of the Programme were introduced mainly as funding arrangement through which donor assistance were to be channeled to cover a portion of the total expenditure in SAP sectors.

Thus, the Government of Pakistan provides the major chunk of SAPP funding. Unlike other projects where upfront financing is made available, in the case of

SAPP, donor funding is through the mechanism of reimbursement. This means, that the Government first allocates funds for each of SAP sectors in its annual budget which are released to the implementing departments and spent on SAP activities.

After the expenditure is incurred by the government, a portion (about 10 percent) of the total expenditure is reimbursed by the donors as additional funding based on the Statement of Expenditures submitted by the Government. Another 14 percent of SAPP funding is provided through on-going or new projects in the basic social sectors financed by donor agencies. The SAPP, therefore follows a programme approach and not a traditional project based approach, both in terms of funding as well as in terms of its design.

For a more objective assessment of SAP performance, it is important to have a broad understanding of the environment in which SAP was implemented during the last 7 years. Since its inception in 1992/93, SAP has seen ten different governments (including the caretaker setups). Only one of the governments could complete more than 3 years in office. These changes did not augur well for the Programme. Although all the governments continued the Social Action Programme, frequent change in top management affected the pace of implementation.

Another phenomena which coincided with SAP was the heavy politicization of development programme during the 1990s. This resulted in weak management and poor governance in public sector service delivery particularly in the social sectors. Each of the successive governments introduced politically motivated development programmes implemented through elected representatives.

Under these programmes, elected members of the national and provincial assemblies were provided annual grant by the government to implement new schemes in their constituencies. The criteria and procedures followed for selection of these schemes were often in variance with those under SAP. This policy adversely affected the implementation of SAP particularly the selection of sites for new schools or RWSS schemes, recruitment of staff and procurement of goods and civil works.

Frequent change in governments also resulted in excessive staff turnover particularly at top, and senior management in the line departments. Lack of continuity of staff was another obstacle faced by SAP. Finally, severe deterioration in the country's macro-economic position since 1996/97 badly affected the funding of SAP as the Government was unable to maintain investments in basic social sectors at the agreed minimum level of 1.8 percent of GDP.

The principal agreement on financing was to gradually increase total expenditures in the SAP sectors with emphasis on increasing the government's contribution in SAP over the life of the Programme. Specific policies were agreed to be pursued during the Social Action Programme/Project in this regard.

These, mainly consisted of:

(i) increase in government's contribution (net of foreign assistance and SAP reimbursements) in basic social services from 1.6 percent of GDP in 1993/94 to 1.95 percent by the end of the SAP Project in 2001-02;

(ii) increase in share of non-salary budget in the total recurrent budget;

(iii) protection of SAP budget in comparison to non-SAP portion of the budget especially during resource crunch; and

(iv) improvements in the flow of SAP funds.

Financing of SAPP started facing problems during the second phase of the Project as macro-economic situation in the country deteriorated. Subsequently, governments' contribution to SAPP declined from 1996/97 onwards and reached a low of 1.46 percent of GDP in 1998/99 as against the 1 target of 1.85 percent.

Within the provinces, spending on SAP during the period 1992/93 to 1998/99 has grown at a higher rate as compared to 9.1 percent annual growth in the total provincial Non-SAP expenditures. However, data of the last two years show that this trend has reversed since 1997/98 when growth in SAP expenditures started declining with an accompanied increase in non-SAP spending by the government.

One of major objectives of SAP was to improve the quality of services. This was to be achieved, among others, through increase in non-salary budget in the education, and health sectors so that critical inputs required at the facility level can be provided. The purpose of this increase was to ensure that textbooks, education material, furniture, chalk, blackboard etc are supplied in adequate quantities to all government schools.

Similarly, in the health sector, the increase was for provision of sufficient quantities of medicines, injections, vaccines, contraceptives etc for primary health care facilities. The non-salary component which is part of the recurrent budget had generally remained low in the education and health sectors prior to SAP.

At the start of the Programme in 1992/93, only 1.4 percent of the recurrent expenditure in the education sector in all provinces went for purchase of non-salary items while the remaining was spent on salary of staff. This share increased to 5.1 percent by 1998/99. Non-salary expenditure increased consistently in education departments in all provinces.

In the health sector, total provincial expenditure on non-salary items increased from 25.2 percent of the recurrent budget to 34.9 percent during the same period. The overall increase in spending on non-salary items reflects the importance given by the government to redress the past neglect. Whether this increase is adequate to purchase sufficient quantities of required items for schools and health units is another issue.

Although, non-salary budget was increased substantially, delay in release of the allocated amount continued to remain a problem during most part of SAP. This was contrary to the SAP policy of improving flow of funds particularly for non-salary component so that critical items required for schools and health units can be procured and distributed on time.

The government generally followed the practice of releasing major chunk of non-salary funds towards the end of the fiscal year. This affected the quality of expenditure as funds had to be utilized in a very short span of time to avoid lapsing of the budget before the end of year. Delay in release of non-salary budget in the education and health sectors emerged as the most common issue raised by the SAPP missions throughout the duration of the Project.

To address the endemic issues in the social sectors, a series of policy and institutional reforms were planned and introduced under SAP in all provinces and areas in the four sectors. Of these, only the main policies pursued under SAP are assessed here. These included: increase in funding for basic social sectors; improved planning, implementation and monitoring; improvements in governance; greater community participation and strengthening of public private partnership, better staffing practices, and addressing gender imbalances.

The overall design of SAP was to support the creation of an enabling environment for the social sectors growth and development in the country. A number of adjustments in the planning process of the government were made to achieve the objectives of SAP. Improvements in the planning process under SAP centered on a greater focus to primary services in the social sectors as opposed to tertiary, increased sectoral allocations particularly for the non-salary budget, emphasis on consolidation of existing services to make them more effective as opposed to only expansion, focus on involving communities and non-government sector in service delivery, and introducing specific interventions to address gender imbalances.

This was complemented by instituting monitoring mechanisms within the line departments, and at the provincial and federal levels to ascertain timely implementation of the agreed policies and plans. Within the planning process, SAP focused on developing long term vision and institutional reform for each sector by the provinces/areas.

These were to be contained in the sector-specific Annual Operational Plans (AOPs) which were developed both as planning and monitoring tools and included development as well as non-development/routine operational activities. This was a departure from the traditional approach followed by the line departments which required total compartmentalization of development and non-development/operational activities funded by two different portions of annual budget.

As the major emphasis of SAP was on consolidation of services, it discouraged construction of new facilities (which are funded through the development budget) and promoted initiatives to improve the quality of services delivered by existing facilities. The priority, therefore, was given to strengthening of operational activities financed under the non-development budget.

The system of preparing Annual Operational Plans (AOPs) was introduced under SAP to improve the planning of operational/non-development activities and to link it with the development programme. These Plans were to be prepared annually by each of the five SAP implementing departments in each province and federal area.

The AOPs provide an update on achievements during the preceding year and present the next year targets for expenditure, and monitoring indicators, in addition to an implementation plan describing the policy reforms and other development and operational activities to be carried out during the year.

The AOPs, introduced as a requirement by SAPP donors, are being prepared by each line department since 1993/94 without exception. During the initial years, the line departments were provided assistance in preparing Operational Plans, however, as their capacities improved, the AOPs are now being prepared independently by most of the departments.

The Operational Plans, to some extent, have brought some discipline in the planning process of the line departments in terms of increasing their focus on operational activities within each sector. However, there is not much evidence to suggest that the process of AOP is fully institutionalized and would continue within each department even after the completion of SAP. Based on the experience so far, it appears that the AOPs are prepared by the line departments primarily for the donors for their review and for reaching agreements on funding by the donors.

SAP starting with the Social Sector Coordination Committee of the Cabinet (SSCCC) chaired by the Prime Minister. This was supported by the SAP National Steering Committee (NSC) chaired by the Deputy Chairman, Planning Commission. The NSC is supposed to meet twice a year to review progress of SAP in the provinces/areas and ministries and address any institutional or structural issues impeding the Programme.

Since its inception in November 1993, the Committee has met on nine occasions in the past six and half years. The last meeting of NSC was held on December 4, 1999. Similar arrangements were established at the provincial/ area level where SAP Provincial Steering Committees (PSC) consisting of Secretaries of Finance and line departments, and headed by Additional Chief Secretary were setup. The PSCs were to convene on a quarterly basis, however their performance varied across provinces. The PSCs met on a more regular basis in Punjab, NWFP and FATA particularly during SAPP-II.

In terms of system development, special efforts were made in SAP to strengthen existing MIS and M&E

systems and to introduce new systems where required. Systems for monitoring input, output, impact, quality and governance in SAP were strengthened at various levels and departments. For input and output monitoring, the main instruments are the MIS and M&E systems in the implementing departments in each province and area.

These systems are at various stages of development and maturity. Of the four SAP sectors, education has the most well established MIS in the shape of Education Management Information System (EMIS) which has been operational for the last 6-8 years in all provinces and at the national level. It is based on annual school census which collects information on vital statistics such as enrolment, number of teachers and schools, dropout and repeaters, and physical status of school building.

The Education Departments in three provinces (Sindh, NWFP, and Balochistan) also have School Mapping System. Student Assessment System for monitoring the learning outcomes of students has been operational in NWFP for the last 4 years, while in Punjab it was established last year. The Health Management Information System (HMIS) is functional in the Health Departments across the country. It is based on monthly reporting by primary health care facilities (RHC, BHU and MCH center).

In addition to the above systems, another area of focus to establish a regular system of spot checks or field visits to facilities. Each of the line departments even prior to SAP had supervision arrangements under which different levels of functionaries were required to visit the field/facilities and report on qualitative aspects such as staff absenteeism, availability of supplies, and quality of service in their tour notes.

A greater emphasis was placed in SAP to develop it into a more systematic, regular and action oriented arrangement. While the departments issued fresh instructions on spot checks and follow-up actions, there was limited success in evolving a regular and effective system of field monitoring. This was partly because of lack of funding made available by the line departments to cover the cost of field visits.

For monitoring the activities included in the Operational Plans, a system of Quarterly Monitoring and Reporting was introduced during the second phase of SAP (SAPP-II). This was aimed at establishing a mechanism within the government for monitoring the progress of SAP on a quarterly basis. The QMRs are being prepared by several line departments, albeit with delays. The process of quarterly reviews by the provincial governments on the basis of QMRs is yet to be fully institutionalized.

The experience of provinces such as Punjab where it has been used on a more regular basis, shows its utility and contribution in improving the implementation of SAP. For impact monitoring of SAP, the system of Pakistan Integrated Household Survey (PIHS) was established as an annual exercise (later reverted to a bi-annual survey).

PIHS has a sample size of 16,000 households across the country and is implemented by the Federal Bureau of Statistics. It covers all four sectors of SAP and also includes a detailed consumption module to assess the distributional impact of SAP across various income groups and to measure poverty levels. The PIHS conducted by the Federal Bureau of Statistics has completed three rounds during SAP while the last and fourth round will start next year to coincide with the completion of SAPP-II.

Biannual national surveys on health and fertility conducted by the National Institute of Population Studies, Pakistan Medical and Research Council and the Population Council are used for monitoring the outcomes and impact in population and health sectors. For governance monitoring, a system of Third Party Validation (TPV) by the Department of Auditor General was introduced in SAPP-II to monitor four governance areas (site selection, procurement, recruitment and staff absenteeism).

In addition to TPV, the annual audit of SAP expenditures are also conducted by the Auditor General's Department since the start of the Programme. In terms of utilization of the available MIS/M&E systems for planning and management functions, the experience in SAP shows limited success as it remained much below the potential.

The Education departments did use EMIS for identifying schools which required repair, rehabilitation, physical facilities or furniture. In Punjab and Sindh, it was also used to prepare teachers redeployment plan to rationalize their distribution. However, it was not fully used by the provincial education departments for planning purposes such as setting provincial and district targets on enrolment rates or other indicators and assessing the achievements at the end of the year; or for identification of under-enrolled or low performing schools/districts and formulation of initiatives to bring improvements.

In the health sector, very limited attempts were made to integrate HMIS in the planning and management process of the department. Improving transparency and governance in the line departments was also one of the key strategies in SAP to enhance efficiency and quality of expenditures and of services. However, the major thrust to improve governance came during the second phase of SAP (SAPP-II).

It was only in SAPP-II that greater emphasis was given to SAPP audit reports particularly by the donor agencies, and a number of concrete steps were initiated to improve governance including the Third Party Validation exercise. The areas focussed for improving governance were financial management and internal controls, procurement, site selection, staff absenteeism, recruitment and other staffing practices.

The annual audit conducted by the Department of Auditor General remains one of the pillars on which financial discipline in the public sector rests. The annual audit reports in Pakistan had generally lagged behind by more than three years. This resulted in diluting the impact of audit as most of the key players would have been transferred after the publication of audit reports thus making it difficult to fix responsibility and initiate any action.

The situation was further compounded by a general lack of interest or importance shown by the line departments on audit observations. During SAPP-II, the government agreed with donors to finalize the SAPP audit reports within 6 months after the completion of the fiscal year. The Department of Auditor General has successfully adhered to this agreement for the last two years. This has brought more relevance and importance to the audit process.

The Departmental Accounts Committees have also been activated as compared to the past and are discussing audit observations with the auditors on a more regular basis. A number of steps have been and are planned to be taken by the line departments to improve financial management and internal controls during SAPP-II. Most significant among these is the establishment and/or strengthening of internal audit.

For this purpose, qualified accounts staff will be assigned in the departments and follow-up of internal and external audit will instituted. One of the most important exercise introduced during the second phase of SAP to systematically monitor and improve governance is the Third Party Validation of recruitment, procurement, site selection and absenteeism monitoring systems. Under this exercise, the A.G. Department, on an annual basis, reviews the cases of recruitment, procurement and site selection across the country in the SAP implementing line departments and validates whether existing procedures and criteria were adhered to in these cases.

It also validates the adequacy and implementation status of systems for monitoring staff absenteeism within the line departments. Three rounds of TPV have been successfully completed with the publication and launching of its annual reports in March 1998, 1999, and 2000. The TPV arrangement also entails follow-up as the line departments are required to take corrective actions on the findings of validation.

These may include disciplinary actions against staff responsible for non-compliance as well as actions to improve overall systems and procedures so that non-compliance is minimized in future. The important question is whether TPV mechanism or other initiatives have contributed to improving compliance and better governance in the SAP implementing line departments. Ironically, the results of the three rounds of validation do not show much signs of improvements.

In the other three governance areas, the percentage of cases in compliance has decreased. Under governance monitoring, it is also pertinent to examine the results of SAP audits to assess if proper procedures are being followed by the departments while incurring expenditures. Unfortunately due to methodological problems in sample selection and in the auditing process, it was not possible to develop a clean set of data which could be analyzed systematically to monitor any change in governance, based on audit findings.

Involvement of beneficiaries or local communities was envisaged as a key mechanism in SAP to improve the quality, efficiency and coverage of social services. Specific policies were developed and implemented by the government in the education and RWSS sectors to involve beneficiaries. In the education sector, the central activity in this area was the formation of school management committees (SMCs) in all provinces and areas since 1995/96.

The Education Departments also decided to provide funds to the committees for minor repair and for purchase of furniture and education material for classrooms. In addition, the SMCs were given some role to support the functioning of school. At present, approximately 74 percent of the 133,727 elementary schools in Pakistan have a school committee consisting of parents, teachers and other members of the community. These committees were mostly established through executive order by the line departments.

The Education departments in all provinces have been providing funds to the committees since the last 2-3 years. However, provision of funds to SMCs has remained a problematic area as often the cheques given to committees were withdrawn by the government or were given after substantial delay. In the rural water supply and sanitation sectors, a uniform policy was developed during SAP and notified by all provincial governments to ensure full involvement of communities in identification, planning, and management of schemes.

According to the Policy, a scheme would be approved only if a request comes from the community and the community agrees to operate and maintain the scheme through its own resources. The Public Health Engineering Departments also prepared a plan to hand over all pre-SAP schemes to communities. Out of a total of 8,990 schemes constructed by PHED to date, about 2,293 have been transferred to communities.

Considering the concept of community involvement was almost non-existent in the education and PHE departments prior to SAP, the fact that 74 percent schools have management committees of local members and about one-fourth rural water supply schemes have been transferred to communities is a substantial move forward. However, the manner in which the school management committees have been established raises serious questions on their representativeness.

The process of community participation has also faced several snags particularly in the Education sector in Punjab where the provincial government reconstituted the committees on atleast two occasions during the last 3 years. This action by the government coupled with withdrawal of funds adversely affected the course of community participation in the province. The process of community involvement in SAP still has a long way to go.

A major problem encountered by the government departments was lack of skills needed for community mobilization. This was further compounded by a certain degree of reluctance shown by the departments in taking steps to address this weakness by setting up community development units or by entering into partnership with non-governmental organizations.

The overall experience so far suggests the need for a much higher level of commitment from the government on implementation of this policy. Focus on Gender: A major objective of SAP has been to redress the gross gender imbalance against women both in terms of staffing as well as access to services. Although, it can be safely said that all interventions in SAP were focussed primarily on women and children, in addition, specific steps were taken as part of SAP agenda to address this particular issue.

For increasing access of female in education, a policy decision on giving priority to opening girls schools and introducing co-education at primary level was taken in all provinces. Steps were taken to increase the number of female service delivery personnel as it was expected to lead to a larger coverage of women and girls by the social services. Qualification criteria for female teacher was relaxed to facilitate recruitment of women from the same locality.

In primary health sector, the government introduced the Lady Health Workers Programme to reach larger number of women. Seats in paramedical schools were increased to accommodate more women, and career paths for the Lady Health Visitors were improved. Priority was given by the government to fill vacant posts for females and a decision was taken to provide atleast one female staff to all basic health facilities. Policy reform under SAP has as yet only touched upon the gender imbalance in service delivery personnel, and do not address the imbalance in management positions.

A study by MSU reveals that barely 5 percent of the positions at top, senior or mid-level management in the provincial offices of the SAP implementing departments have been occupied by women . This issue is of great significance because women in decision making positions could provide institutional support to the process of gender sensitive reforms.

As part of improving governance, a key emphasis in SAP was to improve staffing practice related to recruitment, posting and transfers. The SAP agenda stressed on waiving bans on recruitment of service delivery staff, recruitment preferably from the local area (to reduce chances of absenteeism), merit based recruitment, and continuity of staff as per the rules of business.

The government, to a large extent did manage to enforce the policy of recruitment of service delivery staff from local area. In fact, the position of teachers in the provinces was made a tehsil cadre post which meant that teachers cannot be posted out of the tehsil to which they belong. Similar steps were taken in the health sector in Punjab and NWFP where government introduced the practice of recruiting doctors on contract.

These were non-transferable, district and facility based positions created with the objective of reducing absenteeism of doctors at the facility level. Although ban on recruitment of service delivery staff in the SAP sectors was lifted, achievement against this objective has been mixed. Lack of staff continuity remained a perennial issue in SAP in all line departments across the provinces. According to an analysis by MSU, none of the federal Secretaries of P&D, Education, Health or Population could complete the minimum tenure of 36 months of continuous service in the same position since the start of SAP.

In Sindh, none of the Secretaries of the five line departments could complete the tenure while in Punjab, only one Secretary could achieve this during the last 6-8 years. The PHE department of Punjab saw 14 Secretaries from 1993-2000 while there were 13 transitions in the position of Secretary Education in Balochistan during the same period. Staff turnover was maximum in top management, followed by senior management. Comparatively, it was lesser in mid-level positions.

While the success of a programme hinges on many factors, continuity of staff especially at the top management is always considered to be a major factor in this regard. This is more important in environment where management is centralized, systems are relatively weak and accountability is low as in the case of Pakistan. Among other reasons, frequent transfer in the SAP implementing departments has seriously impacted on programme ownership, motivation, accountability, capacity building and host of related issues with a cumulative effect of impeding the progress of Social Action Programme.

The major focus of SAP in the health sector was to improve the health status of women and children particularly in rural areas. This was to be done among others, through increased coverage of immunization leading to reduction in infant mortality, increased access to pre and post natal services to women, and better quality of services through health outlets.

In terms of expanding immunization coverage, substantial gains were made during the first phase of SAP (SAPP-I) as the percentage of children under 5 who were fully immunized as reported by PIHS doubled within four years - from 25 percent in 1991-92 to 54 percent in 1995-96. However, it is the immunization rate of children between 12-23 months which is a better indicator and prescribed by the World Health Organization to measure the coverage of immunization programme. Results of the 1998 round of PIHS show an increase in the percentage of 12-23 months children who are fully immunized.

One of the reasons often cited by women for not using a government health facility was the non-availability of female staff. To address this issue, a policy decision was taken during SAP that each of the basic health facility should have atleast one female paramedic. The decision was implemented by the government during the course of SAP, though still close to one-fifth of the basic health facilities are without a female staff. Unfortunately, due to non-availability of similar data for baseline year, it is not possible to assess the achievement in addressing gender imbalance in staffing at the facility level.

In the population welfare sector, the strategy under SAP was to expand and improve family planning services leading to greater awareness and use of contraceptives. The end objective of the Programme was to reduced fertility and population growth leading to smaller and healthier family. The SAP target envisaged in the Eighth Five Year Plan was to increase the contraceptive prevalence from 12 percent in 1990 to 22 percent by 1996-97.

The main instruments for monitoring the output and impact of family planning programmes in the country are the national surveys conducted by the National Institute of Population Studies (NIPS), and the Population Council in collaboration with the Ministry of Population Welfare. Although PIHS includes a module on family planning practices, the primary systems for monitoring the population sector are the surveys of NIPS and the Ministry of Population.

Government remains the main supplier of contraceptive with private sector catering to about one-third of the users. In urban areas, this ratio is higher. There is still a large unmet need as reflected by the difference in contraceptive use (24 percent) and desire to use. This calls for substantial improvement in the delivery of family planning services to cater to potential users.

Data from the surveys conducted during the last 10 years show that Pakistan is experiencing a decline in fertility. This could be due to greater use of contraceptives in the last 6-8 years. Fertility rates (among women aged 15-49 years) dropped from 5.4 during the period 1986/91 to 5.26 in the next four years (1992/96). Compared to other countries in South Asia, fertility rates in Pakistan are much higher.

In terms of population growth rate, Pakistan appears to have made some inroads as reflected by the 1998 census figures, according to which the population growth rate reduced from 2.9 percent in 1981 to an estimated 2.2 percent by 1998. In the rural water supply sector, the government adopted a uniform policy under SAP on the advise of the donors.

According to this policy no new scheme was to be constructed by the PHE and LG&RD departments unless the beneficiary community agreed to operate and maintain the scheme after completion. The government also agreed to transfer all previously completed schemes to the communities. Piped water is available to only 12 percent of the rural population. These ratios have remained constant since 1995/96. This could be due to a reduction in the number of new schemes taken up by PHED during the second phase of SAPP.

In fact the government imposed a moratorium on new schemes since 1997/98. This was done to complete the backlog of on-going schemes and to transfer the completed schemes to communities. The PIHS data does not make a distinction in source of drinking water by provider of service, hence it is difficult to gauge the coverage provided by the two government departments (PHED and LG&RDD) responsible for providing rural water supply and sanitation facilities.

The general perception is that handpump or motorized pump which are the main source of water have mostly been installed privately by the households. The government's share in providing access to water supply in rural areas is estimated to be around 40 percent. As per the sectoral policy in SAP, the Public Health Engineering Departments in the four provinces started the process of community mobilization and transfer of schemes since 1993-94.

Political Economy

More than seventy-five percent of the world's population lives in developing countries. Of the world's some six billion people, about a third live in India and China, two countries which also have among the highest annual GDP growth rates in the world. Almost one-and-a-half billion people live in South Asia. This is about one person in five.

The developing world has experienced varying patterns of economic growth. Latin America, having emerged from colonialism in the 19th century, had a head-start over the rest of the developing world. In the 1980s, however, Latin American development slowed significantly, though there are signs of recovery in some places. East Asia underwent a different trajectory. Primarily agrarian in the late 1940s and 1950s, East Asia developed into one of the world's most dynamic regions in the first half of the 1990s, but some of these "tigers" have recently hit hard times.

South Asia, emerging from colonialism after the Second World War, was also primarily agrarian in the late 1940s and it experienced very low rates of annual GDP growth rates during the colonial period. Following independence, the major economies of the region grew slowly at first, but began to pick up momentum in the mid-1980s and may now be in the early phases of sustainable high growth, perhaps equaling the rates of China in the 1980s and Southeast Asia in the 1970s.

The economic growth rates in South Asia increased significantly in the 1990s with the more aggressive implementation of market reforms, but slowed down in the first few years of this century. There are signs that the economies throughout the region (with the prominent exception of Afghanistan) may be moving again toward the higher grown rates of the 1990s. In fact, India may be growing at an even faster pace.

The explanations for what has been a temporary slow-down are many: the impact of the Southeast Asian slowdown, lack of a sufficient infrastructure, unstable politics, etc. Unstable politics may have been the major factor and instability still poses a considerable threat; for that reason we shall spend considerable time looking at the challenges facing the various political systems, which have various forms, including a virtually absolute monarchy, constitutional democracies, a militarized democracy.

Virtual civil war exists in two of the regions eight states. Uneven accommodation of ethnic aspirations exists in almost all the countries of the region. Part of the instability is rooted in significant social changes that have taken place over the past two decades. In India, for example, groups historically discriminated against have become major political players whose demands must be serious considered. This is a political economy course, meaning that it combines elements of political science and economics, with the emphasis put on the former.

Political economy as an academic discipline possessing a career; after its "invention" in the eighteenth century it kept changing. The intellectual history of its theory and practice reveals major contests among varying views more than it does academic certainty. The gold standard, once considered an economic and political necessity for a stable order, has been abandoned.

The concepts of "market" and "interest" have undergone changes influenced by political compulsions.

Environmental and global processes, to take another example, make economies defined and bounded by territorially sovereign nation states increasingly obsolescent. Globalization comes in many forms, all which play a role in economic and political development. Its sinister face is evident in the terrorist destruction on September 11, 2001 of the figurative and literal heart of world capitalism, the twin towers of the World Trade Center, an event which dramatically illustrates the intimate relationship between political and economic life.

So too does the US government bail-out of an already ailing airline industry. The huge - and economically indefensible-subsidies provided by India for its agriculture underscores the power of the farm lobby in that country. Economists say that these subsidies must be drastically reduced for the economy to grow at the faster pace that the present government says is its goal; however politicians cringe at offending the powerful farm lobby.

Development thus is not simply an economic phenomenon and this course will try to make the connections among the various processes.

Sustainable Development

Since the United Nations Conference on Environment and Development, held at Rio de Janeiro, Brazil in 1992, the region has made significant gains in many areas of sustainable development, including the provision of the basic physical and social infrastructure for promoting economic activity and alleviating poverty, the development of environmental policies, institutions and legislation and the conservation and management of natural resources and ecosystems, but the region's environment continues to deteriorate and the number of poor people continues to increase, outpacing the best efforts of many countries in the region.

The widespread poverty prevailing in the region and inadequate financial resources have been among the most serious constraints to effective implementation. The key issues and priorities for sustainable development in the region are multisectoral and cross-cutting, embracing the environmental, economic and social spheres. These multifarious issues and priorities will require promoting economic growth and social deve lopment, making globalization a positive force for all the world's people, with special emphasis on poverty eradication, environmental protection and management.

The economic and social issues is essential to sustainable development in the region:

— chronic and persistent poverty, the impact of globalization, sustainable energy development, sustainable agriculture for food.

— security, human settlements development, unsustainable consumption and production patterns, human development and coping with natural disasters.

Asia is the largest developing region in the world in terms of land mass and population, but it is the poorest of all regions, with about two thirds of the world's poor, or almost one billion people. The nexus between poverty, environment and development is apparent in the region. Poverty reduction and sustainable economic growth are essential elements of sustainable development and that success in this area will require the combined efforts of

Governments and civil society and strong and sustained support from the international community.

Globalization has both positive and negative impacts on the sustainability of development. Globalization has brought about positive changes in increasing the volume of trade, foreign investment and local employment and integrating the economy and the environment by employing market-based instruments. However, economic globalization has also brought negative impacts that are evident in the trade-related loss of natural resources, and abrupt investment shifts that have negative consequences.

To make globalization work for sustainable development, the urgency of fully integrating developing countries and economies in transition into the world economic and trade system, taking into account national requirements and the need for a level playing field between developed and developing countries, promoting capacity-building and providing technical assistance to developing countries and economies in transition, enhancing the role of information and communications technology as a factor for development, and promoting trade and investment to attain a fair and broad-based distribution of the benefits of globalization.

The least developed countries are among the most vulnerable to the negative impacts of globalization. The least developed countries require increased technical assistance and less restrictions for access to their products in the global markets and for progressive integration in global trade. That energy is vital to economic development and that the rapid growth in the demand for energy in the region has given rise to critical issues that include indoor and urban air pollution caused by fossil-fuel burning and urban transport; the availability and accessibility of energy to the poor; the development of cost-effective and socially acceptable sources of renewable energy; and increasing energy efficiency by demand-side management and the prevention of system loss.

To achieve sustainable energy development, measures need to be taken to increase the cost effectiveness and effic iency of energy production and consumption, develop and use affordable clean energy technologies, increase the use of renewable energy, and implement policies to reduce the material and energy intensity of production and consumption.

Since agricultural production depends on natural resources such as land, water, and biological resources, agricultural activities affect the environment in both positive and negative ways. For example, some activities, such as overexploitation of land for agriculture, could damage the environment, while agricultural activities done in a.6 sustainable manner could provide various goods and services such as food, wood and environmental services sustainably at a lower cost.

In order to lessen the degradation of natural resources and to achieve food security, the pursuit of sustainable agriculture and rural development, while reducing trade distortion, is essential. The provision of livelihood and the basic infrastructure to sustain a good quality of life and maintain a healthy environment are the main challenges in the development and management of human settlements in the region.

Underemployment and unemployment in rural areas are resulting in migration to cities, transplanting rural poverty to urban areas and increasing the pressure on already deficient urban infrastructure and services. The megacities are also beset with traffic congestion, problems of solid and hazardous waste management, air and water pollution and associated health hazards, and improper constructions.

Since most urban and rural local governments in the region have insufficient resources and capacity to address effectively the range and magnitude of the problems facing them and to promote urban and rural linkages, it is urgent to enhance the institutional capacity of local authorities in terms of human, technical and financial resources. Measures to address these issues, including cooperation between local governments for disseminating know-how to overcome these problems, should also be strengthened.

In most subregions there is rapid population growth and large differences in progress in terms of human development between ethnic groups and genders and between urban and rural areas. In general, women fare worse than men; minority ethnic groups fare worse than majority groups; and rural areas fare worse than urban areas. Infectious diseases are not only a public health issue that threatens people's lives in developing countries but also creates serious obstacles to the economic and social development of developing countries.

Environmental education is particularly important; therefore such programmes in schools and enterprises should be improved. The natural disasters, which take heavy tolls in terms of human lives, suffering, displacement of poor communities and economic losses, are major concerns for sustainable development. The rich biodiversity of the region, which claims more than two thirds of the global biological resources, is under serious threat from habitat alteration, the introduction of exotic species, pollution, global warming and other human activities.

International efforts are needed in promoting sustainable management of all types of forests, in particular, mobilization of financial resources, transfer of technology and capacity-building. The discharge of hazardous and toxic wastes, land-based sources of pollution, the destruction of corals and mangroves, offshore oil drilling and mineral exploration and exploitation, oil spills, marine accidents, excessive coastal tourism and overfishing have been identified as some of the main causes of marine environmental degradation.

Economic growth, urbanization, industrialization, population growth, overuse and system losses, and the limited availability of freshwater resources in some countries of the region have all contributed to water scarcity in the region. Arsenic contamination in water resources is also a severe problem, causing serious health hazards in some parts of the region.

Access to energy resources for the poor segment of our community is therefore instrumental in alleviating their poverty. Special consideration should be taken to ensure sustainable practices in extracting energy and mineral resources and to foster renewable energy development. Climate change is expected to increase the frequency and intensity of extreme events, such as storms, floods, high temperature, drought and sea-level rise.

There is a need to assist developing countries, especially least developed countries and small island developing States and economies in transition, in capitalizing on funding opportunities. It is important to improve the accuracy of seasonal forecasting of monsoons and the understanding of the regional water cycle and promote regional cooperation in joint research on climate observation.

Another concern is the effective implementation and enforcement of legislative and policy measures to address issues related to atmospheric and climate change. Sustainable developmet policy should be based on a set of principles of economic sustainability, poverty alleviation and human development, environmental stewardship, including ecosystem-based approaches, respect for effective traditional resources management, and institutional safeguards, with a special focus on poverty reduction. At the global level the key institutional issue is to strengthen existing global institutional mechanisms that Governments need to coordinate and to support the implementation of regional platforms for the next decade to make them more responsive to the demands of sustainable development in all countries.

There is a need to promote the development of local technologies, improvement of capacity for technology assessment, particularly of new and imported technologies, private sector participation in research and development and bigger national allocations for science and technology. The technologies of particular relevance to the region are biotechnology, information and communications technology, environmentally sound technology and renewable energy and desalination technologies, and resource-efficient low-waste and no-waste technologies.

The vital role of major groups in sustainable development and call on all Governments in the region to recognize fully their crucial role and promote their active participation in sustainable development. Major groups, including community-based organizations, non-governmental organizations (NGOs), industry, agriculture and business associations need to be encouraged and nurtured, particularly because they have the capability of delivering social services, often in partnership with Governments.

The development and early implementation of a regional initiative on capacity-building for sustainable development that will build on existing programmes in the region and be closely linked up with all the other regional initiatives on sustainable development. Its primary goal is to develop the capacity in the region to address effectively the policy challenges and the necessary institutional reform and governance and promote effective partnerships for sustainable development.

It may include promoting awareness of sustainable development; strengthening networks of civil society organizations involved in sustainable development; developing capacity, expertise and skills in integrating sustainable development principles into planning, implementation and assessment; building capacity in multilateral environmental agreements and international negotiations; enhancing capability for coping with natural disasters; and improving capacity to cope with the challenges of globalization, including developing skills in trade-environment policy analysis, planning and evaluation.

It may also include building capacity for the promotion and use of traditional knowledge and practices, local and modern technologies and advanced sciences to address sustainable development problems. Equally important is the strengthening and capacity-building of subregional organizations working to promote environmental management and sustainable development.

The implementation of the regional strategy on poverty reduction, which basically demands sustainable economic growth, inclusive social development, effective policies and institutions and increased investment in both physical and social infrastructure to meet the basic needs of the poor and the promotion of equitable access by all to assets, opportunities and decision-making.

The importance of mobilizing in a coherent manner all available resources, especially domestic, for financing for sustainable development. However, developing countries, economies in transition and small island developing countries will continue to need international financial assistance in order to achieve sustainable development. Better access to export markets, private financial flows, especially foreign direct investment, can play a substantial role in generating resources for sustainable.26 development in developing countries and economies in transition.

Civil society is an important partner in improving environmental management and accountability. The business sector is a potent catalyst for development and a critical partner in the pursuit of eco-efficiency. Regional and subregional cooperation could significantly facilitate resource mobilization and the transfer of environmentally sound.technologies and know-how. Strengthening regional and subregional cooperation is particularly important for activities that enhance national capacity-building processes.

District Poverty Initiative Project

The District Poverty Initiative Project is to be implemented in the six poorest districts of Andhra Pradesh (Adilabad, Anantapur, Chitoor, Mahabubnagar, Srikakulam, and Vizianagaram). The basic approach to poverty alleviation adopted by the project is to assist poor rural communities in mobilizing for effective self-representation, and to thereby initiate a process of participatory, demand driven, sustainable, and equitable rural development. The broad contours of this approach are increasingly familiar. The objective is to enable village communities and institutions to undertake a pivotal role in the determination of their priority needs, in the identification of sustainable investments to provide for and/or service these needs, and in channeling resources to identified projects.

DPIP-AP intends to accomplish this objective by providing three types of inputs: (1) Building local institutional capacity; (2) Providing a community investment fund (CIF) for three broad categories of investment: (a) community infrastructure; (b) vocational training for the provision of social needs; and (c) training for farm and off-farm income generating activities; and, (3) Initiating a process of re-integrating girl child laborers into the regular school system by providing bridge schools.

The project intends to create/strengthen several tiers of effective local institutions at the sub-village, village, and supra-village level, and to link such institutions with each other, with local government institutions (Gram Panchayat and provincial line departments), and with private formal institutions, such as banks, to which the poor typically have little access. The structure of local institutions envisaged by the project has, at its base, the concept of a thrift and credit self-help group (SHG).

This is referred to as a Common Interest Group (CIG) in project documents and constitutes its basic instrument for social mobilization and demand identification. A CIG is envisaged as a thrift and credit self help group which also shares a common occupational or developmental objective. The project will set up a community support cell at the mandal level (MCSC) to assist in the formation and strengthening of SHGs and CIGs. The MCSC will also help CIGs in preparing sub-1 projects which reflect local priorities. During its lifetime, DPIP will fund competitively chosen micro-projects through the community investment fund (CIF), which will be managed at the district level.

It is expected, however, that eventually communities will be able to raise funds for sub-projects independently, through their linkages with other institutions, including local government institutions and banks, as well as by mobilizing their own resources. In fact, this will constitute a critical test of a group's long-term sustainability. The project intends to assist in this process at two levels:

1. It will provide training to groups in financial management and conduct a performance rating for each group. The main objectives of a performance rating would be to facilitate linkage with banks for leveraging funds, and to help the groups by designing appropriate capacity building interventions.
2. It will assist in establishing institutional mechanisms for better communication and coordination between

communities and local government bodies through a process of local 'institutional deepening'. First, CIGs and SHGs, once they stabilize and mature, will be encouraged to federate into village level organizations (VOs).

In the early phase of the project, the MCSC will also take on the role of mediating between the CIGs/SHGs, the VOs, and the local government institutions, the Gram Panchayat. As VOs mature, however, they will be further encouraged to federate at the Mandal level forming a Mandal Samkhya (MS) which will be expected to internalize the mediatory and service delivery responsibilities of the MCSC as well as to actively foster the creation and development of new CIGs.

As soon as this is accomplished in a sustainable fashion, it is expected that the MCSC will be dissolved and the project's central objectives in that community will have been achieved. The Community Investment Fund (CIF) will fund three broad categories of investment: (a) Small community infrastructure; (b) Vocational training for social needs; and (c) Training for farm and non-farm income generating activities. The CIF will also assist with the provision of common supporting facilities where necessary. Proposals for the use of CIF funds for vocational training, as well as for training to enhance income generating capacities of group members, would equip members of a CIG or SHG to undertake either group or individual activities.

This is likely to be an important input since a key constraint faced by poor households, and one that is less likely to be satisfied by private providers, is the capacity to absorb productivity enhancing investments. Providing skills and training has the benefit of crowding-in investment funds from private sources, creating the possibility of a synergistic public-private partnership for enhancing productivity and ensuring income generation.

Overlap with other concurrent programs such as SGSY is also eliminated, allowing for a clearer attribution of the net contribution of DPIP in an environment characterized by multiple interventions. A distinct component of the project is a targeted intervention to address the girl child labor problem, which is considerable in some project districts. The specific intervention proposed by the project is an increase in the supply of residential schools for older girls in the 12-14 age group who are otherwise neglected.

The project is expected to fund up to 12 residential 'bridge' and regular residential schools from grade 7 on up. The residential bridge schools will provide remedial courses for girls in the 12-14 age group to prepare them to transfer to a residential or state run day school. It is expected that this intervention will yield immediate benefits in the form of higher school retention rates, and a reduction in girl child labor, as well as longer term benefits due to the enhancement of human capital and attendant effects on the incidence of chronic poverty.

Given the innovative nature of the project, and the enormous learning possibilities inherent in its implementation, a monitoring and evaluation framework that has three components. First, in order to track the process of institutional development at the village level a system of on-going 'process' monitoring will need to be set up. This should ideally have two components.

A computerized 'process MIS' to track information on key indicators of institutional development, and a more qualitative process monitoring system which should elicit feedback from potential beneficiaries on the performance of the project and the viability of local institutional development, as well as provide a mechanism through which beneficiaries can self-evaluate. Second, an MIS system will need to be put in place in order to monitor the routine flow of project inputs and outputs.

This 'financial MIS' must be linked to the 'process MIS' to maximize its use. Third, an assessment of net project impact on culmination outcomes such as the reduction of child labor and increased economic well-being of the poorest will need to be done.

DPIP's integrated approach to poverty alleviation, requires that potential outcomes are also viewed in a comprehensive fashion. In particular, the process by which the 'culmination' outcomes (poverty reduction, rural development) are to be achieved must be as central to an evaluation as the outcomes themselves. In this context, the project's success in creating sustainable local institutions, rooted in the mobilization of traditionally marginalized and vulnerable groups, must be a central component of an evaluation.

This will encompass an assessment of the project's success in building effective institutions at the village level, and in successfully linking such institutions to local government bodies, banks, and other higher tier institutions, as well as an assessment of the ways in which the project has utilized, augmented, or displaced social networks within the community. In tandem with this, an evaluation should attempt to assess the extent to which sub-projects put forward by common interest groups, and eventually funded, actually reflect the priorities of marginalized and vulnerable groups.

To the extent that this objective is realized, the project has the potential for reducing not just poverty but also inequities within rural communities. Since the reduction of poverty and inequality are the overarching objectives of the project, an evaluation must also assess the extent to which these objectives have been realized. The central objective of project monitoring should be to ensure that inputs are delivered in a timely fashion and that the processes through which the stated objectives are to be realized are in place.

If problems are encountered, the monitoring process should serve as an early warning mechanism and be of assistance in implementing corrective measures. The MIS as described is considerably larger in scope and scale than a conventional MIS that focuses only on financial aspects of the project. The State Project Management Unit (SPMU) which will be responsible for the disbursal of project funds will also undertake the task of monitoring the functioning of the project at all levels.

The SPMU will maintain a management information system (MIS). This should be designed to facilitate concurrent and transparent monitoring along various dimensions. Specifically, such a system should:

— Track the delivery of project funds for various inputs of the project and monitor the allocation and use of such funds.

— Monitor the delivery of other targeted inputs such as training of staff and potential clients, the construction of residential schools, and other organizational inputs.

— Monitor the demand for and use of the Community Investment Fund (CIF)

— Calculate notional cost estimates for different types of sub-projects, in order to generate good estimates of funds required to implement winning sub-projects.

— Track progress in the various tiers of institution building (group formation, federations etc) and other process indicators.

This will make it possible to: (i) calculate gross project costs; (ii) ascertain the extent to which funded sub-projects are well targeted, i.e., the proportion of sub-projects submitted by the poorest villages and by geographically isolated and/or economically and socially marginalized groups; the proportion of such sub-projects actually funded; and the overall distribution of the community investment fund (CIF); (iii) determine the extent to which project management is efficient and transparent in selecting and disbursing sub-project funds; (iv) ascertain the sustainability of investments undertaken with the use of project funds.

A well designed monitoring framework (i.e., one with a well designed and maintained Management Information System (MIS)) will also produce an extensive database on the project which should be brought into use in an evaluation of project impact. Specifically, it will obtain direct information on client satisfaction through the use of Participatory Poverty Assessments (PPAs) using rapid and light qualitative methods (including client self-evaluation), and assess the extent to which the poor have been included in the process of project selection, design and implementation at the individual and community levels, as well as the results of this inclusion.

In order to work effectively, it will be important for the independent agency to have access to project data gathered by the MIS and to use it effectively in conjunction with its own assessments in order to ascertain the quality of project implementation. Since the formation of sustainable groups and federated institutions based on such groups is a matter of central concern, it will be important to try and track the degree of volatility (formation, attrition, inclusion and exclusion) within and across such groups, particularly in the early/ formative phase of the project.

As such, the dynamics of CIGs and VOs should be an important focus in process monitoring. This will require information on: the formation and dissolution of groups, member turnover, frequency of meetings, average attendance, diversity of discussion topics, opportunity for equitable participation, rotation and accountability of leadership, the ability of the group and or its leaders to mobilize resources, frequency of conflicts within a group, gender dimensions in the formation of groups, inclusion and exclusion etc. This may require frequent qualitative surveys in random sub-samples of project mandals-perhaps a sub-set of the mandals selected for the baseline.

It should be kept in mind that in the mandals where SHGs are now well established and VOs exist and are functioning, client self-assessments will be particularly important and useful in the early phase of the project. The on-going monitoring of process outcomes, should, in principal, generate a learning and feedback mechanism which would enhance prospects for adaptation, especially in the early stages of the project. In order to facilitate this process, the agency will be expected to provide a report of its assessment to the project every six months.

The central objective of an evaluation is an assessment of the impact of project inputs on a set of outcomes/indicators of performance derived from the development objectives of the project. Since outcomes can depend on a number of factors, some unrelated to the project, an effective impact evaluation must derive the net impact of the project on specific outcomes after controlling, to the extent possible, for such factors.

Andhra Pradesh has a long.history of group based activities, with at least two major types of pre-existing groups. The GOAP's DWACRA groups and the SAPAP (UNDP) groups, some of which are in an advanced stage of federation at the village and mandal level. While, the former are important from the project's perspective because they are composed of the poorest and are widely prevalent in most of the project districts, the latter constitute both a model for the formation of new groups and an existing resource pool on which the project hopes to build.

Since features of existing SAPAP groups and federations will serve as a partial model for the DPIP project, the baseline in the pilot districts could provide a unique learning opportunity. The main source of information for the evaluation of project impact will be household and village/community/facility survey data collected specifically for this purpose. In addition, quite valuable use could be made of the data base created by the enhanced MIS. It is important to clarify right away that given the enormous diversity in the project's objectives and inputs, aggregation across potential project outcomes will not be possible.

However, a first-order approximation could be obtained by aggregating income and/or.consumption gains across households in villages that participate in DPIP. These benefits could then be compared to the total costs of the project (including all project implementation costs, as well as the costs associated with direct investments in sub-projects), in order to get an estimate of the net economic benefits of the program at the village/habitation level. It is also worth noting that, in principal, a project like DPIP could strengthen or undermine existing village networks and organizations, formal and informal.

In order to assess the net impact of the project on existing organizations and networks we need to be able to evaluate the ways in which the project has augmented the quantity and quality of community involvement and cooperation. Indicators that measure the performance of local institutions engendered by the project, as well as their linkages with/absorption of existing community organizations will constitute an important aspect of project impact at both the household and village level.

Anit Trafficking: A Social Action Programme in South Asia

Throughout South Asia men, women, boys and girls are trafficked within their own countries and across international borders against their wills in what is essentially a clandestine slave trade. The number of trafficked persons is difficult to determine as the bribery and corruption surrounding the practice render an estimate of its magnitude virtually impossible.

The Congressional Research Service and the U.S. State Department estimate that between 1 to 2 million people are trafficked each year worldwide with the majority originating in Asia. Its existence in South Asia is certain and the toll of human suffering is evident in cities and villages throughout the region.

The root causes include extreme disparities of wealth, increased awareness of job opportunities far from home resulting from globalization and the penetration of mass media, continuing and pervasive inequality due to caste, class and gender bias throughout the region, lack of transparency in regulations governing labor migration, poor enforcement of internationally agreed-upon human rights standards, and the enormous profitability for traffickers.

The growing international labor market runs into conflict with barriers to lawful migration, creating a demand that is being met by smugglers and traffickers. The lack of distinction between lawful labor migration, irregular migration, smuggling and trafficking has left many legal issues unresolved. The international prohibition on slavery and the slave trade was one of the first rights to be recognized under public international law.

Indeed, the 1927 Convention on Slavery (drafted under the auspices of the League of Nations) is widely recognized as the first modern international treaty for the protection of human rights. The 1948 United Nations Universal Declaration of Human Rights expanded the prohibition against slavery and the 1957 Supplementary Convention on the Elaboration of Slavery, the Slave Trade and Institutions and Practices Similar to Slavery further expanded the prohibition to apply it to the institutions and practices of debt bondage, serfdom, servile forms of marriage and the exploitation of children, which are all held to be "similar to slavery."

The Convention includes additional terms, including prohibitions against placing persons in "servile status" (i.e., a victim of one of the practices referred to as "slave-like" or holding persons in "servitude"). Although many elements of slavery or servitude (e.g., the detention or sale of the victim, degrading treatment, total control over the victim) are present in trafficking, Gallagher made the point that it has been legally difficult to sustain claims that trafficking is included in the jus cogens norm prohibiting slavery and the slave trade.

State parties to the Slavery Convention have undertaken measures to prevent compulsory labor "from developing into conditions analogous to slavery." The 1930 ILO Forced Labor Convention definition of forced labor is still widely accepted today:

> "all work or service which is extracted from any person under the menace of any penalty and for which the said person has not offered himself voluntarily." However, a United Nations body has never formally invoked this international prohibition on forced and compulsory labor in relation to a case of trafficking, forced prostitution or exploitation of prostitution. Debt bondage is a condition related to maintaining a situation of forced labor and has been identified by the ILO Forced Labor Convention as a practice similar to slavery, which defines a victim of debt bondage as "a person of servile status."
>
> ". . . the status or condition arising from a pledge by a debtor of his personal services or those of a person under his control as security for a debt if the value of those services as reasonably assessed is not applied towards the liquidation of the debt or the length and nature of those services are not respectively limited and defined."

Debt bondage is defined as various international conventions dealing with traffic in women and girls (the so-called "white slave" trade) were concluded and in 1949 they were consolidated into one instrument known as the Convention for the Suppression of the Traffic in Persons and of the Exploitation of the Prostitution of Others.

This convention has a number of important provisions dealing with cross-border cooperation and protection of foreign victims, and it has attracted strong measures of political support. The Convention on the Rights of the Child goes further than the ILO Forced Labor Convention or the 1957 Slavery Convention in stipulating the actions that State Parties are to take to prevent the abduction, sale or trafficking of children for any purpose or form (Article 35), including economic or sexual exploitation or abuse.

The prohibition against trafficking and related exploitation of children has been reiterated and extended through the adoption of the ILO Convention on the Worst Forms of Child Labor in 1999. The 1999 UN Crime Commission work and the November 2000 Convention against Transnational Organised Crime are supplemented by two additional protocols, Smuggling of Migrants and Trafficking in Persons Especially Women and Children.

Trafficking in persons is defined as another person for the purposes of exploitation. Exploitation shall include, at a minimum, the exploitation of the prostitution of others or other forms of sexual exploitation, forced labor or services, slavery or practices similar to slavery, servitude or the removal of organs. The critical factor that distinguishes trafficking from smuggling is that trafficking includes the presence of force, coercion or deception for the purpose of exploitation.

Both can occur within a country or inside cross-border movement, but smuggling involves consent, which is a critically important distinction. Several elements of international law pertaining to trafficking were reviewed in her paper with special attention to the position of non-citizens as being one of the most highly politicized and central issues to protecting the rights of trafficked persons.

Although traditional international law recognizes that a host state owes "equal treatment" or an "international minimum standard" to aliens within its territory, Gallagher noted that such protection is uneven and uncertain, although core rights such as the prohibition on slavery, forced labor and debt bondage do appear to be protected consistently. Despite these well-recognized rights, the distinction between trafficking and migration for work are rarely made, with the result that the rights of the trafficked person as a worker are rarely articulated or protected.

Although the International Convention on the Protection of the Rights of All Migrant Workers and Members of Their Families that was adopted by the UN General Assembly in 1990 clearly stipulates many protections for non-citizen migrant workers, it has been ratified by only 16 States to date and is thus not in effect. The failure to gain widespread support for this convention is indicative of the difficulties in securing rights for non-citizens.

However, there is a marked reluctance (in general) on the part of States to recognize any but the most fundamental rights as being applicable to this group. The most recent and relevant international instrument for trafficking is the Trafficking Protocol. It was opened for signature in December 2000 and 81 countries having signed it to date. The protocol represents a significant step forward in the fight against trafficking, most notably in the emerging consensus that it is time to end debate about conceptual issues surrounding trafficking and use the existing frameworks to develop national policies and programs that prevent trafficking but do not inhibit labor migration.

As a result of the consensus on what constitutes a definition of trafficking, attention is now shifted towards the application of the agreed upon international covenants on trafficking and their effects on national and regional law reform in South Application of International Covenants to the South Asia Region Asia. Although new international covenants on trafficking complemented by national legislation such as the United States' recent Victims of Trafficking and Violence Protection Act of 2000 have created a sense of workable definitions among anti-trafficking constituents, the application of these definitions into state laws and services has not advanced.

The interpretation of agreed upon definitions is frustrated by class and gender biases, as well as reluctance (or inability) of states to ensure the rights of all persons within their borders. These impasses result in misrepresentations on the incidence and nature of trafficking, the conflation of trafficking and irregular migration, and the conflation of trafficking and prostitution. The latter gives rise to unproductive debate about whether commercial sex work is a valid occupation and detracts attention from the larger issue of ensuring that a person's right to work is not condential upon the type of labor.

Although the intention motivating these reforms is benevolent, the resulting actions are a cause of grave concern. It is recognized that because they have limited access to the public world and safe channels of mobility, coupled with fewer measures of legal and social protection in many societies, women and minors throughout South Asia are highly vulnerable to trafficking.

The gender-sensitive analysis of migration developed by Joyti Sanghera illustrates how trafficking transforms an agent into a victim, and how national anti-trafficking legislation in South Asia that prevents mobility and limits access to new forms of livelihood serves to disempower women and restrict their rights. Recent developments in anti-trafficking legislation from Bangladesh, India and Nepal were drawn upon to illustrate these points.

In all three settings there is a clear trend in national legislation to draft increasingly draconian laws on trafficking with stiff penalties, including application of the death penalty in Bangladesh for a range of crimes against women, including trafficking. Legislation pending in Nepal contains a strongly moralistic approach that emphasizes safeguarding the "interest of the general public" and maintaining "good conduct" by bringing together wide-ranging offenses, especially sexual offenses into one general anti-trafficking law.

Language used to describe trafficking is often lumped together with crimes against women. For example, Indian and Nepali legislation deals simultaneously with issues of rape, pornography, child sexual abuse, prostitution, abduction, wrongful confinement, battering and trafficking. These and other laws do not differentiate between women and children and provide for severe penalties, including capital punishment and life imprisonment. Ironically, these extreme penalties have led to less rather than more protection for women and children.

Many courts are reluctant to convict people based on imperfect investigations and evidentiary procedures when mandatory life imprisonment or the death penalty will be imposed. This results in high acquittal rates, which are sending clear signals to societies in the South Asian region that perpetrators of trafficking will likely escape punishment. Anecdotal evidence suggests that another outcome of legislation mandating stiff penalties is an increase in the amount and frequency of bribes, as wealthy traffickers seek to avoid prosecution of crimes with harsh penalties.

For example, the Nepali "Foreign Employment Act of 1985," the "Foreign Employment Order" issued by the Ministry of Labor, and the "Passport Order" all restrict the mobility of single Nepali women seeking to move and work across the border. These legal restrictions are negative indicators of development that link a woman's ability to voluntarily migrate with measures of empowerment and self-determination.

National legislation in Bangladesh, India and Nepal that criminalizes prostitution results in criminalizing the prostitute as well, regardless if she has been trafficked. A trafficked woman's criminal status will overshadow her victim status under the terms of this legislation. Commonly, only women are arrested on charges of prostitution, and only adolescent minors are considered exempt from being criminalized. According to this common line of thought, the only way a trafficked woman's victim status can be protected is to treat her as a child and assume that she could not know where her best interest lay when she decided to practice sex work.

The socio-legal construction of an innocent victim of trafficking is one of a disempowered subject whose autonomy and agency have been criminalized. Sanghera concluded that despite new developments in the international legal framework that defines trafficking, there is a pressing need for national law reform to move away from a moralistic stance of protecting women to measures that reflect a genuine human rights model, celebrating the autonomy and agency of South Asian women.

The analysis of trafficking from within a human rights framework draws upon standards and principles of rights that have been encoded with United Nations treaties and conventions and which can form a basis for analyzing any social issue. In addition to these conventions-based mechanisms, the United Nations possesses extra-conventional offices and working groups that investigate cases of trafficking, communicate with governments, and make recommendations to other bodies for redress or actions to protect against future violations.

Although trafficked persons suffer serious criminal violations at the hands of traffickers, more often than not, once they are released from the slavery-like or forced labor conditions they are . . . treated more like a criminal than a victim". Often trafficked persons do not have the opportunity to lodge complaints, seek damages, assess whether it is safe to return home, collect their belongings or seek asylum before being taken into custody and deported.

In all such cases state parties can be held directly responsible for these violations of trafficked victims' human rights. The Trafficking Protocol contains strong law enforcement provisions designed to assist governments to organize and share information linked to identifying and prosecuting traffickers. While the Trafficking Protocol's focus on prevention is positive, it has an over-emphasis on criminal prosecution that can detract from protecting the human rights of victims.

Specifically, the Trafficking Protocol's provisions are limited to protecting and assisting trafficking victims who agree to become witnesses for the state, and very little attention is given to providing aid to trafficking victims who cannot or will not become witnesses. The law enforcement provisions mandate state obligations for law enforcement while the protection and assistance provisions in the Trafficking Protocol are discretionary. "Trafficking in persons means the recruitment, transportation, purchase, sale, transfer, harbouring or receipt of persons:

(i) by threat or use of violence, abduction, force, fraud, deception or coercion (including the abuse of authority), or debt bondage, for the purpose of:

(ii) placing or holding such person, whether for pay or not, in forced labor or slavery-like practices, in a community other than the one in which such person lived at the time of the original act described in."

Human Rights has enumerated the basic principles that States should follow to combat trafficking. The list includes, among other points, the following:

— Trafficked persons should not be criminalized for the coerced illegality of their entry or residence in countries of transit and destination, or for the coerced activities they perform as a consequence of their status as trafficked persons.

— Victims of trafficking including those with "irregular" immigration status should be granted protection and necessary physical and mental care by the authorities of the receiving country.

Women and children should not be treated the same in the identification, rescue and repatriation process. Efforts must be made to address the root causes of trafficking, including poverty, inequality, discrimination and racism. Rights constitute an abstract principle that needs to be actualized through conscious application of principles such as those described by the UN High Commissioner for Human Rights.

Thus, human rights-oriented programs that seek to prevent trafficking need to work through legal measures that enable women to claim their rights, including the creation of transparent and manageable procedures for legal migration for all kinds of work. Discrimination, in this case discrimination against migrant workers or workers of a particular industry, is the chief obstacle to participating in a process that promotes human rights.

An over-reliance on legal mechanisms can produce results that are counter-productive. When laws are created to be as broadly encompassing as possible, an over-generalization occurs that actually restricts the application of the law and reduces its impact. Legal measures to restrict trafficking that lack specificity in terms of gender and age have been shown to mischaracterize the harm done by trafficking, and actually compound restrictions on the movement and employment of younger women instead of protecting these rights.

Movement in and out of coercive and exploitative circumstances is a dynamic process that is well recognized in irregular migration, smuggling and trafficking. Interventions (legal or programmatic) that intercept trafficking at its outcome point, rather than at the time or place when it first occurs draw attention to identifying when movement within or between countries becomes exploitative and not voluntary, and serve to protect (as proposed to limit) an individual's right to migrate.

A human rights analysis draws attention to the protection of equality and the promotion of non-discriminatory migration. The definitions of trafficking employed by the UN Trafficking Protocol and the United States Victims of Trafficking and Violence Protection Act of 2000 deconstruct trafficking into three aspects: "(1) movement and trade/sale of a person, (2) techniques used to bring about a condition for this movement (e.g., deception, fraud, violence), and (3) a listing that relates to the "purpose" of movement (e.g., forced labor, prostitution, servitude or debt bondage)".

These three elements draw attention to the movement of people, but do not directly address the conditions of the outcome or end point of the movement. The use of this type of language is not restricted to the UN or the United States Government. The term "trafficking," which itself connotes movement is not always translated into other languages in a manner that promotes a wider understanding of the issues that are involved.

For example, in Bangla the term is commonly translated to mean "movement of women across borders." The emphasis on movement has several drawbacks. It shifts attention to prevention and rescue in transit, activities that are more closely aligned with stopping irregular migration than investigating violations of human rights in the workplace.

Furthermore, voluntarism is a status that individuals may enter into only after a substantial period of being entrapped. The decision to remain in an exploitative working conditions when other options become available, or to return to servitude after being "rescued" by an anti-trafficking program is commonly encountered by programs. The interplay between an individual's exercise of self-determination and his or her psychological health after being trafficked is a complex issue.

The ILO Convention Number 182 of 1999, Article 3 (Worst Forms of Child Labour) declares that "all forms of slavery or practices similar to slavery, such as the sale and trafficking of children, debt bondage, serfdom and forced or compulsory labour, including forced or compulsory recruitment of children for use in armed conflict" represent a set of practices prohibited by the convention.

ILO Convention 158 guidelines protect children from exploitation Degrees of Vulnerability through the application of minimum age criteria (e.g., light work for ages 13-15 years if education is continued), compulsory education up to 15 years, and proscription of certain types of hazardous labor for children up to age 17 years. The ILO Conventions govern actions that can be taken in the workplace, even though interventions take place in the family setting and public venues.

Activities conducted in public venues are, by comparison with social services directed towards families, relatively more straightforward. For example, the identification of "free floating" or unaccompanied, abandoned children in a market place can be undertaken by the government and NGO programs.

Intervening to protect a child from a dysfunctional family setting is more problematic. A first step is for programs to acknowledge that all families do not necessarily provide a protective environment against trafficking, and that relatives of the trafficked child may in fact be responsible for selling the child into servitude. This recognition carries implications for programs that strive to rehabilitate victims of trafficking and then reintegrate individuals back into their communities.

The sub-text behind many governmental programs is to simply stop people from migrating and, in the process, to stop individuals from becoming victims of traffickers. Thus "success" in preventing trafficking actually means stopping migration. The prevention of irregular migration is principally being addressed by the receiving countries, not the countries of origin.

Children are more expensive and difficult to care for once they are rescued and more problematic to reintegrate or repatriate. States experience many difficulties in assuming responsibility for non-citizen minors and are therefore often reluctant to assume any responsibility for their protection and care. NGOs can play an important role providing humanitarian services for this (sometimes) will-fully neglected group of trafficking victims.

The Convention on the Rights of the Child defines anyone under the age of 18 as being a child and subject to special measures of protection. However, the Convention on the Rights of the Child mentions trafficking only in a general prohibition in Article 35, which says that states "shall take all appropriate national, bilateral and multilateral measures to prevent the abduction of, the sale of, or traffic in children for any purpose or in any form".

This instrument, when coupled with the combined effect of the Convention on the Rights of the Child, Trafficking Protocol, and the ILO Convention 182 on the Worst Forms of Child Labour, provides sufficient international legal precedent instruments to regulate state responsibility for the prevention of child trafficking. Issues of consent are integral to understanding the protection of minors, and the Trafficking Protocol addresses this concern in a positive manner for all parties, particularly for children. Because the victim is a minor, any transfer without the consent of the parent or guardian is illegal.

The lasting damage to children by trafficking is a concern for society. Children are being trafficked for sexual exploitation, domestic and farm labor, and are brought into forced conscription in armed conflicts. They are more vulnerable to HIV/AIDS and are also more likely to suffer emotional deprivation and psychological abuse that will shape them into dysfunctional adults, thereby perpetuating crimes against humanity in societies worldwide.

In this arena the role of NGOs has become critically important and the role of international legal instruments to guide the formulation of their programs is essential. The pre-movement phase describes the forces that compel individuals to migrate and fall into trafficked situations.

Many misconceptions or over-simplifications of the underlying causes of migration obscure the resources that are available to trafficked persons and their resiliency.

For example, poverty is often cited as the reason for migration or accepting employment conditions of debt bondage, despite the common occurrence of migrants actually paying for transportation or transit services. A more refined analysis suggests that in many circumstances large disparities of income and wealth entice individuals to migrate, rather than absolute poverty that pushes individuals away from their home communities. Clearly a number of "push" factors do exist that encourage individuals to migrate, including human nature and a breakdown of family or social structure, in addition to the more frequently cited reason of "poverty."

Marshall described two types of anti-migration approaches that emerge in anti-trafficking policies that act to prevent or discourage movement: 1) prohibitive measures to constrain migration (e.g., lack of transparent immigration policies or procedures), and 2) expansion of choices to curb the desire to move (e.g., improving local circumstances through livelihoods and micro-enterprise development programs). The first approach limits human rights and is ineffective in stopping irregular migration or trafficking. The second approach is more constructive yet ultimately will have limited impact given the large disparities of economic opportunities that motivate migration for employment.

Programs that combat exploitation in the workplace are sometimes confounded by changes in the degree of control exercised by an individual over the exploitative circumstance. For example, circumstances that are forced upon an individual may become more accepted or benign over time, and ultimately may no longer be perceived as entrapment or servitude. Indeed, context-specific definitions of servitude or servile status are elusive for many settings, while overly generalized laws do little to promote a sense of rights and protection.

After the exploitation has been stopped anti-trafficking programs are confronted with the difficult, and time-consuming task of rehabilitating the victim and then ensuring his or her reintegration into society. In this area of anti-trafficking activities, the experience gained by HIV/AIDS control programs can provide guidance.

For example, lessons learned from conducting advocacy work to reduce stigmatization and creating support groups for HIV positive persons have direct parallels to creating conditions for ensuring the rights of returned persons. Contemporary border protection activities sometimes fail to manage illegal or irregular migration simply because agents have limited training and are only able to manage clearly defined migrant categories.

Suspected trafficking cases are in fact quite difficult to identify at border crossings particularly if the trafficked person is not yet aware of the deception or fraud. The application of a definition of trafficking (such as contained in the Trafficking Protocol) requires specific parameters for identifying victims that can be linked with appropriate operational responses by border agents.

Anti-trafficking programs conducted in Bangladesh and Nepal were the subject of papers presented by Rina Sen Gupta (IOM, Dhaka) and Durga Ghimire (ABC, Nepal), and commented upon by Celine Costello Daly. Many NGOs in the South Asian region are working in the areas of prevention, rescue, care and support either as a principal activity or as an important aspect of a broader social development project.

Activities to improve local conditions for women and children that also incorporate messages to reduce vulnerability to trafficking are being implemented by NGOs throughout South Asia, with varying levels of government support. For example, a number of NGOs in Nepal, India and Bangladesh are conducting women's leadership training courses, family life education, livelihoods skill building programs for adolescent girls and the formation of women's cooperatives (for group savings and credit activities).

These programs seek to improve conditions that have often been identified as being the underlying causes of trafficking. NGOs in the region are also implementing programs that directly address the vulnerability of persons to trafficking. Awareness-raising activities directed at the general public (through street theatres, rallies and community meetings) and community leaders are common elements in many of the prevention programs.

Unfortunately, some community awareness-raising activities have inadvertently equated trafficking with HIV/AIDS and commercial sex work and exacerbated the stigma and discrimination of persons living with HIV/AIDS. Negative messages and scare-tactics, particularly content that conflates trafficking with HIV/AIDS need to be avoided. In general, more work needs to be done on creating localized definitions of people "vulnerable to trafficking."

Several programs address the needs of trafficked persons by providing services that take place either during rescue, rehabilitation or reintegration. Rescue-related activities are extremely problematic to implement due to the difficulties in evaluating ambiguous migrant categories, coupled with the use of fraud and deception by the trafficker. As a result, programs that attempt to seize trafficking victims at the border invariably restrict women's rights or encourage corruption.

Rescuing victims at the end point of the trafficked movement (e.g., workplace) reduces the risk of stopping legitimate migration. Rehabilitation-related activities are, by comparison, easier to implement. Unfortunately, the creation of shelters and safe areas has been found, in some instances, to isolate trafficked persons and contribute to (instead of reducing) stigmatization. Moving a trafficked person out of rehabilitation and back into society can be complicated if a dysfunctional family or failed social support system in the communities contributed to the original trafficking event.

This is particularly the case with minors, but is alsc an important consideration for older victims. Clear, operational definitions of successful reintegration are generally lacking: this may be a contributing reason foı the scarcity of effective reintegration models in the South Asian region, particularly for children who may have been sold into servitude by their families. In addition there are other concerns about the capacity of NGOs tc provide needed services.

As NGOs become more individualized in th delivery of the rehabilitation and reintegration services their programs become smaller and the impact is limitec to relatively few beneficiaries. Rehabilitation progran models that can provide individualized attention t larger numbers of trafficked persons need to b developed. The creation of networks of localized NGO and linkages with government schemes was indicated as a promising approach.

The dilemma of how to reach large numbers of trafficked persons with personalized care and support and reintegration services is an outstanding issue that has not been adequately resolved in South Asian programs. In contrast to the task of moving the highly individualized but limited work of NGOs to a larger scale, legal efforts to identify and prosecute traffickers suffer from problems associated with over-generalization and need to shift attention to a narrower spectrum of specific violations of a person's rights.

There are two broad themes that hinder the development of effective law reform and prosecution in South Asia: 1) the widespread tendency to equate trafficking with irregular migration, and 2) the tendency to equate trafficking with sex work. Both are the consequence of pervasive gender biases in the region. When trafficking is equated with irregular migration, estimates of trafficked persons are substantially inflated and unreliable.

When trafficking is equated with sex work, legal initiatives assume moralistic tones. Both instances of conflation serve to restrict, rather than to promote the human rights of trafficked persons and hinder the development of appropriate legal responses by states in the region. Gender bias also affects the manner in which laws are interpreted and prosecution-related investigations are conducted.

The pervasive pro-male bias in South Asia creates a context that assumes women and girls need both control and protection from either an adult male or the state (which is male dominated). Furthermore, certain women's rights (e.g., freedom of movement) may be willfully sacrificed for perceptions of their greater good. These are not abstract concerns but are in response to actual state laws and regional conventions.

For example, the South Asian Association for Regional Cooperation (SAARC) draft Convention on Trafficking treats consent as irrelevant and criminalizes any movement related to the sale or procurement of women, even when an adult woman may have given her consent and even payment for the purposes of migration or debt bonded labor. Human Rights Watch recently advised the governments of Nepal and India to establish a strict system of border patrol to "guard against the trafficking in women and girls," despite the obvious risks of stopping the voluntary migration of women as a consequence of state-sponsored punitive measures.

The Nepali Human Trafficking (Control) Act of 1986 was intended to expedite action on what was perceived as a grave problem. This legislation includes the formulation of a special court in Kathmandu. However, the special court and women's crime cells have served to isolate the legal venues where cases can be investigated and brought forward, and have actually resulted in fewer, not more, cases being brought to successful prosecution.

In addition, there has been a perceptible shift in the burden of proof to the victim in Nepali trafficking cases, with public testimony required for conviction. The socio-legal environment is such that all trafficked women are labelled as prostitutes, with victims commonly reporting that they have suffered harassment in police stations and even in courts. The experience reported on from Nepal indicates the importance of developing local law enforcement capacity to adequately investigate trafficking.

Police and state attorneys need training to increase their skills and abilities to identify and act in suspected trafficking cases in a manner that protects the victims' rights while at the same time expediting prosecution of the implicated agents. The management of trafficked children is at once a more straightforward and more complex issue than it is for older victims. The limited ability of children to provide consent for themselves coupled with agreed-upon international guidelines governing child labor make it easier to identify situations where children (as opposed to adults) are living and working in servile status.

For example, while an adult woman may or may not be in a position to voluntarily engage in commercial sex work, a girl of 15 or 16 is legally incapable of making that decision. In contrast to adults, the dependency of children and their vulnerabilities make the provision of care and support services more demanding, and their reintegration into the community more challenging.

Forced sexual exploitation of both girls and boys occurs in most cases of trafficking, even in settings where children are working for other purposes. Although pedophiles have always existed there is a perception among agencies working in the region, particularly in Sri Lanka, that recently the problem is acknowledged more openly by state and civil society actors than it has in the past. Detection and reporting of cases in many settings is clearly increasing, adding to the media reports of a rise in the incidence of child trafficking. However, sexual exploitation is not the only outcome of trafficking in children.

The need for coordination and cooperation between agencies working to prevent trafficking became acute in Sri Lanka during the 1990s as the number of agencies and programs increased. Programs began competing for funding and focused on establishing differences in their priorities and activities, with the result that the development of anti-trafficking policy risked set-backs. The National Child Protection Authority (NCPA) in Sri Lanka is a model program of how NGOs, academics, governmental agencies and political leaders can be brought together in a consultative framework to advise the government and undertake complementary activities.

The Sri Lankan NCPA works in four areas: 1) awareness-raising about child trafficking; 2) capacity-building of a variety of professions working with child abuse; 3) legal reforms and monitoring enforcement; and 4) protection and rehabilitation of trafficking victims. International donors have been engaged in supporting activities through the NCPA on a number of issues, including the creation of district child protection committees that increase awareness among communities and develop the capacity of local law enforcement and government officials.

The National Task Force on Trafficking in Sri Lanka is another example of how an effective forum for consolidating policy advice from highly credible sources can be created. The emphasis on awareness-raising among local constituencies in Bangladesh is necessary because, in contrast to Sri Lanka, trafficking of children in Bangladesh is relatively unacknowledged or seldom discussed in public discourse.

While the rescue of trafficked children is a primarily a state responsibility, the experience in India demonstrates that NGOs can play an important role in identifying and reporting cases where children are held in servitude. After minors are removed from these settings, NGOs are better equipped than local government services to provide care and shelter.

The care, support and reintegration of the trafficked child require the sustained involvement of caring agencies if programs are to succeed. The girl child needs to choose among the options of seeking social legitimacy through marriage, while being placed in a setting that provides protection from a brothel owner. She cannot be returned to the dysfunctional family or community that sold her into trafficking in the first place.

Long-term programs are needed that permit rescued children to engage in the process of developing social and livelihood skills; these skills will eventually act as protective factors as children grow and mature. For this process to work, however, sufficient resources are necessary to sustain skill-building and nurturing programs over time without interruption. In addition, agencies working in the field of child trafficking require an ideological orientation to uphold human rights and combat gender and caste-based discrimination.

The monitoring and evaluation of anti-trafficking programs is a complex undertaking. Program interventions operate in multiple sectors (law, health, social, vocational) and at different stages of the trafficking continuum (before, during, after; prevention, seizure, care and support, reintegration). Minors and adults are involved, as are citizens and non-citizens. These complexities not withstanding, certain principles of program design and operations do apply to the implementation of anti-trafficking activities and facilitate their evaluation.

In general, clearly defined objectives that are linked to specific activities greatly facilitate program operation and serve as evaluation indicators. To the extent that South Asian NGOs incorporate clear objectives into their operations, their activities will also benefit from more effective management and reporting.

Monitoring and evaluation activities need to be developed that are specific to the intervention and setting, and are appropriate to the amount of resources expended on evaluation vis-a-vis the program and its anticipated impact. The use of qualitative or participatory research methods is encouraged, for some activities, in addition to standardized survey techniques.

The small-scale, highly individualized context of care and support and reintegration activities undertaken by many NGOs indicate that qualitative, or even participatory, research methods are appropriate. Another proposed research method is the use of mico-economic data collection and analysis techniques. Methods to estimate the costs of program elements will be needed when successful interventions begin to be replicated and scaled up.

The conceptual framework and research methods for evaluating anti-trafficking programs has not been field tested with South Asian NGOs, although the general relevance of the model to a wide variety of public health and social development programs is well recognized.

Bibliography

Abecassis, David, "Identity, Islam and Human Development in Rural Bangladesh", University Press Limited, Haka, 135 pp, 1990.

Afridi, M. A. Zaheer, Catch 22: The Poverty of Politics. A Study of Social Welfare Planning and Policy Analysis, Pakistan Academy for Rural Development, Peshawar, 219 pp, 1989.

Alamgir, Mohiuddin and Sadiq Ahmed, "Poverty and Income Distribution in Bangladesh", in T. N. Srinivasan and P. K. Bardhan (eds.), pp. 11-38, 1988.

Amhad, R., "Impact of Workers Remittances from the Middle East on Pakistan's Economy: Some Selected Issues", *in The Pakistan Development Review*, Vol. XXV, No. 4, Winter, 1986.

Banerjee, Nirmala, "Women Workers in the Unorganized Sector", *The Calcutta Experience*, Sangam Books, Hyderabad, 1985.

Bhalla, S., "Is Sri Lanka an Exception? A Comparative Study in Living Standards", in T. N. Srinivasan and P. K. Bardhan, pp. 89-117, 1988.

Cain, M.T., "The Consequences of Reproductive Failure: Dependence, Mobility and Mortality Among the Elderly of Rural South Asia", in Population Studies, Vol. 40, No. 3, 1986.

Cain, M.T. and A. Mozumdar, "Labour Market Structure and Reproductive Behaviour in Rural South Asia", in G.

Rodgers and G. Standing (eds.): *Work, Poverty and Under-Development, ILO*, Geneva, 1981

Chaudhry, M. Ghaffar, "Green revolution and Redistribution of Rural Incomes: Pakistan's Experience", in Pakistan Development Review, 31, 3, pp. 173-205, 1982.

Gavan, J. and I. Chandrasekera, "The Impact of Public Foodgrain Distribution on Food Consumption and Welfare in Sri Lanka", *Research Report* No.13, International Food Policy Research Institute, Washington, DC, 1979.

Hewavitharana, B., "Industrialisation, Employment and Basic Needs: The Case of Sri Lanka", *ILO, World Employment Programme Research, Basic Needs and Employment Programme,* Working Paper 60, Geneva, 124 pp, 1986.

Kohli, Atul, "The State and Poverty in India", *The Politics of Reform,* Cambridge University Press, Cambridge, 260 pp, 1987.

Krishnan, T.N., "Population, Poverty and Employment in India", Economic and Political Weekly, November 14, pp. 2479-97, 1992.

Levine, Nancy E., "Webs of Dependence in Rural Nepal: Debts, Poverty and Depopulation in the Far Northwest", Contributions to Nepalese Studies, Vol.15, No.2, July, pp. 213-45, 1988.

Rodgers, Gerry (ed.), "Population Growth and Poverty in Rural South Asia", (ILO/WEP), Sage, 249 pp, 1989.

Shaw, Annapurna, "Wage Labour in Slum Households of Calcutta", Labour, Capital and Society, 17, 1, April, pp. 26-42, 1984.

World Bank, Nepal, Policies for Improving Growth and Alleviating Poverty, A World Bank Country Study, The World Bank, Washington, DC, 150 pp, 1989.

Index